the

parent s☕up ®

A-to-Z Guide
to Your
Toddler

practical advice from parents who've been there
on everything from activities to potty training to whining

Kate Hanley & the Parents of Parent Soup
Medical Information from Alan Greene, M.D.
Foreword by Nancy Evans

CB
CONTEMPORARY BOOKS

Library of Congress Cataloging-in-Publication Data

The Parent Soup A-to-Z guide to your toddler : practical advice from
    parents who've been there on everything from activities to potty
    training to whining / Kate Hanley & the parents of Parent Soup ;
    medical information from Alan Greene ; foreword by Nancy Evans.
        p.   cm.
   ISBN 0-8092-2959-5
     1. Toddlers—Miscellanea.   2. Child rearing—Miscellanea.
  I. Hanley, Kate.   II. Parent Soup (Organization)
  HQ774.5.P35   1999
  649'.1—dc21
                                                     98-35478
                                                             CIP

Interior and cover design by Maria Garcia-Palencia
Interior production by Susan H. Hartman

Published by Contemporary Books
A division of NTC/Contemporary Publishing Group, Inc.
4255 West Touhy Avenue, Lincolnwood (Chicago), Illinois 60646-1975 U.S.A.
Copyright © 1999 by iVillage Inc.
Printed in the United States of America
International Standard Book Number: 0-8092-2959-5
98   99   00   01   02   03   QP   11   10   9   8   7   6   5   4   3   2   1

![parent soup]

foreword

Parent Soup debuted on the Internet in January 1996 as the ultimate watering hole for parents. It is a place where parents can come seven days a week, 24 hours a day to ask for help, compare notes, or find a soul mate. While Parent Soup has thousands of articles and resources to help parents, what parents seem to like best is talking to one another. And one way they talk is in message boards, where a mom can post a question and other moms will come to the rescue with solutions that have worked for them.

Think of those posts as letters to and from friends. Some are a pithy few lines; others are a heartfelt few pages. They are almost always helpful, and sometimes they are truly moving in their awesome clarity. Like parenting itself, the discussion ranges from the brass tacks of how to get your child to bed to the bigger picture of learning what being a parent is all about. Humor and kindness abound.

In this book you will find the best of these posts. We read every message in the Parents of Toddlers message boards to find advice and wisdom that can make you realize that, no matter what challenges you face while raising your toddler, you are not alone. You've got a whole community of support in Parent Soup.

As I write this, more parents are coming into Parent Soup to add even more lived wisdom. It is a daily accumulation. So if it happens that there's an answer you can't find in this book, log onto Parent Soup (www.parentsoup.com

on the Web or Keyword: ParentSoup on AOL), click on the Parents of Toddlers icon, and get ready to meet your new friends. As one mom says of her son's debut at nursery school, "Imagine how different your life would be if you went into a strange situation and viewed it not as a situation where you encounter strangers, but as a situation where you meet friends whose names you don't know yet." That's a pretty good description of the people in Parent Soup, friends whose names you don't know yet. But you soon will. You'll meet many of them in this book.

As of November 1997, Parent Soup has joined other channels of interest to women in an online destination called iVillage.com: The Women's Network. Along with Parent Soup, you'll find channels on health, work, fitness—all the things you care about, in addition to your children. The Web, which not very long ago was a decidedly male place, has now become a place of true usefulness to women. After all, nobody knows better than a mother how difficult it is to find time for anything. The Web, with its 24-hour access and information literally at your fingertips, has become an unexpected ally to women. And the numbers show it: when we first started iVillage in 1995, less than 19 percent of the people online were women. Today women constitute almost half of the people using the Internet.

This book will give you a solid sampling of what women talk about when they go online. Far from idle chat, these women are helping one another as women always have. I hope that the women you'll meet in this book can help you begin to answer the question, "What does the Internet have to offer me?" May this be the beginning of a beautiful friendship.

~ Nancy Evans   nancy@iVillage.com

parent soup is part of
iVillage.com
THE WOMEN'S NETWORK

parent soup

acknowledgments

i'd like to thank the parents of Parent Soup for being so wise, so witty, and so human. They have so much good information to share that this book practically wrote itself.

Many thanks also to Kait Simpson for her resourcefulness in scouring the message boards; Felicia Jones for her calm project management; Maria Garcia-Palencia for her enthusiastic help in designing the book; Dr. Alan and Cheryl Greene for their diligent and insightful contributions; the entire Parent Soup staff for helping assemble the various elements of the book; and Nancy Evans for her unending support and editorial expertise.

There are certain members of the Parent Soup staff—Susan Hahn, Tarrant Figlio, Monica Hixson, and Chris Mattoni—who are featured prominently in the book. These women contribute a lot of hard work to Parent Soup, and their combination of parenting know-how and good old-fashioned kindness help make the Soup such a resource and a comfort to parents. I am thankful for them and their willingness to share their talents.

~ K.H.

v

introduction

did you ever wish you could peek into other people's houses and see how they deal with the many challenges that parenting brings? So you could find out how the Joneses potty-train, or how the Garcias deal with temper tantrums?

If you've ever asked yourself, "How do other parents deal with this situation?" this book is a dream come true. Here you'll find the voices of parents from all across America offering ideas on how to get your kids to sleep in their own beds, how to handle anger, even how to revive your sex life.

The parents featured on these pages are all members of Parent Soup, an online gathering place for parents on AOL (Keyword: ParentSoup) and the Web (www.parentsoup.com). Every day, thousands of parents come to Parent Soup to talk to each other and to get answers to the many questions they face every day. Parent Soup also has parenting experts on hand to offer a professional point of view on a range of topics. But the thing that makes the Soup special is the sense of community the parents share. No matter how old your kids are, or what type of parent you are, you can find a friend in the Soup to lend an ear, share a laugh, or reassure you that you're not alone in your parenting journey.

This book incorporates the best of the Soup—collective wisdom from parents, expert advice, eye-opening poll questions, and brain-teasing trivia questions. Inside these pages, you'll meet Dr. Alan Greene, our resident pediatrician, and learn his thoughtful, sensible approach to parenting (for his bio, turn to page 10). You'll also hear from Don and Jeanne Elium, Parent Soup's resident family counselors and behavior therapists, for insight into your toddler's sometimes baffling behavior (for their bio, turn to page 16). And best of all, this book can give you the sense that you have a community that you can draw on, whether you need information or solace.

The information is organized so that this book is as easy to use as possible, because we know that living with a toddler doesn't leave you with much time to read a book at your leisure. If you don't see what you're looking for in the A-to-Z format, just turn to the index for more ideas on where to look.

Everything you see in this book has worked for some parent out there. Dr. Greene has also read all the tips to make sure that the ideas the parents suggest are safe. But we have to advise you that while all remedies suggested in this book have worked for someone, we cannot promise that they will all work for you. Some of the main beliefs that Parent Soup is built on are that what works for one family might not work for another, and that there is no *one* right way to parent. So here are some ideas to help you become the best parent that you can be. We hope that you'll be inspired to visit Parent Soup and share your lived wisdom, and help us build our community of passionate parents.

~ Kate Hanley   hanley@iVillage.com

ACTIVITIES *(See also Toys)*

Now that your child is no longer a baby, he can talk, he can walk, he can run you silly as you try to keep up with him. The challenge is to keep him happy, stimulated, and directed so that he can discover the world in a way that will teach him and keep him safe. The problem is, one day, he

 may be more than happy to sit and play with socks while you do laundry. The next, he may launch a screaming attack if you try to involve him in your daily routine. So your best solution is to have an arsenal of activity ideas. Below are some suggestions to stimulate your toddler's imagination and keep you at the ready when an old standby reaches its expiration date.

ART
Fun for Budding Impressionists
Cut or rip up various colors of tissue paper, then give the children the tissue paper and a piece of blank white paper. Have them lay the pieces of tissue down on the white paper and then "paint" over them with a paintbrush and water. The tissue paper will bleed through and when dry it will just fall off, leaving a really neat effect.
   ~ *Tarrant F., Gainesville, Florida*

Magna Doodle Dandy
I got my two-year-old a Magna Doodle. She will sit and doodle a long time with that one. Sometimes she does crazy haphazard scribbles, looks at

HOMEMADE PLAY DOH

1 cup white flour
¼ cup salt
2 tablespoons cream of tartar
1 cup water
1 tablespoon oil
Paste food coloring

Mix flour, salt, and cream of tartar in a medium pot. Add water and oil. Cook and stir over medium heat. Mixture will look like a globby mess, and you will be sure it won't turn out but it will. When it forms a ball in the center of the pot, turn it out and knead it on a lightly floured surface. Add paste food coloring to suit your taste (the

me, and says, "Picture of mommy." I look at it and say, "Yeah kiddo, some days that's right on target!"

~ *Carla L., Baltimore, Maryland*

Set Them Loose with a Bucket of "Paint"

Is your child bored? Ask her to "paint" the house or the floors—give her a bucket of plain water and a big paintbrush. Kids love this activity!

~ *Monica H., Evanston, Illinois*

Displaying Their Efforts

I use plain clothespins and hang my children's artwork on the dining room curtains. That way, we don't ruin the wall, or the art. When a new project comes in, we take down the oldest work and display the new.

~ *Parent Soup member Mamabev*

COOKING

Shake It Up

My son and I like to make homemade butter. All you need is a small jar and a lid (I use a baby food jar), a couple of ounces of heavy cream, and a dash of salt. You pour the cream into the jar, add the salt, and shake, shake, shake! After about three minutes of pretty hearty shaking, it suddenly balls up and you have enough for a few pieces of toast, or some muffins. We also bought some butter molds recently, and once the butter forms, we spread them in the mold. This morning we had clover-shaped pats of butter with our breakfast.

~ *Lara H., Las Vegas, Nevada*

The Mix Master

My son loves mixing potions. Every morning he saves a bit of milk from his cereal bowl and some orange juice from his cup and mixes them with the water sitting in a bowl in the sink. One day I gave him four small containers filled with water and two drops of four different food colorings. I also provided four empty containers, an eyedropper, and a spoon. He mixed potions to his heart's content. It's easy to set up, not very messy, and keeps him glued to his seat for at least an hour.

~ *Parent Soup member Wendy061*

OUTINGS

Exploring the Great Outdoors

One outing my kids (nine years old and almost three) enjoy is a hike in our local canyon area. Living in Los Angeles, there are not too many places nearby to do a little hiking and experience nature. Luckily, I found a place not far from home, and the kids and I take bread with us and we feed the ducks at the pond. I have to hold my three-year-old because he would love to go in the water and touch the ducks. We do a little hiking and I point out different types of trees, foliage, we listen for bird sounds, stuff like that. We have a wonderful time and the kids really enjoy it.

~ *Pieri L., Burbank, California*

Variety Is the Spice of Life

I have three-and-a-half-year-old twin girls. Our outings are many and varied. Some of our favorite destinations are: playgrounds, feeding the

key to really bright wonderful colors, it is available at cake supply stores and many craft places, and nationwide at Lechters, which is in many malls; one assortment of it will last years!). Store in an airtight container or plastic bag. Edible, but not tasty!

~ *Tarrant F.,*
Eugene, Oregon

3

FINGER PAINTS

1 cup all-purpose flour
4 cups cold water
Food coloring

In a large saucepan combine flour and one cup cold water. Stir until smooth. Add three cups additional cold water. Cook and stir over medium heat until mixture thickens and bubbles. Reduce heat. Cook and stir one minute more. Pour into three heat-proof bowls. Use food coloring to tint to desired color. Cover with plastic wrap at room temperature until cool. Spoon paint on paper; paint. You could also use Kool-Aid or icing paste or dry tempera paints to tint.

~ *Rebecca G.,*
  Montgomery City,
  Missouri

ducks, visiting the airport observation area, going to indoor play areas (such as Discovery Zone or a children's museum), taking a tour of the fire station, going to a paint-your-own pottery place, or even going to the grocery store (we bring along our own little shopping carts).

~ *Dawn M., Odenton, Maryland*

Walking out the Door on a Moment's Notice

I have two toddlers, ages one and two and a half, and getting out of the house even to play in the backyard is always a chore. I have to make sure I have everything in one trip or I have to bring both kids back in with me. And you know that getting a toddler indoors isn't easy. What has really made my life easier is a wicker picnic basket that I keep near the back door. It is always packed with a few necessities: diapers, wipes, sunscreen, two baseball hats, a bag of pretzels for snacking, some of my small gardening tools (Mommy likes to play outside too), and a tablecloth. That way it is always ready and convenient. And the basket is pretty, so it never looks messy sitting on our shelf. I just have to add the drinks for the toddlers and my coffee in a travel mug, and we are out the door to the yard. And one arm is still free. The basket also makes it easy to pack everything back up to come inside.

~ *Tammy H., Buffalo, New York*

PLAYING

Look and Learn

My two-year-old loves anything where there's something hidden underneath something else, such as wooden puzzles. I found a great one with the alphabet, and each letter has pictures underneath of words that start with those letters. We sit together and she shows me the letter and I will tell her what letter it is and say, "A is for apple," and she will look for the apple and put the piece in. We also found these Fisher Price peekaboo books (really sturdy) where you lift the flaps and there are colors, shapes, opposites, etc. It's become a nightly "story/game" where we go through the book and open all the doors and talk about what's underneath.

~ *Laura B., Vancouver, Washington*

Let Them Entertain You

Children love to put on shows! This seems to defy age limitations; the show just gets more elaborate. Young children can dress up in leotards and tights. Then put classical music on (they always love the snappier Mozart tunes) and watch them work out a dance routine—lots of giggles, hysteria, and banging around. Just make sure they have plenty of room. When they are ready to perform, set up chairs for the parents and any other audience members, set up a lamp spotlight, put on the music, and let the show begin! Lots of applause at the end. (When my five-year-old daughter did her ballet show, at the end her three-year-old brother stood up, flung his arms wide, and shouted "This is a disaster!" I told her to always ignore critics.) After the show, have a "cocktail" party with soda in champagne glasses and cheese-and-cracker hors d'oeuvres. Enjoy your children, they're free entertainment!

~ *Parent Soup member*
Midge

PARENT POLL

Do you think it's OK for kids under the age of two to watch TV?

Of **1,247** total votes

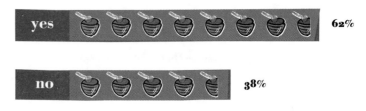

yes — 62%

no — 38%

1 bowl = 100 parents

5

Not Fancy, Just Functional

My three-year-old son was bored yesterday, and I know he likes playing bow and arrow. So I got into my "project box" and made him a cardboard bow and arrow out of a paper-towel middle, a shoelace, and some other cardboard for arrows. He hasn't let it out of his sight. When I finished it, he said, "Mommy, you make the best bow and arrow in the world! I love it." Makes you realize how the simple things give them the most pleasure.

~ *Erin C., Lacon, Illinois*

READING

When You Don't Think You Can Read Pooh One More Time

My daughter is two and a half now, and has always had a love of being read to. Reading the same books to her repeatedly can get a little old, so I take her to the public library. It has a wonderful kids' room, where they don't have to be quiet. She gets to pick new books out as often as she wants, and I don't have to read the same old books day after day. Try starting a library day with your child once a month. Reading helps so much with language development, and gives them a longer attention span. Encourage that passion in your child and you will be amazed at the things he will do in life.

~ *Charla C., Birmingham, Alabama*

I agree that reading the same books over and over and over can be boring, but it does have its payoff. My daughter is two and a half, and she now "reads" these books to her dolls and stuffed animals word for word! It shows me that she's learning, *and* it keeps her busy for a long time!

~ *Deborah P., Andover, Minnesota*

No matter how often you read the same book or how often you have to play Hi Ho Cherrio or Candy Land (been there), remember that kids like the same old same old. Don't be surprised when she sits down and reads you the book. Repetition is how they learn.

~ *Parent Soup member BrandyM*

If at First You Don't Succeed . . .
I can only suggest to keep trying new things, inside and out. If one thing doesn't catch his interest, try another. By the way, that doesn't mean he won't be interested in the thing he rejected the last time, so don't throw out the ideas, just cycle through them.

~ *Amy A., Costa Mesa, California*

SPECIAL DAYS
Go with a Theme
Once a week (usually Mondays, when my daughter is often grumpy due to switching gears after the weekend), I try to institute a "theme" day. Here are some examples:

Farm Day: dress her in overalls, go visit a farm. Read books that contain farm animals, sing songs like "Old MacDonald," give her paint or crayons and let her draw farm pictures.

Teddy Bear Day: gather up the teddy bears, have a teddy-bear tea party, read books with bears in them, let her help you bake cookies shaped like bears (my daughter loves to pour in the ingredients and "stir" them up, plus decorate with frosting).

The possibilities are endless, and often this makes the usual toys and books a little more exciting. And you'll be surprised how creative you really are.

~ *Mary K., Catonsville, Maryland*

Give Them Something to Look Forward To

I have three children. On the first day of each month we all huddle around my very large calendar. One by one the children close their eyes and select a day on the calendar to be "King" or "Queen" for that day. For that day they choose what we will have for dinner and just get a little special attention. It's a small sacrifice (or none at all) on the parent's part and a big thrill to the kids.

    ~ *Cindy W., Winston-Salem, North Carolina*

PARENTS' FAVORITE COMPUTER SOFTWARE FOR TODDLERS

Jumpstart (Preschool, Kindergarten)

These are wonderful learning tools. They have a report card that you can pull up to see where your child needs help. I would recommend them to anybody.

    ~ *Linda G., Aurora, Colorado*

Living Books

My three-year-old son received the Living Book *Dr. Seuss's ABC* as a gift. He has had more fun, as he says, "working" on the computer. The CD reads the story, highlighting words as it reads, and allows children to interact with the characters, words, and hidden surprises.

    ~ *Parent Soup member Rammatt*

Memory Matching

My 25-month-old son's favorite programs are his Memory Matching games. He can sit for up to an hour on the computer (just about the only time he'll sit still). He knows how to use it very well, so he can do it by himself, I just have to load the program.

~ *Parent Soup member Porks2*

My First Dictionary

My two-year-old loves this program. It's educational and fun. What more could you ask for?

~ *Parent Soup member Tjaz99*

Creative Wonders

We have the Creative Wonders software *Elmo's Preschool, Letters,* and *Art Workshop*. Our daughter has been playing on them since the age of two (for eight months now). They each have enough activities in them to keep different levels and ages interested and challenged.

~ *Parent Soup member LORISSTC*

Rabbit Reader's Preschool

Our three-year-old loves *Rabbit Reader's Preschool*. He has the best time with this! It has lots of music and he loves to dance, so he will play for a while then dance around the room.

~ *JoEllyn M., San Diego, California*

KIDS SAY THE DARNEDEST THINGS

I asked my four-year-old daughter how to spell her name. She replied, "K-R-I-S-T-E-N.com." Too much computer?!

~ *Kellie G., Lodi, California*

9

ALLERGIES

Allergies can be a chronic source of stuffiness for your child. Determining the source of those allergies can be a long process. In the meantime, how do you give your child relief? Here, Dr. Alan Greene, Parent Soup's resident pediatrician, explains the best treatment for childhood allergies. But first, a word about Dr. Greene and his impeccable qualifications:

Dr. Greene is a practicing pediatrician in San Mateo, California, who views each child as an individual and encourages parents and child-care providers to see children as unique and deserving of individualized care and attention. Dr. Greene attended Princeton University (undergraduate) and top-ranked medical school the University of California at San Francisco; after completing his pediatric residency at the Children's Hospital Medical Center of Northern California, he served as chief resident there and passed the Pediatric Boards in the top 5 percent of the nation. He is also on the Voluntary Clinical Faculty at Stanford University and was awarded the Physician's Recognition Award by the American Medical Association. He's the author of *The Parent's Complete Guide to Ear Infections* and and has his own Web site at www.DrGreene.com. He was also the medical expert for *The Parent Soup A-to-Z Guide to Your New Baby.* His love of children is evident—he has four healthy kids of his own. Dr. Greene appears regularly on Parent Soup to chat and swap messages with parents. And in his spare time (you may be saying, "What spare time?"), Dr. Greene is teaching each of his children to play chess!

Is It Allergies, or Is It Just a Cold?

Q: If a child has cold symptoms that go on and on, is it really allergies? Or is it just one long cold? Are the treatments the same?

~ *Shirley, Mill Valley, California*

DR. GREENE'S INSIGHT

A: The lining of our noses contains tiny guardians called mast cells, whose purpose is to protect us from harmful particles in the air we breathe. People with allergies have hypersensitive mast cells that sound the alert in response to relatively harmless particles such as pollen, dust, or pet dander.

When pollen sticks to the membrane of a mast cell of someone with pollen allergies, the cell begins to swell and swell. Finally the mast cell bursts, spilling histamine and many other potent chemicals into the surrounding tissue. As a result, allergies typically feature a clear nasal discharge with sneezing. There may be itchy, watery eyes and/or a dry cough. Often parents notice a "rabbit nose"—a child crinkling her nose to relieve the itchy sensation inside. The "allergic salute"—rubbing the nose with the hand, sometimes leaving a horizontal crease on the nose—is another common sign. "Allergic shiners"—dark circles under the eyes—have long been associated with allergies, but are less predictive than the other symptoms.

Colds will often begin with a clear nasal discharge, but after several days it usually turns creamy, yellow, or green for a time. Sneezes tend to be more productive, and coughs sound wetter than with allergies. If the eyes are involved, one or both of them usually turn pink, with a discharge that matches that in the nose. A fever may be present.

A sinus infection in a child often begins like a cold but lasts for greater than 10 to 14 days with no period of improvement. Sometimes a sinus infection begins with a high fever (greater than 103 degrees Fahrenheit), facial swelling, or facial pain. Since children with allergies often get more colds, sinus infections, and ear infections than their counterparts, it can be difficult to figure out exactly what is going on. The experience of other family members offers a big clue: Allergies often run in families. Eczema and asthma are also more common in allergic families.

What if Your Child Does Have Allergies?

Walking into a drugstore, you are confronted with an overwhelming display of allergy products. Many of these products can actually harm your child and make the effects of allergies even worse. The right choices, however, used in the right ways, can dramatically improve your child's springtime.

For years, the centerpieces of over-the-counter allergy therapy have been decongestants and antihistamines. Decongestants are caffeinelike compounds that work by constricting blood vessels throughout the body, including the nose. By limiting blood flow to the nose, nasal congestion and swelling are somewhat decreased, providing a measure of relief.

Decongestants temporarily raise the blood pressure and make extra work for the heart. Since most kids have strong, healthy hearts this is usually not a problem. Rather, the tendency for kids on decongestants to experience irritability or sleeplessness is a more practical concern. Allergy preparations advertised as "nondrowsy" are typically decongestant preparations. Multisymptom allergy or cold medicines usually contain one of the two main decongestants found in oral over-the-counter preparations: pseudoephedrine and phenylpropanolamine. If you decide to use a decongestant for your child, pseudoephedrine gives better relief with fewer side effects. Topical decongestants (nose drops or nasal sprays) provide far greater relief with fewer side effects, but these powerful medicines should not be used for more than three days at a time (or they begin to work backward and can also be habit-forming). These may be a great option for a night or two while another strategy is beginning to work but are a poor choice for beating the effects of the allergy season.

Antihistamines reduce allergy symptoms by blocking the action of the histamine released by mast cells in response to allergic triggers such as pollen. These can be very effective, but all of the over-the-counter antihistamines cause some change in kids' levels of alertness. Most of the time, they produce drowsiness in children (which can be quite welcome, especially at night), but about 5 percent of kids will act hyper instead.

Of far greater concern is the effect of antihistamines on thinking and learning. We know that kids who are experiencing allergy symptoms don't think or learn or remember as well as kids who are feeling well (*Annals of Allergy*, August 1993). Careful studies have now been performed to determine whether this reduction in learning ability could be reversed by using over-the-counter antihistamines to relieve the allergy symptoms. The surprising results were that even though kids felt better on the antihistamines, their learning abilities were even worse than with no treatment (*Annals of Allergy, Asthma, and Immunology*, March 1996). Children are better off congested than drugged. (Better yet is having the symptoms relieved in less problematic ways!)

Over-the-counter antihistamines are a reasonable choice for nighttime use, or for an occasional day or two when a child is home from school. I do not recommend them, however, as a long-term solution. Learning—even during play—is too important a part of childhood to blunt with drugs.

Antihistamines are found in almost all allergy preparations that are not specifically advertised as nondrowsy. Diphenhydramine is the most powerful, but it also makes kids the sleepiest (or most wired). Chlorpheniramine and brompheniramine both are a little less potent but have fewer side effects.

Nasalcrom is an exciting, new, over-the-counter allergy medicine that is more effective and far safer than either decongestants or antihistamines. Nasalcrom is a nasal spray that creates a protective barrier around the allergy cells in the nose so that pollen, mold, dust, and animal dander can't stick to them. It stops the allergic response before it starts—without causing any drowsiness, irritability, or decreased learning. It doesn't reverse allergy symptoms that are already present, but it prevents new allergen exposures from causing symptoms. Unlike decongestant nasal sprays, this gentle medicine can be used for weeks or months at a time with no fear of rebound effects or addiction. After 14 years as a prescription-only medicine, Nasalcrom is poised to revolutionize the over-the-counter treatment of allergies.

Preventing exposure to airborne allergies is another powerful way to treat allergies at home. To this end, a High Efficiency Particulate Arresting (HEPA) filter can be an excellent investment. These filters, available at discount drugstores for about $60 to $100, can remove 99.97 percent of the pollen, dust, and animal dander from the air. I highly recommend placing one in the room where a child with hay fever sleeps.

When kids are playing outside during hay-fever season, pollen from grasses, weeds, and trees clings to their clothes and hair. Taking off the outside clothes as they enter the house, and perhaps rinsing the hair, can greatly reduce the pollen they are exposed to that night as they sleep. Every little bit of exposure reduction helps.

The *Old Farmer's Almanac* advises tying a bag of onions around the neck or around the bedpost as a good home remedy for allergies. My guess is that this works by stimulating tear production, which naturally washes pollen particles out of the eyes and nose. A less smelly way to accomplish the same thing is the liberal use of saline nose drops or saline eyedrops (artificial tears). Saline drops are not the same as the eyedrops that are advertised to "get the red out." While "get the red out" drops do help to reduce the red appearance of irritated eyes, they are not a good choice for preventing or treating allergies.

The *Almanac* also suggests turning a piece of orange rind inside out and inserting it in the nose. We now know that some of the ingredients in citrus fruits (including vitamin C) block the histamine response in a safe and natural way. The most potent of these appears to be a vitamin-like compound called quercitin that is found in citrus fruits and buckwheat. Increasing these foods in the diet makes sense. Quercitin/vitamin C supplements are available in health-food stores. We know that these reduce hay-fever symptoms in rats, but their effect on human children has not been established. They do appear to be safe and gentle, however, and many people report success with them.

Stinging nettle is the other natural remedy that shows a lot of promise. Also available in health food stores, this herbal supplement is now known to reduce the histamine response in test-tube experiments. But again, although I have heard many testimonials, the scientific evidence in support of its effectiveness in humans is sparse.

ANGER *(See also Behavior and Sanity Savers)*

Children inspire a range of intense emotions in their parents, and anger is no exception. Toddlers are learning the accepted rules of human behavior, and they are bound to make some mistakes along the way. For example: You ask them not to do something. They do it anyway. Or, you make their favorite meal, spaghetti. They scream "Hot dog! I want hot dog!" Aargh.

Everyone knows that getting angry with your kids isn't the best way to deal with your frustration. And by learning how to keep a lid on your anger, you are not only defusing any tense situations with your kids, you are showing them—by example—how to handle their anger. Not only will you feel better, but your kids will feel better (since you won't be yelling at them), and they'll learn how to make themselves feel better the next time they get angry. Well, maybe not the next time, but someday.

In this section you'll also get the Eliums' point of view. Don and Jeanne Elium—Parent Soup's resident family counselors and behavior therapists—are therapists, advisors, authors, and most important, experienced parents who have raised kids themselves. The Eliums answer questions from parents every week on Parent Soup, offering plenty of time- (and sanity-!) saving tips that are guaranteed to foster better communication within the family. They are also authors of three books: *Raising a Son*, *Raising a Daughter*, and *Raising a Family: Living on Planet Parenthood*. Later in this section they offer an expert opinion on healthy ways to deal with anger.

Change the Way They Act by Changing the Way You React

I have a three-year-old and a two-year-old. Believe me, they can get to me. I have learned to use my quiet times (such as before I go to bed) to take some really deep breaths and pray for patience. When you are frustrated and are acting out-of-control, the situation only gets worse for the kids. Try whispering instead of yelling. Try hugging instead of hitting. Let your child know he is loved unconditionally no matter what. It takes work, but I find that the more I love my kids, the better their behavior becomes. I have also given them ways to deal with their frustrations. When they want to throw, bite, or scream, I talk to them in a calm voice and tell them to hit a pillow. It does get better, but only if you can learn better ways to react. Remember, they learn more by example than all the yelling or even talking you could ever do.

~ *Dianna W., South Bend, Indiana*

Step Away from the Situation

I got this advice from our family doctor (an enlightened man who had hands-on experience with his own children). The doctor told me that it was better for a child to cry for a few minutes if it meant Mom was getting a much-needed breather and would be better able to deal with the situation after taking a minute to calm down. Luckily, when I first needed to take a breather it was summer and I would not only put on music—Jonathan Livingston Seagull, which also helped calm my daughter—but could go sit on the steps and soak up the sunshine and fresh air. I could come back inside and deal with everything so much better after a break.

~ *Charlotte O., Fort Wayne, Indiana*

Time-Out for Mom

I used to be a screamer and hitter. The more I screamed the madder I got. I used wooden spoons to swat little butts. Occasionally, I would hit the counter with the spoon for emphasis. One night, after a stressful day at work and coming home to a toddler and two school-age children and no spouse, I cracked. I was screaming and banging on the counter with the wooden spoon when it broke, flew across the room, and landed in the dog's dish. The kids just stood there terrified of me. What a terrible feeling to have as a parent—the kids were scared of their mom. I didn't know what to do. I stood there and thought a while. Then, I told the kids that Mom was not behaving herself and was going to take time-out in her room for 15 minutes. They didn't know what to do—Mom in time-out? Well, it worked. I used that time to cry and think. I realized that I wasn't accomplishing anything and was making things worse. So, from that day on, when I felt that I was not acting appropriately I went to time-out. When everyone is calm we then sit down and talk about what happened and how to deal with it. Time-outs give all of us time to think.

~ *Charlotte O., Fort Wayne, Indiana*

When I can't take it anymore, I tell my girls I am getting ready to throw a tantrum and need a time-out. I go to my room, lock the door, and scream. The kids are usually so surprised that they stop the unwanted behavior and check to make sure I'm OK! I tell them I will be out when my time-out is over and to go to the playroom. Then I take five minutes to myself.

~ *Yvonne W., San Jose, California*

Sweat It Out

Q: Has anyone found exercise to be a good anger-buster? For me, any exercise will do: a one-hour run with the dog or a 30-minute exercise session with my favorite exercise tape or several jumping jacks with the little ones (followed by something a little more intense). I know that finding the time to exercise can be tough for lots of people, especially those with little, little kids. Does anyone have great ideas for fitting exercise into your busy day?

~ *Christine S., Kansas City, Missouri*

A: I exercise about four times per week. I joined a gym about four years ago, and it's so much better to get out of the house and go exercise there. It helps enormously when I'm feeling angry or resentful for various reasons. The gym has child care, or I wait till my kids are in (pre) school, then I go. On weekends I leave the kids with my husband or another family member and make the time to work out even if it's just for an hour. It's not always easy when you have babies. So vacuum and dust later, and go exercise to ease some of your frustrations.

~ *Mia S., San Dimas, California*

Ending the Cycle of Abuse

Q: I am a proud father of three-and-a-half-year-old twin boys. I love my children with all my heart, but I have a hard time controlling my temper. I grew up in a very abusive atmosphere, both physically and mentally. I can see a lot of my parents' traits in me as I try and discipline or even interact with my children. I tend to yell at my kids even when they do something so insignificant it shouldn't even warrant a response. I hear that the punishment should fit the crime. I was wondering if someone could give me some examples or suggestions. I don't want to continue the cycle, nor do I want my kids resenting me. I love them with all my heart and want nothing more than for our family to have a loving and nourishing relationship.

~ *Parent Soup member Jjacquez*

A: I think you should look into a discipline/parenting class for birth to three, offered through your community college, Red Cross, or other community agency. They go into things in a concrete way and can answer your particular questions. Also call the Parent Helpline of Parents Anonymous at 1-800-345-5044. They can help you out, whether you have lost control or think you might or just want help learning how to handle anger and discipline issues.

~ *Tarrant F., Gainesville, Florida*

19

a anger

A: My youngest son is almost two and he does the whining, crying bit. I go to a parent support group called Parents Anonymous. It helps a lot. Everybody talks about their week and what they went through. I've gotten some good ideas from them that really work. My Parents Anonymous chapter also offers free child care.

~ *Parent Soup member Griffshaus*

Anger Forecast

I give my children "storm warnings"—a sort of graduated scale of my feelings. I use the warnings in the same sequence every time, so that my children will know exactly how what they're doing is affecting me. But the trick is to start when you first notice something bothering you. So for the first level, you say, "What you are doing is annoying to me." Second level, "What you are doing is really irritating me." Third, "What you are doing is making me cross, and if you don't stop right now, I will get very angry." Finally, fourth, "Now, I am really angry and" (impose an appropriate consequence like grounding or time-out). Children naturally push your limits, but they are usually too inexperienced to know from tone of voice or body language when they're going too far. Verbalizing just how far they're going will help them to learn this better. Eventually, they learn that they don't want to get to stage four.

~ *Mary K. H., East Lansing, Michigan*

Healthy Releases

There are some appropriate ways to let the anger out. Using them will not only make you feel better, it'll provide your children with good modeling. First, tell them that you are angry (you don't have to explain why) and you need to let off steam. You can tear up old telephone books. You can go to a recycling center and throw cans and bottles—they make a great noise when thrown hard! You can punch pillows. You can go to an airport and scream when a noisy plane takes off. You can jog (and push a stroller), you can bike (put the kids in a kid carrier on the back), and you can make bread dough and punch the daylights out of it when you knead it. What I'm trying to say is, there are many ways to take out your anger without inflicting it on anybody else.

~ *Mary K. H., East Lansing, Michigan*

Mellow Out to Music

When I need to get some perspective on a situation, I listen to blasting music. Then I address the situation with a clear head.

~ *Parent Soup member Wildcatmum*

Sing Out Loud, Sing Out Strong

When I am at my wits' end and know that I am going to lash out in a screaming fury, I sing. Doesn't matter if I'm in the car, in the kitchen, or watching television, I sing the same song (hasn't changed in 13 years) at the top of my lungs, from the bottom of my stomach and with every inch of heart I have. I belt that song out. At the end of my song, I am relaxed, smiling, and the house is blessedly quiet. The bickering, the whining, the pestering, and negative-attention-seeking behavior has ended. What can possibly compete with my truly terrible voice and its awe-inspiring volume? It works. My flash of anger is gone, and the children have a few moments to realign their behavior. Oftentimes, they'll even join in. Now my children have learned to use this trick. When being mercilessly teased or badgered by a sibling, they start to sing and don't stop until their tormentor is gone. Best of all, with this tactic, there is never any guilt. Sometimes, it's fun to be angry.

~ *Parent Soup member Corrykg*

Accentuate the Positive

I try to focus on the positive side of being two. At this age, our kids are becoming little individuals and must make a place for themselves in this crazy world of ours. Sure, my son is impossible when he's tired, screams and runs the other way when we're dressing him, and insists on possessing everything, but he's also developing a great sense of humor, loves deciding what he's going to eat for dinner or watch on TV, and helps Mom and Dad do grown-up things like mop the kitchen floor. I know it's hard not to lose your temper, but try focusing on the positive achievements your children are making during this often frustrating and always exciting time.

~ *Parent Soup member Varula*

The Payoff

When you least expect it your kids will say or do something that you've been drumming into their heads. Then you'll feel like a million, because believe it or not they do absorb some things you try and teach them in life. When those moments happen, save them, like pearls or diamonds or shooting stars, and remember them for days when you feel overwhelmed. Just remember, for every step back there are two forward. The problem is, when you get the steps forward is a crapshoot.

~ *Parent Soup member MasIM35*

A Mother's Mantra

I have a two-and-a-half-year-old son and a six-month-old son. We've gone through all kinds of adjustments, tears, tantrums, the whole bit. I mean all of us, not just my toddler! Through it all, I keep in mind this quote: "God, help me endure my blessings."

~ *Parent Soup member Ckhunter2*

When Single Parenting Adds Extra Frustration

Q: I'm a single mom of a sweet little boy who just turned three. You're probably wondering why I'm writing you if he is so sweet. Well, I guess the problem is: how do I learn to let the small stuff slide? I stress out over things I can't control. Then when I'm at my stress limit my sweet adorable son starts whining (a sound that triggers the urge to scream and strangle). Any suggestions? There is no family close by.

~ *Cari M., Fairmont, West Virginia*

THE ELIUMS' POINT OF VIEW

A: You are experiencing a common single-parent syndrome. Parenting alone is demanding, and when you have reached your stress limit, you want to blow. This is when a partner would take your son to give you some time off. How do you create time off as a single mom? Creating a parenting team is vital for you to be able to feel good about your mothering and the other parts of your life. Join a mothers' support group or start one if there are none in your area. These groups provide support, advice, and co-op day care, so you can have a few hours for a nap or shopping alone. To find one, check your local newspaper, library, grocery store, elementary school, church, or temple. You might find other mothers who need a break in your apartment complex or down the block. We know mothers who met other moms at the park where their kids played together while they talked, ate, and even took turns napping. With no family nearby, you'll want to create your own family of friends who will support and relieve you and take a role in your son's life.

The other issue to tackle is your reaction to stress, i.e., your urge to scream and strangle somebody. Let us assure you that these are normal urges for parents. We just do not want to act on them! Talking with someone about your feelings and stresses would help a lot. There may be past, unresolved traumas or issues that come up for you now that you are a mother. This is very common for many people. Our children can sometimes bring out the worst in us, and always the best! Seek out a good friend, therapist, minister, or other trusted person for solutions to deal with your stress. Many church and city educational programs offer classes in meditation, yoga, dance, painting, and other relaxation tools you may find helpful. It is important that you develop a personal life of your own to balance your challenging work as a mother. We recommend a delightful book by Shoshana Alexander called *In Praise of Single Parents: Mothers and Fathers Embracing the Challenge*. You may also find insight about your son in our book called *Raising a Son: Parents and the Making of a Healthy Man*. Best wishes!

When Patience Just Flies out the Window

Q: I am a 26-year-old mother of a three-and-a-half-year-old. I try to always be there for her. I come up with games to play, encourage her to write, and read her stories whenever she wants. I have raised her alone for three years (her father thinks it's the woman's role to raise children), and for the past six months I have had household help. My problem is that I seem to be getting less and less patient with her. She will do something—like spill her paint on the floor or not write her name properly or just generally be a child—and I seem not to be able to handle it. Someone told me that I expect her to grow up too fast, or, because I have raised her almost alone with no help day and night, I need a major vacation. I don't believe in dumping my child with someone. I chose to have her, and I will take responsibility. My husband just says I'm just too strict. Am I losing my motherly instincts, or am I turning into one of those horrible mothers?

~ *Parent Soup member Diahanne*

THE ELIUMS' POINT OF VIEW

A: Even the most wonderful and dedicated of mothers needs regular time away from her children to pursue adult interests and activities. Without this refreshment, we all become burned out, more impatient, more demanding, exhausted, and bored. Our children also begin to tune us out, and they, too, become bored with the same old routine. Depending upon their ages, of course, our children benefit from learning to trust other adults who care for them, and from playing with their peers. Your daughter is still very young, and needs to not be away from you for very long periods of time, but she may enjoy an afternoon of play with the children of other mothers that you enjoy talking with. Have a tea and invite other young mothers you know, or want to know better, for a play date; or meet friends you know with children for an afternoon in the park. Taking a class, or doing something you love, with a friend or on your own, such as shopping, painting, golfing, or swimming, once or twice a week, can do wonders to lift your spirits and renew your enthusiasm for the wonderful mothering job that you have been doing. Of course, you do not want to dump your child on someone else to care for her, but giving yourself the breaks that you need, so that you can be more fully present to mother your daughter, is vital. You owe it to yourself and your daughter. Do something fun for yourself, right away!

ASTHMA

Asthma is one of the most common disorders affecting children.

Thankfully, medical advances have made it possible for children with asthma to lead normal lives. But the search for the perfect combination of medicine for these children can be long and winding, even scary. Here, Dr. Greene shares his reasoned approach to treating asthma. So you—and your child—can breathe easily.

DR. GREENE'S INSIGHT

As many as 10 percent of children have some degree of asthma, and the number has been rising steadily since about 1980. Thankfully, advances in the diagnosis and treatment of asthma have dramatically improved life for these children. Today most children with properly managed asthma can lead a life unhindered by their disease. It shouldn't hold them back from even the highest levels of athletic competition, as recent Olympic gold medalists have shown.

Having said that, the death rate from asthma increased 46 percent in the last decade in spite of these treatment advances. A major cause of this increase in mortality is improper use of inhalers. Often children are handed several inhalers and never really understand the different functions and uses of each one.

Asthma is a chronic lung disease characterized by tight airways—a result of airway hyper-responsiveness. Our airways are designed to be responsive to harmful substances in the air. If we walk through clouds of smoke, our airways will shrink, protecting our delicate lung tissues from the noxious ingredients in the smoke. They should return to normal when we begin to breathe fresh air. People with asthma have an exaggerated tightening response.

Different people with asthma respond to different "triggers" such as smoke, allergens, environmental irritants, viral infections, or cold air. When we exercise, we breathe rapidly and are unable to bring air temperature all the way up to 98.6 degrees—particularly if we breathe through the mouth. Thus, asthmatics who are sensitive to cold air will often wheeze with exercise. (Wheezing, the classic asthma symptom, is the noise made by air moving through these tight airways.) Because asthmatics respond differently to different triggers, their airways are tighter at some times than at others.

Hyper-responsive airways tighten in three ways in response to triggers. First and most immediately, smooth muscle surrounding the airways constricts, narrowing the caliber of the airways. Second, the airways are narrowed by inflammation and swelling of the airway lining. This leads to the third component of airway narrowing, which is the accumulation of mucus and other fluids, which can plug the airways.

The goal of asthma therapy is for children to maintain their normal activity levels while free from symptoms such as wheezing, coughing, or breathlessness. There are different basic types of inhalers, albuterol (Proventil or Ventolin) and cromolyn (Intal). They belong to two different classes of asthma medications, which work entirely differently. Albuterol (Ventolin or Proventil) works almost instantly to relax the smooth muscles surrounding the airways. It quickly opens the airways and reduces symptoms. Unfortunately, its success is its greatest danger. All too often, children with wheezing will use a Proventil inhaler alone to treat the symptoms. Each time they use a puff of the inhaler they feel better, but all the while the airway lining is swelling and filling with mucus and fluid. Finally the symptoms come back, but the Proventil inhaler is no longer effective since the airway muscles are already as relaxed as they can get. At that point it is too late to relieve the swelling and inflammation, and the child suffocates.

Cromolyn (Intal) is an anti-inflammatory agent that works slowly to prevent inflammation and swelling. It helps blunt the airways' hyper-responsiveness. It is not useful as an emergency drug.

The National Asthma Education Program convened an expert panel to propose guidelines for the stepwise management of asthma. They defined mild asthma as brief wheezing, coughing, or shortness of breath with exercise (less than half an hour of symptoms). Mild asthma can include additional intermittent, brief (less than one hour) wheezing, coughing, shortness of breath, or tightness up to two times weekly, and infrequent (less than two times a month) nocturnal coughing and wheezing. Children with mild asthma are completely asymptomatic between exacerbations. For these children they recommended pretreating with one or two puffs of albuterol (Proventil or Ventolin) before exercise or exposure to other triggers and using two puffs of albuterol (Proventil or Ventolin) up to every four to six hours as needed for symptoms, not to exceed four times per day.

If albuterol is required daily, the child should be classed as having moderate asthma, and an anti-inflammatory agent should be the mainstay of therapy. For these children the panel recommended using an inhaler such as cromolyn (Intal) to prevent inflammation and swelling of the airways. The proper dosage is two puffs, two to four times per day. (This is a very safe medication that will help control symptoms and reduce the need for albuterol.) In addition, an albuterol inhaler (Proventil or Ventolin) should be used as needed to keep the child symptom-free. It may be used safely up to three or four times daily.

If a child is taking Intal regularly and still needs the Proventil three or four times per day on most days, he should see an asthma specialist. He will probably need an additional anti-inflammatory inhaler (such as an inhaled corticosteroid) as well as the Intal.

For a child with moderate asthma, Intal is the steady mainstay of treatment, and the Proventil should be used with one to two puffs whenever your child feels wheezing, coughing, shortness of breath, or chest tightness. It may also be used before exposure to any known trigger. It may be used up to three or four times per day.

There is no virtue to holding off treatment with albuterol if your child has symptoms. It is better to go ahead and use the Proventil. If the use becomes frequent, an additional anti-inflammatory medicine is needed. For some children, a home peak-flow meter is used to assess the amount of airway obstruction and the amount and type of medications needed. I would recommend this for anyone with moderate or severe asthma.

All too many families are given the mistaken understanding that all inhalers are interchangeable. The more you and your child understand about asthma and its treatment, the less it will impact his life.

ATTENTION SPAN

As you watch your child pick up one toy after another only to put them down and look for the next activity, it's hard not to hear the words *Attention Deficit Disorder* bouncing around your head. ADD has become a parenting buzzword, and its causes and effects are frequently misunderstood. Here, Dr. Greene explains this commonly diagnosed phenomenon.

A Cause for Concern?

Q: We have a three-and-a-half-year-old, and his attention span for anything is nil. He does know some of the alphabet and can count to seven. I am worried that he might have ADD because of his inability to concentrate on anything. The longest anything will hold his attention is for about 15 minutes, and that is usually when a program on television has someone singing. I would rather he not watch too much television, but his toys do not interest him—except to take them apart. Does anyone have any advice?

    ~ Parent Soup member LeaAnn0223

DR. GREENE'S INSIGHT

A: After a long day in the office, when I am ready to wind down with a quiet evening, my youngest son, almost three, is switching on his turbo jets! Where does he get that boundless energy?

When a toddler enters that stage of zest and fascination, it's almost a rite of passage of parenthood for the parents to remark, "If only we could bottle that energy and sell it, we would be rich!" A three-year-old's normal fountain of energy delights and exhausts, and sometimes frustrates and concerns, modern-day parents. Today we have heard of the medical condition Attention Deficit Hyperactivity Disorder (ADD or ADHD) and wonder if our children might be hyperactive. Just as some people are very tall, some are short, but most are of average height or close to it, something of a bell-shaped curve also applies when it comes to toddler energy level. There is an average period of extreme energy that lasts about a year and often includes the third birthday. This normal phase in normal children actually fits the official definition of ADD (*Diagnostic and Statistic Manual of Mental Disorders*, 3rd edition, revised) as a disturbance of at least six months during which at least eight of the following are present:

1. often fidgets with hands or feet or squirms in seat

2. has difficulty remaining seated when required to do so

3. is easily distracted by extraneous stimuli

4. has difficulty awaiting turns in games or group situations

5. often blurts out answers to questions before they have been completed

6. has difficulty following through on instructions from others (not due to oppositional behavior or failure of comprehension), e.g., fails to finish chores

7. has difficulty sustaining attention in tasks or play activities

8. often shifts from one uncompleted activity to another

9. has difficulty playing quietly

10. often talks excessively

11. often interrupts or intrudes on others, e.g., butts into other children's games

12. often does not seem to be listening to what is being said to him or her

13. often loses things necessary for tasks or activities at school or at home

14. often engages in physically dangerous activities without considering possible consequences (not for the purpose of thrill-seeking), e.g., runs into the street without looking

(Note: According to this definition, the farther up on the list one of these items is, the more important it is for diagnosing ADD.)

Parents who have tried to take a three-year-old out for a leisurely dinner in a quiet restaurant quickly learn that normal children at this age can exhibit all of these behaviors. Since these diagnostic characteristics are normal in young children, the cutoff should be at least 10 of these items, for at least one year in the preschool age group. Even so, the definition is not a totally accurate tool for pinpointing the child with ADD.

Perhaps a good way to tell whether a child's development is normal would be to ask his day-care providers, preschool teachers, or religious teachers. These adults see at close range a larger sampling of children. If your child is more active, more restless, less attentive, and more impulsive than the rest of the class, this will be a clue for you. But keep in mind that less than half of those actually diagnosed with ADD at age three, and only 10 percent of those who concern their early teachers, will be the ones who turn out to have ADD in the long run (*Journal of Child Psychology and Psychiatry*, September 1990). The toddler's full-tilt exuberance usually gives way to the dawning self-control of a preschooler at about age four. Different children go through this energetic stage at different ages. Those who still have 10 or more ADD symptoms at age four, though, have a much greater chance of truly having ADD.

There is still no reliable way to make the diagnosis of ADD in a three-year-old, but we now know that symptoms of impulsivity are more important than symptoms of restlessness or inattention. Thus, I would be more concerned about problems of social interactions with peers than with a short attention span, more concerned with those for whom it is difficult to obtain a babysitter than with those who are always on the go, and more concerned with those who consistently disrupt other children's play than with those who fail to listen. If you'd like more information, the best relevant book I have seen is *Attention Deficit Hyperactivity Disorder, A Handbook for Diagnosis and Treatment*, by Russell A. Barkley, Ph.D.

As much energy as it takes to keep up with my now three-year-old son, I shall dearly miss these days when they are over.

A Fellow Parent Answers

A: My three-year-old sounds just like yours, and I used to be concerned, too. But I've learned that it's pretty typical for this age. A suggestion—make sure he gets lots of physical activity throughout the day. Running, climbing, jumping, dancing, and just acting silly will help make sure he burns off energy so he's not so restless when it's time to play indoors. Do you have a park nearby where he can play with other kids? You may want to look into age-appropriate classes such as swim lessons, dancing, or gymnastics to help keep him active through the cold-weather months. You can also see if your library has any books or videos on activities for preschoolers. You may also want to limit the number of toys available at one time. Pack up a box with stuff he hasn't used for awhile, then bring some of it out at a later date. When you bring out the new toys, pack away the current toys for awhile. Sometimes kids just get overstimulated with too much stuff. It's really tough having a busybody, but be grateful he's healthy and inquisitive. You probably have a future engineer/inventor/ scientist on your hands!

~ *Laura F., Cicero, Indiana*

BATH TIME

You may have a toddler who's part fish and more than willing to rip off his clothes and jump in the tub at the merest whisper of "bath time." But if your toddler is part cat, and bristles and hisses when it's time to bathe, you're not alone. Try some of the ingenious suggestions below for wheedling a reluctant child into the tub.

The Problem

Q: My son has never liked his hair washed, but we have always managed to get through bath time. This week, bath time is like putting a cat in water, screaming, kicking, and hitting. Any suggestions on how to get my son back in the water? He is 16 months old.

~ *Parent Soup member Nrsegdbdy*

Bubble Power

A: I used to have a hard time bathing my son, until my sister gave him a bath with lots of bubbles. For some reason he feels safer if he can't see the bottom of the tub.

~ *Lisa W., Hudson, New Hampshire*

A Tub of a Different Color

A: My two-year-old son went through a phase where he refused to take a
bath. Luckily it was summer, so I bought a plastic child's pool. Every
day I put it on the patio and filled it with warm water and bubbles.
He never knew it was bath time. By the time it got too cold for a pool,
he had outgrown the stubbornness.

~ *Shelly B., Walnut Creek, California*

Help for the Shampoo Phobic

A: Cabbage Patch has bath pals. Each one has a little hair. You can have
your daughter wash the doll's hair while you wash hers. The doll
comes with a shower too—it could help with another transition later,
who knows.

~ *Parent Soup member L84work2*

Hose Them Down

A: Have you tried one of those bath hoses that hooks to the water spout
and sprays water like a shower? Ours is shaped like a turtle, and both
kids (ages 2½ and 13 months) love it. This hose also makes it a lot
easier to control the flow of water and keep it from running down
their faces.

~ *Lisa K., Tucker, Georgia*

The Old Hand-Off

A: I got so sick of the bath-time battle that my solution was this—my son
goes in the shower with Daddy! Now this does not always work, but if
you're quick in the morning you can get him in there before Daddy

knows what's going on. Then hand him the shampoo and say by the way he needs his hair washed! When I tried it, there was no noise, not one peep from the kid. (Daddy had something to say, but at least I can reason with him.)

~ *Gigi T., Providence, Rhode Island*

BEHAVIOR *(See also Biting, No!, Sanity Savers, Tantrums, Time-Out, and Whining)*

To a toddler, the world is a very exciting place. The baby who used to be content to do whatever you felt like doing is now only too eager to run from one activity to the next. Every situation is an opportunity to learn and to assert his newly developed concept of free will. His job is to learn how to navigate the world on his own, while your responsibility is to help him do so safely and enjoyably. As any parent of a toddler can tell you, this can be quite a challenge.

This chapter is not about really bad behavior, such as tantrums, biting, or screaming "No!" at whatever you say (there are separate entries on those). The information here will help you understand *why* your toddler behaves the way he does when he defies you, or ignores you, or breaks down into tears at the slightest little thing. It will also help you figure out how best to ease your toddler through the transition to a decision-making individual. Despite what you may be thinking, the parents of Parent Soup attest that yes, it is possible.

The Way They Do the Things They Do
Defiance seems to be part of the three-year-old's job requirement. There is always a lot of "No" screamed loudly, and "I don't want it" or "I don't like it anyway." On those days, it's particularly exhausting and I feel like pulling out my hair strand by strand. It seems he wants to push the envelope as much as possible. I know he's just trying to test to see how much power he has. All I have been able to do is to try to talk to him, explain why he can't do or shouldn't have something. I try to give him choices so that he feels like he has control over some aspects of his life, and it does help. The truth is, it's a hard learning process for them and us at this stage.

~ *Parent Soup member JustTeeezn*

Understanding the Mind of a Toddler
Toddlers are, by nature, very self-centered. They don't understand that other people have feelings, and no amount of hitting and yelling is going to teach them. Learning about the feelings of others takes time and a lot of patience on the part of the parents. It is very frustrating to be a toddler, especially if the child is not very verbal. Children who can't express their feelings in words may lash out because it is the only way they know to get attention. The best way to stop negative, attention-seeking behavior is to deny the attention.

~ *Parent Soup member JulJimEvKy*

The thing that helps me most in those terrible-twos moments is to always look at things from my daughter's perspective. She's just a little bundle of emerging emotions with little or no control over herself or anything else, yet she's driven to explore and learn as much as possible. I always try to do more than just say no to her, and it works beautifully. For instance,

37

she started pitching a fit every time I tried to clear her plate from the table (even though she was finished and playing in the other room). "Mine! Mine! Mine!" she would bellow. So after a few negative confrontations, I took an extra moment after the meal to ask her if she was done, and if so, could she please clear her plate, scrape the leftover food into the garbage, and put her dish in the dishwasher, and guess what—she loves doing it! It makes her part of the family rather than just a little baby who gets no respect. I think it's a basic instinct we all have to feel like we're important and needed, toddlers included. It's amazing how many tantrums we've circumvented simply by asking her to be part of the solution instead of just saying no.

~ *Lisa C., Petaluma, California*

Putting It into Perspective
Consider how many times a child must fall off a bike before he is able to ride it, or how many times he'll swing at a ball before he hits it with the bat. Whether a child is learning physical control or emotional control, mastering these skills takes time.

~ *Parent Soup member marisa*

Taking the "Struggle" out of Power Struggle
My husband and I make every possible effort to diffuse, diffuse, diffuse. All my daughter wants is the opportunity to be in control, and if no one is being hurt and no rules are being broken we try to let her have her say. That is not to say that we sacrifice our needs or our comfort. We don't, but she is capable of negotiating with us, and we get beautiful behavior out of her whenever we engage in calm conversations that offer her a bit of the power. So we give her choices: She wants a popsicle for breakfast? No, we won't be having popsicles this morning, but you can make a

choice between yogurt or cereal. It usually works. Other key concepts to remember are respect and gentle voices and touches.

~ *Parent Soup member GODCC*

When to Offer a Choice

I have a two-and-a-half-year-old, and I have some advice. Never *ask* a toddler to do something if it's something he must do (such as "Do you want to eat lunch?" or, "Do you want to go to bed?"). Just tell him it's lunchtime or bedtime. However, if you can give him a choice, do (such as "Do you want to read this book or that one?"). Also, I only offer a choice of two things.

~ *Julie K., Powder Springs, Georgia*

I say, "It's time to make a choice, would you like _____ or _____?" The decision made by my child is the final word. If a crying spell occurs, I quietly remind that we can "try again" another time. This has been really helpful, because I don't believe a parent should have to keep changing whatever it is the child wants, over and over. After all, we are parents, not slaves.

~ *Parent Soup member Skiinaz*

Casting a Positive Light

I have a two-and-a-half-year-old who is very "spirited." When his behavior starts to get the best of me, I try to keep a positive attitude and to see him and his traits in a positive light. I tell myself he's not obnoxious, he's persistent, he can really "stick to" something. I went so far as to describe him on a piece of paper, and then next to all the things I had written (they were not flattering) I wrote what is positive about that trait. I stuck it to the refrigerator and remind myself often, because yes, I do have to remind myself. I also have been somewhat successful lately in telling him about himself. I say to him, "You have difficulty calming down so you can go to bed, so we need to sit quietly for awhile, ОК?" Or, "Screaming makes you feel bad, doesn't it? It makes me feel bad, too." Sometimes he'll even say, "Mommy, I'm too excited and I need book time." He is getting better, even if the improvement is incremental.

~ *Parent Soup member Sarkan2353*

Watch how you word it! Positive phrases work wonders. Instead of saying, "You have to go to bed at 8:30," say, "You get to stay up as late as 8:30."

~ *Christina M., Galion, Ohio*

Give Them Room to Breathe

I find that when I just sort of ignore my kids, meaning not jumping on them about every little thing and constantly correcting them, they actually behave better anyway. It's like when my boss isn't looking over my shoulder all day, I do really good work, but I'm constantly defensive if he's right there to criticize me. Maybe that's how kids feel too. There's nothing worse than a nagging and bored and frustrated mother screaming at you all day, I would imagine. So, just let the child be a child—and let yourself be one too sometimes!

~ *Tracy R., Englewood, Ohio*

Catch Them Being Good

I have found that praising my kids when they are doing what I like encourages more of the same behavior. I try to ignore when they are really grating on my nerves (which can be very hard to do). Kids love attention, and they will do whatever they can to get it. If they get the most attention when they are doing "acceptable" things, then they will do more of that behavior in order to continue getting attention.

~ *Susan G., Calabasas, Georgia*

Rewarding Good Behavior

Something that helped with my son was a reward system for behavior modification. When he gets through a morning (or other specific time period) without a tantrum or acting out, he gets a star. Post a card on the refrigerator (or other "public place") with a specific number of spaces on it (you decide how many to earn a prize of his choosing, such as a toy or special meal). You can also post the prize next to the card, so that he can see the progress he's making. When he fills the card with stars, he gets the prize. This worked for both my children, and it saved a lot of gray hairs for Mom.

~ *Mary K. H., East Lansing, Michigan*

Consistency Is the Key

I am the mother of a five-year-old and a three-year-old, and I have worked very hard at getting them to behave. When my son was one, I would say "No" and physically get up and redirect him, every time. I would tell him why not, such as, "If you break that, I would feel hurt, I like it." I never raise my voice to him unless it is dangerous. My son takes my "No" very seriously to this day. There is

PARENT POLL

Do you judge people by the way their kids behave?

Of 911 total votes

yes 38%

no 62%

1 bowl = 100 parents

41

no waste of breath for me and no curiosity for him. It took a lot of work and time and burning the chicken, but it all paid off!

~ *Parent Soup member mizzens*

Teaching Compassion

When my toddler son starts acting out and throwing things around the room, I use a combination of things that seem to have helped lessen the throwing fits. First of all, I tell him that I love him, but how unhappy I am about his attitude, which works sometimes and not sometimes (it depends on how feisty he's feeling). If that doesn't work, I try to give the object thrown or hit feelings like a person in an attempt to make him understand that it's not good to throw. For example, when he picks up one of his toy cars and throws it against the wall, I'll say, "Now, that wasn't a very nice way to treat your truck. It doesn't like being thrown against the wall and getting broken." I try to play on his compassion for hurting something else. I'll even go as far as to pick it up and cradle it and tell it how sorry I am that its little boy was mean to it, and a lot of the time he'll come over and hug it himself and tell it he's sorry. Then I have a talk with him about it, and that usually ends the throwing for a while. I have found that appealing to my son's compassion or emotions rather than all-out discipline has helped wonders, and I hope that it will someday teach him to be a more sensitive person.

~ *Parent Soup member JustTeeezn*

"I Wish You Weren't My Mom"

My four-year-old son has started telling me that he wishes I weren't his mom when I either tell him to do something or tell him he can't do something! He has been such an easy child, it sort of shocked me. But I just laugh to myself and tell him, "Well, I'm sorry about that. I still love you." Then he harrumphs and snorts and stomps off.

~ *Kathleen H., Fairfax Station, Virginia*

I think you are handling this in exactly the right manner. Kids say things like this for shock value, and I'm sure it worked the first time you heard it. I think by using the reaction you described you are not only showing that the shock value isn't working, you are showing your child that no matter what he says or does you will always love him and be there for him and that there will always be unbreakable rules because you love him. You must be a great mom.

~ *Angela K., South Bound Brook, New Jersey*

Removing Distractions
What works with us is simplicity. Our house is simple now: our coffee table is clear, so are the end tables (of breakables and tearables). That way our daughter can roam around and be safe and not get yelled at. It's hard at this age because she is just curious, so we try and take away the items she gets a hold of. Out of sight, out of mind seems simple, but it works for us.

~ *Parent Soup member HoneyPup*

Should I Give in to Her Demands?
Q: I have a two-year-old daughter who is occasionally very demanding. She will repeat her demand over and over again, continuing for as long as 10 to 15 minutes, no matter what my wife and I say or do. She only stops if we give in to her demands—"I want ice cream" or "Wanna go to the park." What can we do to stop her from

KIDS SAY THE DARNEDEST THINGS

I have a daughter who will be three and another who will be nine. One day the nine-year-old had a friend over and I jokingly said to this friend, "Pick up this mess, I am not your maid." My three-year-old said, "No Mom, you're mine."

~ *Parent Soup member Ljbowers18*

repeating her demands over and over (other than giving in)? It's driving us crazy.

~ *Parent Soup member Dchun*

THE ELIUMS' POINT OF VIEW

A: When little ones consistently use a behavior that drives us crazy, we have to wonder about it. If we look at your daughter's persistence carefully, her behavior may signal a talent or skill that is too big for her to handle right now, but will serve her well when she is older. If you imagine your daughter 25 years from now, with her ability to demand something over and over again until she gets her way (in a more positive and mature form), what might her gift or career be? An attorney? An environmental activist? A fund-raiser? A legislator? A mom? When we imagine that irritating habit of hers as a potentially useful trait, the next question is, how do we help her manage it now, without going crazy? With a child who makes great demands and who has such persistence in getting them fulfilled, parents must be very clear about what the rules are and when to say "Yes" and "No." Many of us catch ourselves automatically saying "No" to something out of habit, like our parents did, and starting a power struggle. If we think about it a minute, we could just as well say "Yes," with no harm done. So we must be very clear within ourselves about what is OK and not OK. When something is definitely not

PARENT POLL

If someone else's child were misbehaving in front of you and his parents, but the parents weren't doing anything about it, would you correct the child?

Of 900 total votes

yes 52%

no 48%

1 bowl = 100 parents

OK, such as going to the park when dinner is on the table, you must be firm in your resolution to say "No," and find good distraction techniques. Humor often works well—not the cutting, biting form, but kind, gentle humor. Breaking out in a silly song about the situation sometimes helps, too. With someone as young as your daughter, we can be surprised at her tenacity, but her want is real, so we do not imply that you treat it lightly, just that you firmly let her know that you are the leader and you make the decisions. Feeling secure that her parents are taking care of the details while she can explore her world will allow your daughter to grow into this gift that is now driving you crazy.

Why Won't My Son Listen to Me?

Q: My son, four years old, doesn't listen to us. At home, there are times when I have to ask him to do something (or not do something) several times. His preschool teacher says the same thing. She will call him two or three times from the play yard and will finally have to walk over and get him. This concerns me since there may be situations where I may need his immediate attention, and I'm afraid that he will not listen at a critical time. We have tried time-out, yelling, whispering— you name it, we've done it. What do you suggest?

~ *Susan W., Covina, California*

DR. GREENE'S INSIGHT

A: Sometimes when we talk to our children, it feels like a surrealistic play, where we repeat ourselves over and over, and no one seems to hear. Imagine this scenario: Your son is jumping on the sofa. You say, "Stop jumping on the sofa!" No response. "I said stop jumping on the sofa!!!" No response. "How many times do I have to tell you? If you don't stop

45

right now you'll get a spanking!" No response. "Why can't you be more like your sister?" No response. "Stop that!" He shrugs and walks away. Sound familiar?

Occasionally, there is a physical problem. If you are concerned that your son is unable to hear, understand, or attend well, take him to his pediatrician for evaluation. Otherwise, you are experiencing a trial faced in varying degrees by most parents. But why do children who can hear perfectly well tune us out? Kids are passionate about a great many things. They are full of energy, always wanting to play, to move, to explore. As adults, we are anchored by responsibilities, wanting peace, courtesy, safety, order. These agendas collide. We feel frustrated; they feel nagged; we all grumble. The grand adventure of parenting is learning to bring these two worlds together in a creative union, using what I like to call bi-empathic vision. Practice seeing events from both perspectives. Let your focus soften with your son so that one "eye" continues to see what you as a wise parent sees, while the other tries to see what your child sees. With this dual vision, let's look at how you both feel after the sofa scenario: You are frustrated, angry, concerned that you're losing control, and worried that he won't respond in an emergency. He feels hurt, squelched, misunderstood, and angry. He thinks the sofa is more important to you than he is, he resents his sister, and he wants you to leave him alone. Worst of all, he learns nothing positive.

Now let's try the sofa scenario again, using bi-empathic vision: You might say, "Jumping on the sofa is so fun! I love to jump, but jumping hurts the sofa and it might hurt you. Let's go jump on an old pillow!" (You scoop him up, or take him by the hand, put an old pillow on the floor, and jump together, giggling.) How do you both feel this time? You enjoy your son, and you spend less time and energy than in scenario one. He is giggling, feels understood, and realizes you think he's important. This time he learns that jumping hurts the sofa, there are better places to jump, and "Mom loves me." This is a long process. There will be many moments of exasperation. But, nothing compares to the thrill of bringing your two worlds together in a burst of creativity. Not only will you raise your son well, but he will raise you to new levels of empathy, compassion, and wisdom.

BIRTHDAY PARTIES

Birthday parties are prime memory-making opportunities. Most folks have at least one picture of themselves as a tot blowing out candles, or ripping open presents, or smearing frosting over anything that stands still. With toddlers, who are still learning the art of playing together, a successful party with smiling guests and a giddy guest of honor is not a given. Here are some ideas for simple parties that are high on fun, low on cost, and that have delighted toddlers. Just pick the idea that corresponds most to your toddler's age and idea of fun, and get that camera ready.

Lots of Games Without a Lot of Cost
Toddlers don't have the longest attention span, so keep that in mind and don't get frustrated if they don't all want to play games. You might want to have two or three activities for them to choose from, but you don't have to spend a ton of money to have fun: Have a bubble-blowing contest. Spread butcher paper along a fence or wall and let them color or paint on it, and then save it as a souvenir. Or have them all make funny paper hats and decorate them as an activity.

    ~ Parent Soup member Tickle1245

Simple games are the best for three-year-olds. How about playing musical chairs? Or tossing beanbags into a bucket? (Make the beanbags out of socks filled with beans, tied at the end.) Or glue some Velcro to a "pin the tail on the donkey" game and also on the "tails" for a pin-free game. The most important thing is to have fun and make memories!

    ~ Parent Soup member Teach2mch

Break the Ice

If you don't mind mildly destroying a couple of rooms in your house, I've got a great game idea for those first few moments of a party that can be awkward. Buy a package of sturdy string or twine. With your kids' help, wind it all around your house (living room, wherever), going under furniture, around tables, etc. Attach a prize to the "hidden" end and make sure you have the other end near the front door, or the entry to the party room. Then do it again with enough strings for each guest (and maybe one or two extra in case something weird happens). I would remove anything breakable, including lamps, before doing this, and make sure the furniture can take the abuse this game is bound to cause. I suppose you could do this outside, which might actually be more fun. Anyway, the longer and more "spidery" you make the strings, the longer the game will take.

    ~ Parent Soup member LRTS

Edible Art

One of the best ideas we had for my daughter's fourth birthday party was to have shortbread dough for the kids in various colors with various decorations for them to make their own treats when they arrived. I mixed the dough the day before, and every crumb of it was used.

    ~ Parent Soup member medusa

PARENT POLL

How much do you usually spend on a birthday present for one of your child's friends?

Of **745** total votes

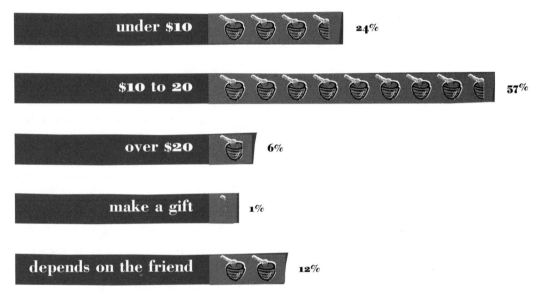

under **$10**   **24**%

$10 to 20   **57**%

over **$20**   6%

make a gift   **1**%

depends on the friend   **12**%

1 bowl = 50 parents

b birthday parties

A Hit with Baseball Fans

My kids' favorite has always been "pin the ____ on the ____," whether it's the tail on Tigger, or the ladder on the fire engine. How about "pin the bat on the baseball player"? Get a big piece of posterboard and draw a baseball player. Then make some bats out of other posterboard and write the kids' names on them. Make a blindfold out of a piece of material, and you're all set.

~ *Kathleen H., Fairfax Station, Virginia*

Get This Party off the Ground

We held my son's third birthday party at the airport, and it was fantastic. The children could watch the planes take off and land, and everyone had a great time. It was my son's idea. A bunch of people I know have had parties there since then.

~ *Tarrant F., Gainesville, Florida*

Welcome to the Dollhouse

I had a doll party for my daughter's fourth birthday. Each girl brought her favorite doll, and we made necklaces for the girls and the dolls. Then we had a doll parade, and each girl received a prize. The awards were for the prettiest hair, shoes, etc. I made awards for them on the computer. We also had a doll piñata and a beauty treasure box. I made the treasure box out of a big gift box and filled it with lipstick, hair supplies, etc. They all had a wonderful time.

~ *Michele B., Bethlehem, Pennsylvania*

Commemorate the Day

At your child's next birthday party, take a picture of each guest with the gift they bring. Make double prints—one for your child, and one to

50

include with his thank-you notes. This way, you'll have a little **memento** to give each guest.

~ Parent Soup member A Souper Mom

Do We Invite Everyone in the Preschool Class?
Have you thought of having a cake party at your son's school? **That way all the kids would feel like they were invited and get some cake. Then you could invite the selected few to the party at your house and not feel guilty.** I used to teach, and one time a mom brought in undecorated cupcakes, white frosting in little cups, and various sprinkles. **The kids had a ball decorating their own cupcakes! (Be sure to check with the teacher first, it is messy.)**

~ Parent Soup member deblee

BITING

As babies grow into toddlers, they are struggling to learn how to communicate their desires. Often, those desires ("I want that toy") bring them into contact with another child who wants that toy too. When this happens, there's a good chance that your toddler won't know how to handle it. She may try to exert her opinion in the most immediate way she knows how ("CHOMP"). So if your child starts biting you or the kids in day care or your evil Aunt Irma, don't hide your head in shame, convinced that she'll grow up to be the female version of Mike Tyson. It's a normal phase that children undergo as they learn to communicate with other people. And it's fixable, with the right approach. Below are some tactics that have worked for others:

b biting

Is My Child Normal?
As a toddler teacher, I can tell you that biting is normal behavior for children this age. Most toddlers do not know how to use their words so when they get upset or angry their first reaction is to bite.

~ *Amy H., San Diego, California*

Change the Subject
My 16-month-old son started biting me about a month ago. If I really reacted (by making a face or saying "Ouch"), he thought it was funny and kept doing it. What I started to do was say "No" very forcefully, pick him up, and try to change the subject by pointing at things outside the window, look at the dog, whatever. I didn't want to make a big deal out of it, and by diverting his attention, he'd soon forgot about it. Now he bites only once in a while, and I handle it the same way.

~ *Lynne A., Endicott, New York*

Give Them the Words to Express Their Anger
When my daughter would bite, I would give her an alternative to her anger (something my parents didn't do) by saying something like "You cannot bite the baby, but you can jump up and down and yell 'I'm angry!'" Then I empathize with her: "You're angry she did this. I'd be angry, too." Punishments didn't work. Instead, I'd try to get her to understand why she has to behave (so she doesn't hurt others) and use lots of feeling phrases like "It sounds like you're angry because . . ."

~ *Parent Soup member BS51S*

Give Them Something to Chew On
I have a son who bites. He would laugh when we tried to discipline him, and the harsher our voices, the funnier it was to him. What we did that

finally worked for us was to find some teething toys or any toys it is OK for him to bite. Every time he bites the wrong thing, we tell him we don't bite that but it's OK to bite this and give him the biting toy. We had about six or seven of them that we kept around so there was always one when we needed one. We carried it out in our normal voices and tried not to pay any more attention to it than that, and the biting stopped shortly after.

~ *Parent Soup member Okizu*

Look for Instigators

My daughter bit her sister constantly. They're 16 months apart. She started at about 22 months. It was just when her sister started becoming mobile. She bit less when we cut out her favorite movie, *The Lion King*. There's a lot of biting in it. And she finally stopped completely as soon as she started talking. I think she was getting frustrated trying to communicate.

~ *Parent Soup member TonyaRosa*

Pay Attention to the Bitee

My oldest daughter was a biter, but it only lasted about a month. She seemed to do it to see the excitement it caused! What we did was to remove her immediately from where she was, tell her no biting, and sit her by herself. Then we gave all our attention to the victim and lavished him with kisses and a treat to make him feel better. She decided it didn't pay and stopped biting pretty quickly.

~ *Donna B., San Bernardino, California*

How Common Is This Behavior?

Q: I am quite bothered by my 19-month-old boy's habit of biting. If I turn my back for a second, he is attempting to bite. One of the

b biting

children that he has bitten has quite a mark on her cheek, and the
child's mother has said I need to get help for my son. I'd like to know
how common this is with other children his age. Any advice that you
could give me would be appreciated.

~ *Elaine C., St. John's, Newfoundland*

DR. GREENE'S INSIGHT

A: What a sinking feeling to see, or hear about, your toddler biting another
child. It may be comforting to know that most parents will go through this at
one time or another as their children explore the wide variety of ways to
interact with others in their search to find the best ways to relate. Your son
is at an age where the urge for exploration and experimentation propels him
forward throughout the day. He is also continually seeking to attract
attention, especially from adults. Once he began to toddle and began
encountering other children, a whole new world of decisions opened up—to
approach or run away, and how to respond if he and another child both want
to play with the same toy or be with the same person. Somewhere in this
time period most children experiment with biting to see how exerting this
power will affect their interactions with other kids—whether it will get them
the things or the attention they want (children want attention even more
than toys and playthings). What your son is going through is quite normal.
The biting behavior can be reinforced by paying lots of attention to it, even
if it is negative attention. To help him grow quickly through the biting stage,
when you observe biting, say, "No!" firmly, so he can tell you are not
pleased, then repeat and name the behavior, "No biting!" Then scoop him up
from the situation, set a timer for about two minutes (the rule of thumb is
one minute for every year he is old), and pay no attention to him for the
next two minutes, even if he acts sorry or angry. Instead, lavish attention on
the bitten child. When the two minutes are up, go right on with your son as

if nothing has happened. You will have to repeat this scenario a number of times, but it will teach him that biting is not the way to get the things he wants. Consistency is important, so if you are going to leave him with other adults in charge, ask them to take the same approach. It is a fine idea to use distraction as well. When you see a situation arising where you think your son might bite, you might want to distract one or another of the parties involved and delay these learning experiments until he is a little older and can learn more quickly.

BOTTLES *(See also Pacifiers and Thumb-Sucking)*

 As your toddler lets go of babyhood, he may cling to some vestiges of his old life as a completely dependent creature—bottles and pacifiers are two obvious examples of this. Sucking is an excellent way for babies to calm themselves, and your toddler is young enough to remember this. So he may come to rely on his bottle as comfort in the face of all the new challenges he encounters on a daily basis. There is something beautiful about having a child who knows how to comfort himself, and you may not want to deprive him of his bottle on the assumption that he will give it up when he's good and ready. There are many parents, some represented here, who agree with you.

There are also other concerns that argue for weaning your child before he weans himself. They include tooth decay from consuming too much milk or any juice (particularly at night), peer pressure (as your child starts interacting more with other children in a day-care or preschool setting), and a future need of orthodontics. The posts below will not only help you decide if you should wean your child from the bottle, but also give you some successful strategies to try if you decide it's time.

Why Children Cling to the Bottle

Like a thumb or pacifier, the bottle is an emotional crutch that a child relies on when tired, scared, stressed, or just needs something to relax him. Two is a hard age for a child. He is feeling his independence, yet at the same time still wants to hold on. These two feelings are constantly doing battle. Think of the bottle as a white flag. I didn't force any of my kids to give it up. They all did it by themselves by age two. They will find out that they can get liquid quicker from a cup and start asking for a cup and refusing the bottle. I always found this sad—good-bye, baby. Kids are a lot smarter than we think they are. It took me three kids to figure this out.

~ *Parent Soup member Kwhita8852*

Never Mind the Naysayers

Honestly, I think the bottle bothers people a lot more than it should. If your child brushes her teeth well and has a good appetite for solid food, what's the hurry? My sister's daughter stayed on the bottle until she was over three. One day she came home from preschool and said, "No more bottles, I am a big girl." If you can tolerate the criticism from others and just let your child enjoy this comfort, you may feel a great weight lifted from your shoulders. I've never heard of a five-year-old starting kindergarten with a bottle in her lunch box!

~ *Parent Soup member Amoskb*

From Bottle to Cup

Have you tried substituting the bottle for a no-spill cup with water in it? We weaned our son at 19 months from a bottle this way. He just turned two, and he still has to go to sleep with his water every night. But since it's water, it can't hurt anything, so why not?

~ *Debra G., Tuscon, Arizona*

Switch to a Sports Bottle

I had success by switching my son to a sports water bottle, with the spout you suck on, not the straw. Another idea: give him only water in the bottle and milk or juice from a cup.

~ *Parent Soup member MNKYDU*

Remove Temptation

Make sure you get the bottles out of the house so it isn't an option to give her one. We have already spent over $1,500 on dental bills making up for that mistake. You also need to provide a substitute security object. If she has a blanket, keep giving that to her when she cries for her bottle.

~ *Parent Soup member Xccow*

Involve Your Child in the Process

This is what I did with my oldest son when he was around two. After he got used to drinking from his cup—he wasn't very good at it, but good enough—I had him take all of his bottles and put them in a trash bag, then I walked him to the garbage can, and he put them in it. He did not ask for his bottle until that night, when he wanted his "nite-nite" bottle. I explained to him what he did so he could be a big boy. He did cry a little the first few nights, but it wasn't too bad.

~ *Jennifer G., Salt Lake City, Utah*

b bottles

Stop the Suction

Try using a straight razor to shave a little off the top of the nipple. Continue every day until the top of the nipple is a hole that your child can drink from, but not suck. Once the sucking satisfaction is gone, she may be more willing to take the milk from the cup.

~ Kristine S., Port Reading, New Jersey

The Old Switch-A-Roo

Start diluting the milk with water, gradually, until you change it over to all water without him knowing. My daughter had a bottle we couldn't wean her from, until we tried this.

~ Tara L., Glenshaw, Pennsylvania

Sounds like a Job for the Bottle Fairy

My daughter got used to going to sleep with a bottle of milk. Finally we started to only give her water in her bottle, no matter if she screamed or cried. She soon developed a tolerance to that and then drank a bottle of water each night from the bottle. When my daughter was about two-and-a-half-years-old, I told her that the "bottle fairy" was going to come and collect all of her bottles and take them away to give them to babies who had none. I told her that the bottle fairy would leave a toy in its place. I also told her that I wasn't sure when she was coming, but I was sure it would be soon because she was getting so big. I let this bottle fairy talk go on for about a week before I actually snuck in her room one night and replaced her bottle with a light-up Mickey Mouse doll. She was thrilled. That night, when she asked for her bottle I told her that there was nothing I could do, as the bottle fairy took it and she had no phone. It worked. The important thing is to really build it up, so she is anticipating it. We even had a little celebration when the bottle fairy came, and showed her new toy to everyone and told them who she got it from.

~ *Kathleen C., Winthrop, Massachusetts*

How Old Is Too Old?

Q: My daughter, who is almost four years old, still wants a bottle to go to sleep. What action can I take to finally end this routine?

~ *Wendy K., Washington, District of Columbia*

DR. GREENE'S INSIGHT

A: When a four-year-old is still using a bottle to go to sleep there are two patterns that must be overcome. First, she has chosen the bottle as her lovey, or special comfort object, to help her with the transition from a wakeful state to a sleep state. Secondly, this choice has become a deeply ingrained habit. Weaning her from the bottle will require either finding an effective substitute, or using tremendous force to break the patterns.

Your daughter's insistent urge to grow is a powerful force that can be harnessed to help effect the change. Engage her cooperation. Set a date in the near future, perhaps her fourth birthday, and offer her an exciting opportunity: to celebrate this milestone, she can collect all her bottles, take them to a local store, and trade them in for something that would be thrilling to her (perhaps a bicycle, a pair of roller skates, or a hamster—something that will make her feel more grown-up). If she looks forward to the date, she may be able to sacrifice the bottle in order to enter a new phase. Be sure to communicate in a way that builds her security and self-esteem: you are excited about who she is as a three-year-old; you will be excited about who she becomes as a four-year-old.

If you are not able to enlist her resources directly, weaning the bedtime bottle can be accomplished by substituting the bottle with a more age-appropriate comfort object. Make the alternative as attractive as possible, while making the bottle less attractive. This new transition to sleep might include a consistent bedtime ritual, when you spend about 20 minutes together doing the same nighttime activities in the same order. A large stuffed animal (about the same size she is) or doll that she falls in love with would be good choices. Or you may want to make a tape recording of your voice singing to her or telling her stories to comfort her as she drifts off to sleep. You know your own daughter best. Select comforting measures that will touch her most deeply. To make the bottle less attractive, try adding a drop of "bitter apple" on the nipple or actually in the bottle (available in pet stores to teach pets not to chew). A small amount will give the bottle a mildly bitter or musty taste, making it a less desirable part of the sleep transition. Many children will stop asking for the bottle within one to two weeks. If neither of these approaches work, you will need to energize the process yourself. Offer milk (or something else to drink) in a cup at the beginning of the bedtime ritual—before reading a story, taking a bath, or brushing her teeth. Reduce the amount she gets in her bottle by half an ounce a day until it is empty, then take the bottle away. Respond to requests for the bottle with hugs. It's best to wean her from the bottle before peer pressure steps in. Peer pressure will do the job, but only by threatening her self-esteem.

CAR SEATS

The backseat of your car used to be home to random shoes, old magazines, coffee cups, and perhaps a beat-up road map or two. Now its main purpose is to house that omnipresent indicator of parenthood—the car seat. Gone are the days when little ones would have free roam of the back of the family station wagon. Nowadays, the sight of a footloose toddler in a car is about as unusual (and as much a cause of alarm) as King Kong scaling the Empire State Building. The only problem is, *many toddlers don't like getting strapped in a car seat*. Not even a little bit. Read on to find out how to keep your little one happy and safe in a car seat.

Squirming out of the Car Seat

Q: I am at my wits' end. My daughter is 20 months old and has gotten out of every car seat we have tried—even a booster seat that she is really very small for. She only weighs 32 pounds. She squirms and slides out of everything. If I sit next to her and physically hold her, she screams as if I am killing her. I cannot take her anywhere by myself. I do not know what to do.

    ~ Parent Soup member Kimmie1849

A: Properly installed and adjusted car seats should leave no room for a child to escape. Call your local car seat safety board and ask them to check your adjustment of the straps. And don't give up the battle. Children must *always* be strapped in. However, my other hint is, as soon as she wriggles out, pull over and stop the car. Buckle her back up. Wait until she settles down. And repeat over and over again. You will need to plan several "driving around town" trips, perhaps, to get this point across.

    ~ Tarrant F., Gainesville, Florida

A: I have one of those Houdinis also. We purchased a baby harness from a baby store and secured it to the car seat. This worked for a while, then we couldn't get him in it. When he was two, we had to bribe him

61

into it with toys and candy and other treats. Now he is two years and eight months, and loves to "go bye" and gets mad when it is time to come home.

    ~ Carolyn S., Groton, Connecticut

A: I remember the time that I was driving down a congested road and felt a tap on the shoulder and looked back to see my 14-month-old baby out of her seat. She is now 26 months and still hates the thing. I have tried every car seat, and she got out of each one. So, I stayed with the one that I had originally, a Century that has a clip to hold the shoulder straps together, and tied a sock over the clip. Another thing that worked was when I ran a belt around her and the car seat straps.

    ~ Parent Soup member WhatnotSue

Car Seat Guidelines from the American Academy of Pediatrics
The following excerpt is adapted with permission from the American Academy of Pediatrics Committee on Injury and Poison Prevention "Selecting and Using the Most Appropriate Car Safety Seats for Growing Children: Guidelines for Counseling Parents," *Pediatrics*, Vol. 97, no. 5, May 1996, pp.761–763.

1. Children should face the rear of the vehicle until they are at least 20 pounds and one year of age to reduce the risk of cervical spine injury in the event of a crash. Infants who weigh 20 pounds before one year of age should ride rear-facing in a convertible seat or infant seat approved for higher weights until one year of age.

2. A rear-facing car safety seat must not be placed in the front passenger seat of any vehicle equipped with a passenger-side front air bag. This practice would prevent the risk of death or serious injury from impact of the air bag against the safety seat.

3. Premature and small infants should not be placed in car safety seats with shields, abdominal pads, or armrests that could directly contact an infant's face and neck during an impact.

4. In rear-facing car safety seats for infants, shoulder straps must be in the lowest slots until the infant's shoulders are above the slots; the harness must be snug; and the car safety seat's retainer clip should be positioned at the midpoint of the infant's chest, not on the abdomen or in the neck area.

5. If the vehicle seat slopes so that the infant's head flops forward, the car safety seat should be reclined halfway back, at a 45-degree tilt. Until engineering modifications can be implemented to prevent this problem, a firm roll of cloth or newspaper can be wedged under the car safety seat below the infant's feet to achieve this angle.

6. A convertible safety seat, which is positioned reclined and rear-facing for a child until one year of age and 20 pounds, and semi-upright and forward facing for a child older than one year of age who weighs 20 to 40 pounds, should be used as long as the child fits well (e.g., ears below the top of the back of the seat and shoulders below the seat strap slots).

7. A booster seat should be used when the child has outgrown a convertible safety seat but is too small to fit properly in a vehicle safety belt.

8. There are two types of booster seats. A belt-positioning booster seat that uses a combination lap/shoulder belt, if that type of belt is available, is preferable to a booster seat with a small shield, which can be used when only a lap belt is available.

Companies across the United States have responded to the problem of incompatibility of older children and seat belts by designing after-market add-on devices that attempt to make the shoulder portion of the safety belt fit correctly, thereby giving better protection to passengers who are not tall, notably children and some adults. These products vary in design, yet all claim to solve the problem of poorly fitting shoulder harnesses. However, some of these products actually seem to interfere with proper lap and shoulder harness fit by positioning the lap belt too high on the abdomen and the shoulder harness too low across the shoulder and by allowing too much slack in the shoulder harness. Although in some cases these products may help shoulder harnesses fit as they were designed, the add-on products are usually tested only by their manufacturers, which allows manufacturers to make claims that cannot be substantiated by independent means.

9. Many new vehicles are equipped with integrated child safety seats that are designed for children who weigh at least 20 pounds and are at least one year of age. All infants younger than one year of age or who weigh less than 20 pounds should be positioned rear-facing in separate child safety seats.

10. Read the vehicle owner's manual and child restraint device instructions carefully and test the car safety seat for a safe, snug fit in the vehicle to avoid potentially life-threatening incompatibility problems between the design of the car safety seat, vehicle seat, and seat belt system.

11. The rear vehicle seat is the safest place for children of any age to ride. Any front-seat, front-facing passengers should ride properly restrained and positioned as far back as possible from the passenger-side front air bag. An infant should never be left unattended in a car safety seat.

For the full AAP policy statement, visit the AAP Web site at www.aap.org, or, to receive a copy, send $1.95 to:

> AAP Publications
> P.O. Box 747
> Elk Grove Village, IL 60009-0747

CAR TRIPS

Riding in the car is an unavoidable aspect of modern life (unless you live somewhere with lots of public transportation). Car seats keep toddlers safe, but what can keep them occupied? Luckily, the parents of Parent Soup have all sorts of little tricks for keeping toddlers happy in the car.

KIDS SAY THE DARNEDEST THINGS

Once when we were planning to go visit my husband's parents on the weekend, my son (three years old at the time) was so excited to go he was the first one up. He ran in to us and told us to get up because it was time to "Smack the road." We still use the phrase.

~ Parent Soup
member Faith9297

C car trips

**KIDS SAY THE
DARNEDEST
THINGS**

My two-year-old and I
always practice our
colors. One morning on
the way to the sitter we
came upon a green light.
My daughter yells,
"Gween Mama, go!"
Just then the light
turned yellow and she
yelled, "Wellow Mama,
step on it!"
    ~ *Sandra K., Little
    Chute, Wisconsin*

Car Essentials
A busy book, a chew toy, a snack, and diapers are all I really need to
take care of most toddler emergencies. I keep these four items in a
backpack by the door, so I am ready to go when my toddler finally is.
    ~ *Monica H., Evanston, Illinois*

Keep in your car some snack food that stores well—canned juice or
bottled water, a few toys, a small pack of wipes, Band-Aids, and a change
of dry clothes. If you're stuck in traffic or your car breaks down or your
toddler goes for a swim in the duck pond, you're ready to cope.
    ~ *Parent Soup member A Souper mom*

Keeping Little Hands and Bodies Out of Harm's Way
After my three-year-old is in his car seat, I say "Hands up!" He puts his
hands in the air. Playing this game protects his little fingers when I close
the car door.
    ~ *Parent Soup member SusanahO*

Making Car Travel More Manageable
As we were getting out of the car in parking lots or wherever I didn't
want them straying from the car, I would say, "Hands on the car." This
was a concrete direction and gave them something to actually do. Saying
"Stay here" or "Don't go away" or other ambiguous directions gave them
too much freedom of choice. Also, "Play the car drums" worked very
well. They would be pounding on the side of the car, but I could be
assured they were staying right there.
    ~ *Melody S., San Antonio, Texas*

Before leaving home for a long car trip, prepare little packages for children to open while traveling. This gives them a sense of adventure and a feeling of belonging on the trip.

~ *Christina M., Galion, Ohio*

Sometimes, the Slower the Trip, the Better

My family and I often have to take long car rides, and my 18-month-old gets extremely fidgety after about an hour. Our only solution is to find a place to stop and let her walk around for about 15 minutes. Sure, it slows the trip down a bit, but isn't it better than having them drive you nuts in the car?

~ *Angela F., South San Francisco, California*

Making the Most of a Commute

On our commute to day care, I give my two-year-old a hand-held tape recorder with a tape of nursery rhymes. I watch her develop talking and singing skills through my rearview mirror. This allows me to concentrate on my driving and lets her control the volume on the recorder.

~ *Amy A., Costa Mesa, California*

Traveling on Toddler Time

Q: My family will be taking a trip to Atlanta with our two-year-old daughter in June. We will be traveling by car, and the drive will be about six hours. My daughter is very active, and I need some advice on how to keep her occupied and have a safe, fun trip.

~ *Stephanie H., Flomaton, Alabama*

DR. GREENE'S INSIGHT

A: Ah, yes, family vacations—those times filled with memories of long days being together and having fun, or memories of long days being together with crying, unhappy kids. With all travel, the number one thing you can do to build happy memories and avoid days filled with tears is to anticipate your child's needs. At home, most children have a set routine with fixed mealtimes and nap times. When on the road, this can be easily upset, and little ones may not respond well to the changes. So, first off, try to stay as close as possible to your normal routine in terms of mealtimes and sleeping times. When making a six-hour car trip, it may be more comfortable for you to leave first thing in the morning and drive while you are fresh. Yet this is the worst time to leave for a two-year-old. Instead, spend the morning in active play and preparation for the journey. At this age, most kids take one long afternoon nap. If this is true of your child, plan on leaving just after lunch (so that no one is hungry), which will probably be about an hour before normal nap time. Most two-year-olds can be happy in a car seat for about a half an hour—only five and a half more hours to Atlanta! When your two-year-old starts to get fussy, it's time to start the normal nap time routine, even if it is a little early. This may include a tippy cup of juice, cuddling a blanket, or holding a favorite toy. The motion of a moving car will put most kids to sleep, and you should have a few hours of peace. In order to take advantage of this sleepy time, be sure everyone has used the restroom before getting into the car (I know this sounds obvious, but stopping a moving car is asking a child to wake up). Also, provide a shaded spot for your child's car seat. In advance, purchase excellent child sunshades to cover the windows that might let the sun shine on your child during the ride. If the sun is shining directly on a child, or if a child is too hot or cold, he or she will not sleep nearly as long.

About three hours into your trip, your two-year-old will probably wake up refreshed and ready to play. This is an excellent time to take a park-and-potty break for the entire family. In fact, you may want to plan your travel itinerary so that you have as much freeway driving as possible during the first three hours of the trip and have an excellent play area available at about the halfway point. If possible, plan to have time to let your toddler run! Bring along a ball and play catch. Have a picnic. Whatever you do, don't stick your child in a high chair at this point! After a good long break comes the final push to your destination. Here is the key—distraction, distraction, distraction! Bring along lots of toys and plan on giving your toddler one each time the previous one gets boring. When toys no longer seem to be helping, it's time for an audio tape. We regularly travel with Raffi, Sesame Street, and a variety of other kid-friendly tapes. When one tape isn't doing it anymore, change tapes. Then go back to toys. As much as possible, get involved with your child and get your child involved with the activities—sing with the tapes, play with the toys, make funny faces (this also helps keep the driver awake!). And don't forget fun food. Crackers, fruit, and cheese all make nice car snacks (except for raisins, they get squished into floor mats and upholstery). During this phase of the journey, you may need to stop every hour or so and let your toddler get some pent-up energy out. Your normal six-hour trip will probably take eight to nine hours, but if you are prepared in advance, everyone can be happy!

KIDS SAY THE DARNEDEST THINGS

One day while waiting in heavy traffic, I was trying to be polite and let a fellow motorist in my lane. To signal him that I would wait for him to enter, I gently gave my horn a beep. From the backseat of my van, I heard my three-year-old son's voice say, "Mommy, you forgot to say jerk!"

~ *Shea S.,*
Enterprise,
Alabama

CHORES *(See also Cleanup)*

How can you raise a child who respects responsibility without having to
act like a taskmaster? According to the

parents of Parent Soup, assigning your
children chores is a good place to start.
Of course, there are limits to what you
can ask a toddler to do. But used wisely,
chores can keep your house picked up,
your family close, and your toddler happy
(that's right, happy!).

Chores as a Learning Tool

I have started chores with my soon-to-be three-year-old because I want to
instill in my children that chores are a part of being a family. We can do
them together, have fun, and even learn. For example: I cut the shape of a
plate, fork, knife, spoon, napkin, and cup out of construction paper. My
daughter glued them onto a large piece of paper, which is the place mat. We
hung this picture up in our kitchen, and she uses it as a guideline to setting
the table. It was fun to cut and paste the picture, and she doesn't need me
to correct her or keep telling her the right way to set. I think chores can
be fun for preschoolers and only hope that when my daughters are older
they will want to do their chores because they love me and want to help.
~ *Gail D., Raleigh, North Carolina*

Chores as a Boost to Self-Esteem

I have a three-year-old who has done chores for a long time now. She has
always been responsible for cleaning up her own toys (since she could
cruise), and there are many other little things that she does every day

too. Some things are strictly to benefit her space (making her bed, taking care of her clothes). Other things are to benefit the family (setting the table, serving food, feeding the dogs). Some things she just thinks are fun (cleaning, doing dishes). The main goal that we have is to make her an equal partner in the care of the household—she lives here, she should help! The two rules we have about her chores are: We never ask her to do anything that we don't do (we make our bed too!), and she never does her chores alone. We are always right there with her helping—that way it's a big togetherness thing. She feels very good about herself when she knows that she is helping out.

~ *Everett H., Norwell, Massachusetts*

CLEANUP *(See also Chores)*

How can you keep your house in some semblance of order when you've got a child running around, strewing toys, clothes, and pacifiers in his wake? First, see the Chores entry. It may give you the motivation to delegate some of the cleanup detail to your son or daughter. Then, read the posts below to get some ideas on how to get your child to actually do what you ask him to and to start tackling some of the piles of stuff. Finally, keep reading to find advice from sage parents who have realized that, after a point, keeping the house clean is an exercise in futility. They can help you realize when it's time to put down the broom and pick up one of those toys that's under your foot and go play with your kids.

Getting the Kids to Pitch In
Q: Our three-year-old's room looks like a bomb went off at Toys R Us, with the fallout landing in one toddler's medium-sized bedroom. Does

---

WHEN CRAYON MARKS START MYSTERIOUSLY APPEARING ON YOUR WALL

Q: Does anyone know how to get black ink off of painted walls? My almost three-year-old got ahold of a black pen and wrote all over my living room wall. (How is it possible to write that much in 30 seconds?)
~ *Parent Soup member CyndiR22*

A: Try shaving cream. Shaving cream and Cascade get rid of just about any stain my kids can whip up, including beet juice, crayons, glue, and ground-in peas.
~ *Parent Soup member CDCasey1*

71

A: If you have white or ivory semigloss paint, try a small amount of Soft Scrub with bleach on a sponge. It worked on my walls the time my daughter did it, and it didn't damage the paint.

~ *Angela K., South Bound Brook, New Jersey*

A: There is a product called Goof Off that removes crayon from the wall.

~ *Tarrant F., Gainesville, Florida*

anyone have any advice on how I can get our son to pick up his room? It was sparkling clean the other day—all his toys and animals were on their shelves, books in the bookcase—and he raced in and, within 30 seconds, the room looked like a clip from the movie *Twister*. I have tried cleaning up with him, but he goes crazy if I put an animal on the wrong shelf, or a Lego in the wrong box. Any suggestions?

~ *Wylie S., Rochester, New York*

A: Have you tried making it fun for him? Maybe you could let him set a timer for two minutes and make a race out of it. See how many toys he can put away in that time while you help keep count. Then do it again and see if he can beat his last record while you cheer him on. This way he'll be cleaning, but he'll also feel as if he's playing a game with you. Maybe you could even give him a small prize (a cookie or maybe even just a big hug) at the end of the race for a job well done.

~ *Parent Soup member Porks2*

A: Making things into a game or competition works. When I want my son to pick up, I use the counting to 10 method ("Let's see if you can pick up all those Legos before I can reach 10") or even offer to compete against him ("Let's see if you can pick up more toys than Mommy"). Once I pick up one or two things, he's speeding like a little demon.

~ *Parent Soup member JustTeeezn*

A: One thing I did when my kids were little was to buy a large willow basket for each of them, and since they couldn't read, I cut out a picture of each child and looped it on some string around the handle of the basket so they knew it was theirs. Each child was responsible for putting his toys in his own basket. I also go through their stuff and throw out whatever they're done with. Out of sight, out of mind really works in our house. Any stuff I can't bear to part with gets packed away. They never miss it, and on rainy days we get those boxes out and it's like having a bunch of new stuff, and I'm a hero!

~ *Parent Soup member Nursemom*

A: I devised a system that really helps my son clean up his room. I got individual containers for various toy groups: one container for all his cars, one for his tools, another for all his balls. Then when it's time to clean up his room, I say "Pick up all your cars first." Then we move on to tools. By breaking it down and making it easier for him, I found that I didn't have to fight with him to do it.

~ *Cheryl C., Glenwood Springs, Colorado*

Scaling Mt. Laundry

My sons are responsible for getting their own clothes into their hampers. In order to make it more fun, we actually use toy boxes for laundry hampers. We have a basketball, football, and stacked-tire toy box. Whenever they complain that they don't have a particular article of clothing and it is because it was left on their floor instead of in their basket—tough luck. It usually takes only a couple of times per child before they realize that I refuse to pick up their dirty clothes from off their floor. I take the clothes only from the baskets. Something else that helps is that I buy only one kind of socks—white crew. That way, we don't have to fold socks and matching isn't an issue.

~ *Parent Soup member Gccdcc*

A: Try hair spray—it works on cloth.
~ *Parent Soup member Taamb*

A: Believe it or not, Avon's Skin So Soft removes crayon from painted walls. I tried it, and it works. Just spray it on and rub gently with a damp sponge.
~ *Parent Soup member ALF56*

Sharing the Wealth and Clearing the Clutter
When our stuff (I mean junk) gets too deep, we box lots of it up to donate
to different charities. Some we mail to the Philippines, others go to local
charities and churches, and some goes to a local migrant labor camp.
What we consider junk because we are so spoiled, they really appreciate.
 ~ *Parent Soup member Bob*

Know when to Give up the Fight
I have tried it all. We have rules, we have storage boxes galore, we have
chore charts, and now we even have a house where finally everyone can
have their own rooms. And do you know what? It does not help a bit! I
just give up while I have young children running around. It makes my life
much easier.
 ~ *Parent Soup member blueshel*

"Cleaning a house while children are growing is like shoveling a walk
while it's still snowing." I love that saying! It won't solve the problem, but
it does help my attitude.
 ~ *Parent Soup member mom13*

CLOTHES

Toddlers can have many problems with their clothes: they won't wear
anything but dresses, they take 45 minutes to get themselves dressed, or
they don't seem to want to wear any clothes at all. If you think deciding
what to wear is a problem for them now, wait until they're teens! Seriously
though, clothes are one of those nonvital issues where you can let your

toddler enjoy some control and start exhibiting some self-expression. Your son or daughter may not show up on Mr. Blackwell's best-dressed list, but you will both be happier.

Barefoot and Stubborn

Q: Every time I put shoes on my daughter, she yanks them off. I have wasted so much money on shoes because she will lose one at the mall or at the grocery or wherever. I am getting tired of it; does anyone have any suggestions?

> ~ *Parent Soup member Ssgtmac14*

A: Have you tried those "shoelace keepers," or whatever they're called? They worked great for my son—he couldn't open them at all. We got ours at Baby Superstore.

> ~ *Paula L., Dale City, Virginia*

When Only a Dress Will Do

Q: Does anyone know what to do with a three-and-a-half-year-old girl who only wants to wear dresses during the day and nightgowns at night? Sometimes it's just not practical. But she gets hysterical.

> ~ *Valerie W., Succasunna, New Jersey*

Give Dresses a Twirl

A: Sorry, wish I could help, but my three-and-a-half-year-old is the same way. Not only will she only wear dresses and nightgowns, but she rates them on their "twirlability" and won't wear the ones that don't twirl enough. I gave up about a year ago, and let her wear whatever she wants (as long as it's clean). It's one less battle we have to fight.

> ~ *Melissa B., Linwood, New Jersey*

Dressing to Frill Without Breaking the Bank

A: I also have a four-year-old daughter who'll only wear dresses. Except my daughter has to have the frilly ones, nothing that looks too much "like boy's clothes" (in her words). I have discovered several consignment shops in a neighboring town and make regular stops there. They have the best brands—dresses you'd pay $30 for at retail—for $5 or $10. I have found that these second-hand dresses last longer and look nicer than the ones I buy at the discount stores.

~ *Kathy H., Augusta, Kansas*

A Common Phenomenon

A: And I thought I was the only one with a four-year-old girl who only wants to wear dresses. Whew! I am so relieved to know I'm not.

~ *Parent Soup member Cfreder807*

At Least They Want to Wear Something!

A: You are lucky. My four-year-old son *never* wants to wear clothes. As soon as I put them on, he is in the other room taking them off!

~ *Lori K., Sacramento, California*

Dealing with a Diaper Dropper

Q: My 22-month-old has discovered that he can pull off any pants I can get him into, as well as his diaper. This is getting to be an everyday thing. I am almost ready to put him in a blanket sleeper for his naps, but it takes so long to get him in that, and with my luck he will learn how to do the zipper just to foil me. Please let me know if you have any ideas.

~ *Elly T., Charlottesville, Virginia*

A: Boy, can I relate. I found a cure for this dilemma some time ago—I put my daughter in the sleeper jammies (zip up the front), I cut the feet off, and I put the whole thing on backwards. I guarantee he won't get out of this one!

~ *Lisa L., Jacksonville, Florida*

A: I have heard of people duct-taping diapers to keep them on. Also, we use what we call a zipper locker to keep our two-year-old in her blanket sleepers. It's a safety pin that we pin underneath the zipper head, across the track.

~ *Lisa K., Tucker, Georgia*

A: I had to put my son in a blanket sleeper with a diaper pin through the zipper in front *and* a diaper pin through the neck band in back (he was like Houdini and would wriggle his whole body out through the neck). That stopped the problem for a while. He did eventually (after several months) figure out how to remove the diaper pin, but he doesn't take his diaper off anymore. Also, we figured maybe he was bored being in the crib, so he is now in a toddler bed where he can get up and play till he gets tired, then he gets in his bed.

~ *Rachel S., Springboro, Ohio*

The Naked Truth

I have an expert stripper! She is 20 months old. The first time this happened was nearly six months ago—we were in the mall, she was in the stroller, and my son and I were walking along pushing her and talking about what we were there to buy, and all the folks kept looking at her and grinning from ear to ear. Of course, I thought they just thought she's

KIDS DO THE DARNEDEST THINGS

One morning my son Kyle, then two and a half, had just put his sandals on the wrong feet. I commented that he needed to swap his sandals. Apparently, he thought I said "swat," and obliged me by slapping the bottom of each sandal and then climbing into the car without further comment.

~ *Tracy Z., Lafayette, Louisiana*

as beautiful as I do. Finally, when a woman told me she will be cold soon, I looked down at my daughter only to realize her pants were around her ankles, her shirt was over her head, and she had her diaper tabs undone. I never laughed so hard in all my life! What we have done, and it has curbed it a little bit, is explain that "Now isn't the time to be nudie." Just like that, in a very even tone of voice. We then dress her again, and explain that if she wants to be naked, she has to wait until we go inside, or come home from the mall, or whatever. And we give her a few minutes to be naked at home, in exchange for staying dressed while out. We never tell her, "Shame on you," "That's naughty," or anything else negative, because we don't want her to feel her body is something she should feel shameful or self-conscious about. We choose our words very carefully. Also, before bed, we have started letting her go naked for about half an hour. This seems to make it less of a want during the day. Odd, but it works!

~ *Evelyn E., Scranton, Pennsylvania*

Stripping for Success

My daughter loves to take off her clothes. It used to bother me, until I took her into her 15-month-old check up and undressing herself was one of the developmental milestones the doctor asked me about.

~ *Anne Marie M., Lincoln University, Pennsylvania*

Speeding up the Getting Dressed Process

What worked for us was to tell my daughter the night before what we would be dressing her in the next day—followed up by lengthy explanations of why. We would repeat it again in the morning before anything got started and then dressed her without letting her help with any part of it. The whole time we were doing it we would talk about the next time, when she would be able to dress herself—how she was going to do it, what she was going to wear, which shoes would go with it, etc. Usually by the time she was done talking about the next outfit she was going to put on, we had her completely dressed and she was happy, as she got to look forward to dressing herself the next day. It worked great! Now she's three and she dresses herself, head to toe, with everything matching (she even picks out accessories), in about 15 minutes. We have quite the clotheshorse—the teen years should be fun!

  ~ *Everett H., Norwell, Massachusetts*

Place a small dot of nail polish on the inside edge of the sole of each shoe, near the base of the big toe. If the dots touch, your child will know the shoes are on the correct feet; if not, time to try again!

  ~ *Susan H., Syracuse, New York*

If your child is learning to dress herself, buy stretchy tube socks. Putting on tight cotton socks is frustrating!

  ~ *Parent Soup member Gotche*

To avoid the "you've got it on backward blues" when your child is first learning to dress himself, buy shirts with designs on the front.

  ~ *Christina M., Galion, Ohio*

Teach your child that it's easier to put on pants if she sits on the floor. Getting a foot through a pant leg is hard enough without having to balance at the same time.

  ~ *Parent Soup member SusannahO*

Once your child moves
out of her crib, you need
to be extra sure your
house is safe for any
nighttime explorations.
As with most parenting
issues, the best
childproofing solutions
often rely on common
sense. Below are Parent
Soup's 15 most popular
and practical ways to
make your home safe for
your little one.

1. Crawl through your
   house to get a
   child's-eye view, and
   remove anything
   that is either
   dangerous to your
   child or precious to
   you.

2. Turn down your hot
   water heater to 120

Life Is Not an Emergency

My two-and-a-half-year-old daughter wants to do everything herself, and
I mean everything. She loves to practice getting dressed and putting shoes
on in the morning when I am rushing out the door to get to work. And
when I realize (after 20 minutes) that she needs help getting her shirt on,
I try to help. Big mistake! She'll have a fit and end up tearing all of her
clothes off. But I have learned that life is not an emergency. If my
daughter wants to take 20 minutes to get dressed, I will be a little late for
work. I have learned that the most important job we have is raising our
children, and they should come first.

~ *Angela E., Williamsburg, Virginia*

CRIB TO BED *(See also Sleep)*

One of the significant outward signs that
your toddler is getting older is when she
gets too big to sleep in her crib. Leaving
the security of a well-protected crib to
move into a nonconfining toddler bed can
be a scary leap for a toddler, and your
daughter may experience some difficulty
sleeping until she gets used to her new
arrangement. Try the tips below to ensure that nights in your house
are peaceful.

How to Tell It's Time to Make the Switch

If your son can get out of the crib, it's time for the crib to go! That's a
long fall from the top rail of the crib, and he could get hurt next time.

Why not try a toddler bed? They are inexpensive, and you can use the crib mattress in it. There are all kinds of bed rails that go with them, too. And if that doesn't work, I would let him sleep in the playpen.

~ *Parent Soup member PSHeideR*

Easing the Transition

Q: My two-year-old just recently made the transition from crib to toddler bed. Unfortunately, he has not slept through the night and is driving his parents crazy. Help! What can we do to get him used to sleeping in his bed?

~ *Parent Soup member Cwutley*

A: We moved our son from crib to bed at age 25 months. At first, we put a mattress on the floor and had him play on it for a week or so. Then we asked if he would like to sleep in it. He would sleep in it for an hour or so and then cry for his crib. Finally, we told him the crib had to go bye-bye, and he watched us take it down and pack it up. (We thought we'd get it back out if he seemed too traumatized by it.) Once the crib was out of sight, it was out of mind.

~ *Pauline L., Findlay, Ohio*

A: Our son started sleeping on a futon at 19 months. Since it was low to the floor, we had no fears of him falling out. However, he could easily come and go as he pleased. The first several nights we would go in after he fell asleep and find him on the floor sleeping with a stuffed animal. We soon noticed it was always the same stuffed animal, so we moved it into the bed with him and he's stayed in bed ever since. Mornings he gets up and plays in his room for a short time, then opens the door (new development at 21 months) and comes to see

degrees Fahrenheit to prevent burns.

3. Secure cupboard doors with childproof locks— but don't expect them to work all the time (some children are more wily than others)! Put dangerous items (cleaning solutions, knives) in higher cabinets far out of reach of children. Leave one easy-to-reach cupboard open and fill it with plastic containers, pots, and pans that are safe for your toddler to play with.

4. Cover all electric sockets with childproof cover plates, and never let your child see you remove the plate (such as when

5. Take the edge off your fireplace and furniture with sharp edges by covering them with throw pillows, quilts or blankets, or foam rubber—Murphy's Law dictates that falls will happen in the worst possible places.

6. Put a hook-and-eye latch high up on your doors so that your toddler doesn't end up anywhere he shouldn't be (like the basement or outside).

7. Make sure every area of your house has a smoke detector and a carbon monoxide detector.

you're vacuuming), so he won't know how to take it off.

Mom and Dad. We decided not to prevent his opening the door, as the house is pretty safe.

~ *Peter P., Oak Harbor, Washington*

A: My 23-month-old daughter recently made that transition, as well. The first couple of nights were #$%!, but we decided to give her something she could only have in her "big girl" bed. We bought her a Barney bed set and make a big deal about her sleeping in her bed. If your child is not a Barney fan, try substituting with Mickey, Winnie, Sesame Street . . . pretty much anything the child really loves and can relate to. Also, you may want to purchase a gate to block the entrance of your child's room to prevent the danger of night wandering.

~ *Debi K., Tampa, Florida*

A: We took our daughter to the store and let her pick out brand new sheets for her big-girl bed. Then we colored pictures and posted them over her new bed. We also put a flashlight (kid-sized) in her bed. Finally, we invited her friend and her parents over to show off the new room. She was so proud of it she hasn't given us much trouble at all.

~ *Christine E., Shillington, Pennsylvania*

Into the Family Bed?

I think it is important to remember that each individual family has to do what works for them. I work and get up early. If I find my daughter is "wound-up" and I am exhausted and have to get to sleep, I will then bring her into bed with me, lights out, and it calms her and eventually we both get a good night's sleep. Struggling through half the night trying to get her into her own bed simply would not work for either of us. As I said, you must remember that each family has to do what works for them—not what works for Dr. Spock, her sister, or an absent parent. I believe it is truly a personal (or family) choice.

~ *Jody C., Ipswich, Massachusetts*

Getting Them to Stay in Bed

Q: My son, Jake, is 18 months old and sleeps well all through the night, but we just bought him a new bed that allows him to get in and out as he pleases. How can we teach him to stay in bed when it's bedtime? Is it something that can be taught? Any advice would be appreciated.

~ *John W., Virginia Beach, Virginia*

DR. GREENE'S INSIGHT

A: When our children reach about six months old and the threat of Sudden Infant Death Syndrome (SIDS) is greatly reduced, we breathe a sigh of relief. We begin to think of their cribs as safe havens. While they may not always be happy in their cribs, they won't be able to hurt themselves while in the protection of those four slatted walls. Then it happens. Your son learns to pull himself to standing. Soon he is cruising around the crib, instead of going down for a nap. Then he begins to bounce up and down. Before long, it's time for a big-boy bed.

Your first task in this transition is to make his room as safe as his crib used to be. This means fresh, aggressive childproofing. Check furniture such as bookshelves for stability. If need be, fasten furniture to the wall. Put locks on dresser drawers—toddlers love to pull out drawers and use them as stair steps to the top of a piece of furniture. Replace standard

If you need help or information, call your local fire station.

8. Remove refrigerator magnets. They are small enough to pose a choking risk and frequently fall off the refrigerator when the door is slammed.

9. Program your phone's speed dial with the numbers of your pediatrician, the poison control center, your partner at work, and your ambulance service (if you don't have 911). Let your babysitter know the numbers are there.

10. Keep a bottle of Ipecac syrup (up high and/or in a locked cabinet, of

course) on hand in case of emergency. This syrup is derived from a plant of the same name and triggers vomiting (not all poison cases require vomiting, so be sure to check with a doctor before administering). Also, call your local poison control center for an emergency reference card. Let your babysitter know where the syrup and card are.

11. Keep hot liquids away from your toddler. Whenever you're drinking coffee, tea, or other hot liquids, be sure to keep it far enough away so that if it spills, your child won't get burned.

electrical outlet covers with childproof covers. Make sure miniblind, drapery, and curtain cords are well out of reach. Remove any toys or other small objects that could be a choking hazard. Put any potentially hazardous materials, such as disposable diapers, in the closet and install a childproof latch on the closet door. Next, make his room a place where he feels safe—especially at night. Night lights are important, but at this age many kids want even more light than that. A 15-watt bulb in a lamp can keep the monsters that "live under his bed" at bay. Put the lamp on a timer so that it goes on at bedtime and off when it is time to wake up. This serves two very useful purposes. First, when your son does wake up during the night, he won't be as frightened as he would be in the dark. Also, you can begin telling him that when he wakes up, if his lamp is still on, it's still night-night time.

Kids love stories at this age, so it's a wonderful time to introduce a cassette tape player that your son can learn to turn on and off all by himself. There are lots of great story tapes available now for children, and investing in a few of these is smart. It's an even better investment to make your own tapes. There are no sounds in the world that are as comforting as Mom's and Dad's voices. At first you will need to help your son turn on the tape, but it won't be long before you wake up in the night to hear your own voice coming from the tape player in the next room.

Finally, you might want to install a sturdy, metal child gate that swings open. Do not use a wooden, accordion-style gate—both for your convenience and his safety. Let your son see you assembling the gate. When it's in place, make a game of opening the gate and walking through it, then closing it and opening it again. Next close the door with you and your son inside. Explain to him that the gate is there to help him stay safely in his own room. When he's comfortable with this, leave the room and stand just outside. Remind him that while he is in his room, he will be safe. Walk out of his sight and come back so that he gets used to being alone, inside his room, with the gate in place. You have just re-created the safety of his crib—only larger.

Just before bedtime, tell him again that the lamp will be on as long as it's nighttime. Remind him that while it is on he needs to stay in his room. When you put him to bed, help him turn on his tape player and, after your normal good-night hugs and kisses, leave, closing the gate behind you.

Your son will undoubtedly test you to see if you will enforce the "night-night time in your room" rule. He will probably stand at the gate and call for you to come and let him out—if you are lucky. (He also might cry mercilessly and try to make you feel guilty for confining him to his room.) When this does happen, check on him to make sure he has not been awakened by a bad dream or he is not sick. Feel free to go into his room and help him get comfortable again so that he can go back to sleep. Let him know that he can read a book, listen to a tape, or play with his toys (since you can't stop it, don't make a fuss over it). But he can't leave his room till morning! Leave and be prepared for an unhappy boy. He will probably try to manipulate you into opening the gate and letting him come into your room. Don't give in. Unless you have decided that you want to have a family bed, teaching your child to sleep through the night in his own room is a real gift to the whole family.

DAY CARE *(See also Preschool)*

There will come a time when you are not going to be able to be home with your child. Maybe you need to go back to work, maybe you need to get out of the house for sanity's sake, maybe you want your child to gain the socialization benefits of day care. Over half of families with parents

12. Never leave your toddler alone in the bath. Because young children can drown in just inches of water, always stay next to your baby when you're bathing him (or when you're near a pool, the toilet, or a bucket of water). If the phone rings, let the machine get it or get a cordless phone.

13. Don't expose your child to smoke. Secondhand smoke can cause illness now and serious health problems down the road.

14. Ask a professional. In many areas, professional "childproofers" will come to your home, install protectors

and locks, and notice hazards you might not see. Because they are so quick, they can be inexpensive. Ask your pediatrician if there are any reliable, inexpensive childproofers in your area.

15. Get a good stain stick to clean anything that you didn't childproof.

who can't be home all the time manage to care for their child(ren) without outside help—either alternating schedules so one parent is always home, or relying on relatives. That means half of you who need child care will have to pay someone to take care of your child while you're gone. How do you find someone you can both trust and afford? Here's advice for thinking through your choices and finding the help that's right for you.

Day-Care Checklist

There are never too many questions to ask when looking for a child-care center for *your* child. Use this checklist, provided by the Child Care Action Campaign, when conducting your search. (For more information about the Child Care Action Campaign, please turn to page 173.)

1. **Licensing.** State licensing requirements generally assure the basic health and safety of a facility, but may not guarantee the quality you are looking for. Be sure to check your state's licensing standards and ask any prospective care facility if it complies. If the child-care facility is not licensed, find out why.

2. **Quality.** Some high-quality center-based programs have been accredited by the National Association for the Education of Young Children (NAEYC). Ask about a center's accreditation. Even if it has not been accredited, some key elements of quality to look for include: staff structure; staff training; interactions between children and providers; cleanliness; safety; and adequate, age-appropriate equipment. Visit the program. Talk to other parents; their experiences can help you learn what to look for.

3. **Group Size and Ratios.** The most
important factors contributing to the
quality of a child-care program are group
size—the ratio of staff to children—and
staff training and experience. Studies
show that children benefit the most, both
socially and developmentally, from being
in small child-care groups that allow for a
lot of direct social interaction between
children and caregivers. Although state
regulations vary, the following are optimal
staff-to-child ratios that ensure that
children will receive enough individual
attention:

• **Family day care**—one adult to five
children, including the caregiver's own
(no more than two infants under one year).

• **Day-care centers**—one adult to four to six two-year-olds; one adult
to seven or eight three-year-olds.

4. **Training.** Because there are no consistent standards for child-care
staff training, child-care workers' experience and education vary
widely. Qualified staff may have college degrees in early childhood
education or a Child Development Associates credential. If the
caregivers at a prospective facility do not have such formal training,
ask if the program provides in-service training for staff. Firsthand
observation is the most reliable means of assessing a caregiver's

PARENT POLL

Would you spy on your nanny or day-care
provider to find out what goes on after you leave?

Of 591 total votes

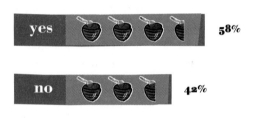

yes — 58%

no — 42%

1 bowl = 100 parents

ability to care for your child. Also ask about staff turnover—low wages for caregivers are the main reason for extremely high turnover in the child-care field, and such turnover negatively affects the quality of care.

5. Adult-to-Child and Child-to-Child Interactions. Watch carefully to see if the children are busy, happy, and absorbed in their activities. Observe the adults. Are they interested, loving, and actively involved with the children?

6. Cleanliness. The spread of infectious diseases can be controlled by cleanliness. Watch to see if teachers or other adults wash their hands frequently, especially after diaper changing. Are the facilities, toys, and equipment cleaned regularly?

> **DR. GREENE'S INSIGHT: If your child is prone to ear infections, moving to a class size of six or smaller during the winter months can dramatically reduce the number of ear infections your child gets. This is especially useful up until age two, when many kids start to outgrow ear infections.**

7. Play Equipment. A variety of interesting play materials and equipment can help your child achieve physical, social, and intellectual growth. In addition, it's important that each age group be provided with enough age-appropriate play materials. For example, jigsaw puzzles and crayons may be fine for preschoolers but are inappropriate for infants. Keeping this in mind, look for appropriate play materials such as books, blocks, wheel toys, balls, puzzles, and musical toys.

8. Safety and Emergency Procedures. There should be an emergency plan clearly posted near the telephone. This should include telephone numbers for a doctor, ambulance, fire department, police, etc. Smoke detectors should be installed and fire extinguishers must be readily available and in working order. The staff should be trained to deal with emergencies.

9. **Price of Care.** Fees for child-care services vary greatly. The price for family day care ranges from $50 to $120 per child, per week. In centers, care for infants (two years old or younger) is usually the most expensive, costing between $50 and $200 per week. (In-home caregivers must be paid at least the minimum wage, and parents are responsible for Social Security and other taxes.) Despite the high fees, child-care providers are among the lowest paid workers in the United States, earning an average of $5.35 per hour. The federal government and some state governments offer tax credit programs to help parents pay for child care; some employers also help out with child-care expenses.

10. **Location.** Transportation and location, like costs, determine whether a program is within a family's reach. When possible, choose child care close to your home or work. Sometimes a center en route to work, near the school that an older child attends, or near a relative, can be a good choice as well.

What You Find Depends on Where You Live

I've looked for day care in two different areas in the country, and I was surprised at the difference in the two regions. Not only did price differ (I now live in the Bay Area, which is very expensive), but the choices were different. Here's what I've learned: The approaches can vary from one place to another. Some of the differences are in structure (everyone has a schedule, but the amount and flexibility change), developmental approach (i.e., play versus formal learning), size, inside versus outside time, the personalities and roles of caregivers, their approach to discipline, etc. I think it helps to have a good idea of what you would like best before you look. As far as variation in price goes, the first place we used was a not-for-profit cozy little center that cost us $350 a month for three days a week in Pittsburgh, Pennsylvania. We absolutely loved it. On the other end of the spectrum I know someone here who is paying $1,000 a month in Silicon Valley, but they are the kind of people who drive me crazy because they want only The Best of everything and think that price is the most reliable indicator of quality. Some tips when visiting centers: if the children seem hungry for your attention when you visit, they are bored and not getting enough attention while there. Arrange to have your child play there for a while to gauge her reaction. Ask questions about how children are disciplined, and get references. Find out how much you can learn about your child's day. Our old place gave us an "infant tracking sheet" that listed everything about my son's day. It was great. I don't feel that I get enough information at our new place, and I'm trying to figure out what to do about it. It is depressing and disheartening to look for day care, but when you find the right place you'll know it.

~ *Parent Soup member khyams*

Determining What Day-Care Situation Is Best for Your Child
Q: My daughter Lily is 13 months old, and I have decided to return to work full-time. I live in an area with only two day-care centers. One is very close to where I live and work. However, it can only take her

three days a week. The other is a 20-minute drive each way, but can take her every day. I am already anxious about the change. Should I be consistent and go with the latter situation or stick with the first day-care center and arrange care for the other two days? My choices are to arrange for the other day care to take her two days, or to hire a babysitter two days a week. In addition, could you give me some pointers for making the transition easier for the both of us. I have left her with a babysitter only a few times since her birth.

~ *Parent Soup member Michelle*

THE ELIUMS' POINT OF VIEW

A: The best way to make this transition easier for your daughter is to provide care for her that is as consistent as possible. Although the day care that can take your daughter every day is farther away, it may provide a more continuous routine. Constant change is often difficult for very young children, although they usually adapt in time. If you did opt for the closer day care, having a sitter come to your home on the "off days" would probably be easier for your daughter, so that she did not have to get used to so many new people all at once. What will help your daughter most is that you are confident within yourself about your decision to return to work. She will pick up any ambivalent feelings and may reflect them back to you in having difficulty with the separation.

Of course, it would be wonderful if you could take advantage of job-sharing—working part-time or telecommuting from home—and just work the three days that the closer day care can take your daughter. These options are not always viable, but you may want to explore them. Regardless of what kind of work schedule you can work out, mothers return to work for all

d day care

At what age do you think a child can begin day care if needed?

Of 1,322 total votes

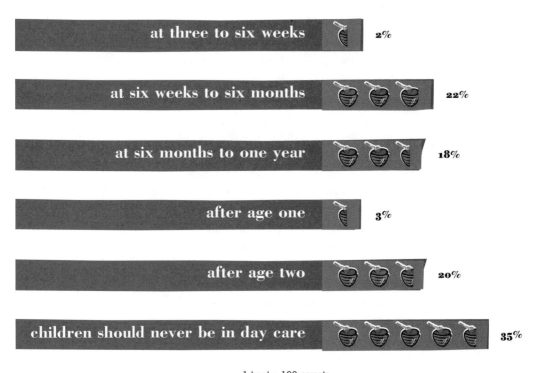

at three to six weeks	2%
at six weeks to six months	22%
at six months to one year	18%
after age one	3%
after age two	20%
children should never be in day care	35%

1 bowl = 100 parents

kinds of reasons and have various feelings about leaving the care of their children to others. Whether you feel good about this transition or not, be prepared for an "adjustment period." Your daughter may truly enjoy being in day care and have no difficulty with this change in her life. Or she may show how hard it is with various behaviors, ranging from crying when you leave her, ignoring you when you pick her up, being extremely demanding and clingy in the evenings at home, and throwing temper tantrums to developing eating problems or difficulty with sleep. Whatever her response is, she is telling you how she feels in the only way she can.

DIARRHEA

Diarrhea is a common ailment for babies, children, and adults alike—each year throughout the world, there are about a billion cases of diarrhea in children alone. For the most part, diarrhea is treatable at home. Dr. Greene explains the best home remedies and tells you when a child with diarrhea should see a doctor.

DR. GREENE'S INSIGHT
The central concern with diarrhea is the possibility of dehydration from loss of body fluids. Treatment is aimed at preventing dehydration, the real culprit. Most children with diarrhea can be treated safely at home. Supplementation with an oral rehydration solution will prevent dehydration. (Pedialyte is the most well-known, but other brands are also effective. Children in my practice seem to like the taste of grape-flavored KaoLectrolyte, chilled, or frozen rehydration pops, such as Pedia-pop popsicles, the best.)

Carrots, rice cereal, bananas, potatoes, and applesauce can help slow down the stools. Avoid fruit juices, peas, pears, peaches, plums, prunes, and apricots until the stools are back to normal—usually within a week or so. Contact your pediatrician right away if your child

- won't drink or appears to be getting dehydrated (dry mouth, lethargic, or going eight hours without producing urine),

- vomits for 24 hours,

- has eight stools in eight hours, or

- has blood, mucus, or pus in the stool.

In addition, if the diarrhea lasts longer than a week, or is accompanied by more than 72 hours of fever, be sure to get in touch with your pediatrician.

Using Food to Treat Diarrhea

There is a diet that doctors prescribe for older babies and young children with diarrhea known as the BRAT diet:

B = Bananas
R = Rice
A = Applesauce
T = Toast

These are binding foods and help firm up runny stools. They are all fairly bland foods too, so it makes them a little more appealing to a tummy that isn't feeling well. It's recommended that anyone experiencing diarrhea stick to this diet until passing at least two well-formed stools.

~ *Lisa K., Tucker, Georgia*

Alternatives to Pedialyte

Q: I bought Pedialyte when my son was having diarrhea. Have you tasted this stuff? It is awful! My son only drank half an ounce before rejecting it. There have to be other ways to stop diarrhea than that.

~ *Parent Soup member JFKluender*

A: Pedialyte is the worst thing I have ever tasted. Neither of my kids would touch the stuff, and I don't blame them. I had to mix half Pedialyte and half juice when my son had diarrhea, just to get him to drink it. Then my pediatrician told me as a substitute, Gatorade was OK. Not great, but nowhere near as bad as Pedialyte.

~ *Tara L., Glenshaw, Pennsylvania*

A: One trick is to freeze the Pedialyte in ice cube trays and then crush it up and spoon-feed it to him. Something about being frozen will make it taste a little better. Also, Gatorade works the same and tastes much better. Both were recommendations from pediatric nurses.

~ *Eva C., Los Angeles, California*

A: Have you ever tried KaoLectrolyte? It also has a grape flavor that tastes 10 times better, and my son has no problem drinking it. The best part is that it comes in little packets, so you can make one bottle at a time and not have to throw away a lot of stuff if you don't use it up.

~ *Dawn K., Norwalk, Connecticut*

EAR INFECTIONS

In the United States, there are over 25 million visits to pediatricians each year related to ear infections, and ear infections are the most common diagnosis in children. Luckily, Parent Soup's own Dr. Greene is an expert on this common ailment—he's written a book of his own on the subject entitled *The Parent's Complete Guide to Ear Infections.*

DR. GREENE'S INSIGHT

There are two basic types of ear infection, which behave very differently. Otitis media with effusion (OME) is the name given to fluid in the middle ear. Acute otitis media (AOM) is fluid in the middle ear plus pain, redness, and a bulging eardrum. Children with OME are often asymptomatic: OME is often discovered at well-child examinations. Children with AOM act sick, especially at night, often with a fever. After an episode of AOM, the child is often left with OME for several weeks.

What Causes an Ear Infection?

Ear infections occur when bacteria enters the middle ear through the eustachian tube, a narrow channel that connects the inside of the ear to the back of the throat, just above the soft palate. The tube is designed to facilitate drainage so that secretions that are normally made in the middle ear don't build up and burst the thin eardrum. Tiny hair cells in the tube propel this mucous blanket like a conveyer belt to carry bacteria down the drain. The tube

96

also functions to keep the air space in the middle ear at the same pressure as the air around us. In this way the eardrum can move freely, and our hearing is most effective.

When all is well, the tube is collapsed most of the time in order to protect the middle ear from the many organisms that live in the nose and mouth. Only when you swallow does a tiny muscle open it briefly to equalize the pressures and drain the ear secretions. If any bacteria make it into the ear, the drainage mechanism, helped by the little hair cells, should flush it out.

Ear infections are the result of the eustachian tube not performing its job. When the tube is partially blocked, fluid accumulates in the middle ear. Bacteria already there are trapped and begin to multiply. If the tiny hair cells are damaged (as by a cold virus), the mucous blanket can't help move the bacteria out.

Respiratory infections, irritants (especially cigarette smoke), and allergies can all inflame the lining of the tube, producing swelling and increased secretions. They can also cause enlargement of the glands near the opening of the tube, blocking flow at the outlet. Sudden increases in air pressure (during descent in an airplane or on a mountain road) can both squeeze the floppy tube closed and create a relative vacuum in the ear. Drinking while lying on one's back can block the slit-like tube opening. The increased mucus and saliva during teething can also get in the way. In addition, the last two decades of the twentieth century have seen a dramatic rise in ear infections largely due to increased pollution and the prevalence of early childhood day care (where children are exposed to many respiratory infections).

Small children get more ear infections than older children or adults for several reasons: the tube is shorter, more horizontal, and straighter—a quick and easy trip for the bacteria; and the tube is floppier, with a tinier opening, and therefore easier to block.

What Are the Best Treatments?

First, a word on antibiotics as a treatment. Although antibiotics are a wonderful, lifesaving tool, we have erred in their overuse. We know this because more and more strains of bacteria are becoming resistant to them and are hence becoming harder to treat. I believe that antibiotics are not always necessary in the treatment of ear infections.

That said, each type of ear infection, OME and AOM, has its own recommended treatment. In otherwise healthy children one to three years old with OME, the Department of Health and Human Services and the American Academy of Pediatrics recommend environmental measures (breastfeeding, avoiding cigarette smoke, and reconsidering day care) and either observation *or* antibiotics. If the fluid is still present six weeks later, they again recommend observation *or* antibiotics. Only if OME is still present after 12 weeks *and* there is a bilateral hearing loss of more than 20 decibels do they recommend treatment either by antibiotics or surgical tube placement, although I would definitely try antibiotics before placing tubes. Millions of cases of OME are needlessly treated with too many rounds of antibiotics.

For children with AOM, new guidelines have been suggested by Jack Paradise, M.D. His ideas are controversial but are an excellent attempt to define the new, wiser middle ground of antibiotic use. He recommends considering five factors when deciding on therapy: the child's age (older children recover more easily than young children), the season (summertime infections clear most easily), the severity of the episode (mild infections rarely cause problems), the child's previous history of ear infections (the fewer episodes of AOM, the more likely each one will clear), and the initial response to antibiotics (prompt improvement is a good sign). If these five factors point to a mild case, he recommends limiting treatment to only five days. If the infection continues to escalate and shows resistance to antibiotics, it might even be possible to withhold antibiotics and follow the infection with frequent ear examinations.

What About Tubes in the Ear?

The surgical procedure for placing tubes in the ears has become one of the most commonly performed operations of any kind. The procedure is a simple one. A tiny tube with a collar on both ends (which looks like this][) is slipped through a tiny incision in the eardrum. This pressure-equalization (PE) tube provides a temporary, extra eustachian tube to allow bacteria and fluid to drain from the middle ear. The procedure has been in widespread use since 1954 and is very safe—probably safer than driving to the hospital for the surgery.

There are four agreed-upon indications for PE tube placement:

1. Children with prolonged OME (or fluid in the ear) will benefit from tube placement. This is the most common reason children get tubes. Tubes are often recommended after 12 weeks of OME, but occasionally as early as 6 weeks. In some situations, which I will discuss below, waiting four to six months is appropriate.

2. Children with recurrent AOM (fluid in the ear accompanied by a red, bulging eardrum, pain, and often a fever) are candidates for tube surgery. These would be children with at least three episodes in six months, who are then placed on prophylactic antibiotics (low-dose antibiotics to prevent ear infections) and who then continue to have more AOM. This is the second most common reason tubes are placed.

3. Children with complicated AOM should get tubes. These complications are not common, but include abscesses, facial nerve problems, or AOM that stays hot, red, painful, and bulging despite antibiotic therapy. Not included is the common situation where after treatment for AOM, the child still has fluid in the ears (OME), which gradually clears on its own.

99

4. Children with complicated OME should get tubes. These complications generally relate to prolonged retraction of the eardrum and its impact on the little bones of the middle ear. This is a very uncommon reason for tube placement.

Early tube placement should be considered for children who have any type of preexisting hearing loss or balance disorder. Children who have any other communication or sensory difficulty (visual, developmental delay, etc.) are also candidates for early tubes. There is no reason to delay tubes for children with known craniofacial, structural problems predisposing them to recurrent infections (cleft palate, Down's syndrome, etc.). Ongoing pain also calls for tubes at the earlier end of the spectrum. Finally, seasonal timing affects the advisability of tubes. In the fall or early winter, the child's ears are likely to get worse over the ensuing months rather than better, and early tube insertion may be warranted.

Some situations suggest further observation rather than rushing to tubes. Children with OME in only one ear at a time (and who have normal language development and balance for their age) should be followed four to six months. The same is true for children with bilateral OME and only mild hearing loss (less than 20 decibels). Children for whom prophylactic antibiotics have resulted in a reduction in the frequency and/or severity of bouts of AOM also warrant further observation before tube placement. Children who are less than one year old should delay tubes if other considerations permit. Many children will have a decrease in the frequency and severity of ear infections in their second year. Finally, in the spring and summer ear infections clear more easily and recur less readily, suggesting a delay, if possible.

FALLS

Toddlerhood is filled with running, skipping, jumping, dancing, and—as all these skills have been recently acquired—falling, lots of falling. Dr. Greene explains how to care for a toddler who's hit his head, and when to call a doctor after a fall.

When Is a Bump on the Head Serious?

Q: My wonderfully active youngster seems to always be "bonking" his head on something. I never know how to respond. Are there some general guidelines for when it is serious and when it isn't? I feel bad about calling my doctor for every little thing, but I certainly don't want to miss something important.

~ *Parent Soup member Anonymous*

DR. GREENE'S INSIGHT

A: Fortunately, most "bonks" are not serious. Nevertheless, when we hear the awful thud of a child's head, our breath catches and for a moment, we fear the worst.

A prompt cry after the injury is reassuring. It is normal for a child to feel sleepy after hitting his head, and it's even OK for him to vomit once or twice. If your toddler has any of the following conditions, call your physician right away:

• unconscious, even briefly

• crying for longer than 10 minutes

101

- repeated vomiting

- blood from the ears or nose

- rapid swelling just above the ear

- inability to walk or talk normally

- unequal pupil size

- severe, worsening headache

- neck pain

- seizures

- severity of injury (car accident, long fall, baseball bat, etc.)

Although your child may be fine, you should be in touch with an expert. If your son is unable to get up by himself immediately after the head injury, don't move him. Call 911 and wait for emergency help to arrive.

If none of these symptoms are present, it is fine to let your son sleep, as long as you wake him every half hour for the first six hours after the fall. After this, awaken your son at your bedtime and again four hours later to check on his status. If at any time your child seems to develop a suspicious symptom, call your doctor.

After reading a list like this, it is tempting to try to protect your son from every situation that might result in an injury. It is appropriate to use good judgment in deciding what activities are safe for your child, but it is also important to allow him the opportunity to express himself through physical activity. Sometimes growth means taking risks, but appropriate risks are worth taking!

FAMILY TIME

With the day-to-day running around of getting little ones cleaned, dressed, and fed (not to mention cleaning, dressing, and feeding yourself), it's easy to forget to spend some time just being a family— enjoying each other's company with no fussing, nowhere to run off to, no goals to accomplish. According to the parents of Parent Soup, setting up family time is not as much of a task as it sounds. Chances are there is some part of your daily or weekly routine that can be expanded into a legitimate family tradition. It might be something as simple as making it a habit to fix your favorite breakfast food once a week. Read the posts below to see how other families have incorporated tradition into their time together. If you don't see one here that appeals to you, perhaps you'll be inspired to create your own.

A Different Kind of Bedtime Story
Children love it when their parents tell them stories from their own childhood or school experiences. It is also a good way to pass on family history and values. My children beg to hear stories about when I was a little boy. I highly recommend it as an occasional alternative to reading books.
   ~ Parent Soup member MarioDrum

Late-Night Talks Work Wonders

I have a nine-year-old boy, but I have found that since he was about three, it was during our late-night talks that I heard about what was really going on in his head. I have found out that many more things bother my son than I ever would have realized. He worries about pollution, animal extinction, nuclear waste, traffic accidents, and drunk driving, to name a few. He certainly keeps me on my toes. When one of those nights occur (and they don't always occur when it is convenient!), I get a blanket and pillow and lie on the floor in his room, and just listen. It is truly amazing the insights this child has. Sometimes he crawls down on the floor with me to snuggle (and feel safe while he talks of these things that scare him). He tells me about school, home, soccer, baseball, then hits the root of the problem. Listen to what they don't say as well. That may tell you far more than what they do say. You may be surprised!

~ *Stephanie C., Phoenix, Arizona*

We struggled for quite some time with our children at bedtime, more specifically, getting them to stay in bed. My husband and I found ourselves dreading bedtimes. We have always done the usual rituals before they get into bed, but they never seemed to help them relax enough to actually stay in bed without getting out of bed three or four times for something. Sometimes it would take them an hour to actually get to sleep because of all the messing around. We finally found something that works to help them relax; we call it "talking time." We give the kids an extra 10 or 15 minutes to tell us three things they were proud of, or that they liked about their day. It helps reduce separation anxiety, helps them to relax, and really boosts their self-esteem. Once in a while they will talk to us about a problem they had that day, and I really enjoy spending time with them listening to their thoughts and feelings.

~ *Parent Soup member Finchfam*

A Great Alternative to Monday Night Football

On Monday nights we always have a special family time. Even though we started it, now our children won't let us miss it! We start it with announcements: who is doing what that week—that way we know what everyone's schedules are—and who did something special the previous week. Then we have a song, led by one of our younger two daughters (they usually pick the song). This is followed by a prayer, which one of the children is asked to give. Then we have a learning time, where Mom or Dad or one of the older children gives a lesson that they've prepared. Then (unless we're too tired) we usually have a game time (board games, ring-around-the-rosies, or duck-duck-goose). Then we have another song, then a closing prayer on our knees. And then some nice treats that we've prepared. And then, finally, it's bedtime. We love the time to get to know our children better, and they love the extra-special attention they get. It is wonderful to see the effort the children put into preparing a lesson or a game for the rest of the family. They feel proud when they've completed it—and it's so much fun to see them enjoying the rest of the family.

~ *Parent Soup member SoftWrit*

Special Breakfast Treats

Any morning that it's snowing, we have French toast for breakfast. You should see my little one run for the window when he wakes up!

~ *Parent Soup member DTAMBURE*

f family time

Making the Family Meal Fun

I have always tried to get the whole family involved in the dinner prep.
With the tiny kitchen I have to work in, too many chefs do indeed spoil
the pot, though! So the little one and Daddy set the table and put on the
drinks. She has been doing this for a long time now, yet hasn't mastered
which side of the plate the silverware goes on. We prefer her logic of
setting the forks on the left side of the plate if you are left-handed and the
right if you are right-handed. And her special folded napkins that look
like paper lumps are a real treat too! I love it that she feels a part of
things. And I can't say that I object to the help, either!

  ~ Kathy O., Pleasanton, California

If you're having trouble getting a conversation started at the dinner
table, how about asking each member of the family to write down on a
piece of paper a topic they would like to talk about. They could be
hobbies, interests, current events, religion, vacation ideas, or the next
birthday party or special occasion. Next, put the pieces of paper in a jar
that comes out only at dinnertime. Each night, a different member of the
family picks a piece of paper, and that's the topic for the night. You can
even do learning topics: history, the Bible, a literary work. Another idea
is deciding in advance—put it on your calendar—which member of the
family is responsible for picking a topic and/or keeping the conversation
going at the table. This will teach young people how to hold and carry a
conversation.

  ~ Patricia M., Anchorage, Alaska

One idea that I heard is from a family that does what they call the
"High/Low Report" every night at dinner. Each member of the family

takes turns saying what was the best thing that happened to them that day and what was the worst. It sounds like a terrific way to keep up to date on any issues your kids might be having.

~ *Laurie M., Merrimac, Massachusetts*

When the Family Dinner Just Won't Happen

We found our way around the difficulty we were having in getting together for a family dinner on a regular basis—Sunday morning breakfast. During the week it's cold cereal, lunch at school, dinner is hit and miss, some eat it hot, some have to reheat, but Sundays it's big breakfast time—homemade biscuits, gravy, pancakes, grits, bacon, eggs, hash browns, milk, and orange juice. I've been doing it for eight years now every Sunday, and it's been worth it! I used to do it by myself. Then as the kids got older, they helped. Now with four kids grown and gone, they still want to come home on Sundays for breakfast and have carried on the family ritual with their new families. I'm still cooking for the three left at home, who are teens now, and what a wonderful surprise when my husband's and my anniversary fell on a Sunday, and we woke up to breakfast in bed with all the fixings. That's when you know the little things you've done in life have paid off.

~ *Collette J., Leawood, Kansas*

Breakfast Alternatives

Eating breakfast in the morning with your children is just one way to have quality time with them. There may be other ways families accomplish this. For example, the way a parent wakes up a child can be an equally warm and fond memory, or singing or listening to music in the car on the way to day care can become a cherished ritual. Some people

just don't like to make a big deal over breakfast. My kids don't always like to eat as soon as they get up.
  ~ Michelle J., Fairfield, Connecticut

As a single parent with two boys, I did what I had to do—go to work every day. To ease my mind and give us some time together every day, we always ate breakfast at home together or sometimes we even went to McDonald's in the morning. I just made time to spend time with them. I now have a day care in my home, and I see other moms running in, dropping off their children, giving me their breakfast, and running out the door. Making time for our children is not always easy, but beginning the day with "nurturing" is not a bad idea.
  ~ Parent Soup member Agape37

FEARS

As one Parent Soup mom said, "Toddlers are quirky little people." One day your daughter can be playing happily in the backyard, the next she can refuse to go outside because of a sudden fear of bugs. As her imagination becomes more and more active, your daughter can dream up wonderful scenarios in her mind. The flip side of that coin is that she can also believe in unexplainable dangers. Getting your daughter over any new fears will require some imagination on your part. Luckily, other parents and Dr. Greene are here to share their tips on walking kids through fears both real and imagined.

Vacuum Cleaner Dread

Q: I have a three-year-old daughter who is scared to death of our new vacuum. If we so much as say the word, she almost goes into a panic, running around and making sure nothing will get sucked up. She has gotten so bad she's scaring her two-year-old sister, who was fine about it. I tried getting her to push, but she won't. She even started wetting her pants again. Does anyone have any ideas?

> ~ *Parent Soup member Beckmom2*

Give Them a Gold Star

A: My nephew was also afraid of the vacuum. My sister gave him a fake gold plastic sheriff's star and told him it was a vacuum repellent star. And she gave him a special place to sit on the couch while the vacuum was running. It sounds silly, but it worked! Before she knew it, he was sitting there yelling, "You missed a spot!"

> ~ *Angela K., South Bound Brook, New Jersey*

When Bugs Become Bad Guys

Q: My three-and-a-half-year-old daughter has an irrational fear of bugs. She never used to be afraid of them. Now she stands and screams and refuses to go wherever there might be bugs. These aren't bugs that sting. We've tried explaining that to her. My husband says I should just force her to face them, that she'll get over it. My mother says I should just ignore her fears. Is this normal? What should I do?

> ~ *Teresa, Kentucky*

f fears

DR. GREENE'S INSIGHT

A: At about age three, most children enter into a magical time when imagination and creativity spring to life. Playtime becomes a setting where wonderful dreams and desires are acted out as kids learn how to pretend. A few props can turn an ordinary rainy afternoon into a trip to a magic castle or the Old West.

But this rich imaginary world is peopled with both heroes and villains, marvels and monsters. New fears are a necessary part of entering the world of possibilities. As the imagination blossoms, kids who never before had problems with the dark are now terrified. Or the neighbor's friendly dog suddenly seems menacing.

Most children will develop one or more deep fears to work through. It might be people in masks, old people, or people with scars. It might be parents leaving or burglars coming. It might be bugs. A natural response for parents who see their children cowering before an inchworm is to try to talk their children out of the fear. Kids respond, though, by cranking up the imagination—the imagined possibilities become worse, not better. Then the children feel disconnected from their parents. Ridiculing or threatening children for their fears is even more damaging (sadly, I hear this from time to time at playgrounds and stores). For these reasons, do not force your daughter to confront the object of her fears.

Instead, the best thing for you to do is to acknowledge the fear while remaining calm yourself. Assure her of your protection and support. When children see that you take their concerns seriously, they feel closer to you and are more ready to work through the fears. One of the fastest ways to help is to provide opportunities to play with *nonthreatening* versions of whatever is frightening your child. I know a little girl who was terrified of all dogs. Her parents took her to visit a litter of newborn puppies. She was delighted. They got her a cute dog stuffed animal—she felt mixed. They watched Snoopy videos. Soon her stuffed dog began chasing her dolls, but her dolls learned how to make the dog friendly. So, in her pretend play she worked through her own fears.

For kids who are afraid of the dark, this might mean lots of play with flashlights and colored lights in a darkened room during the daytime. For kids who are afraid of monsters, monster action figures can be the key (as well as good guys to overcome the monsters).

You might want to take a trip to the toy store to look for nonintimidating critters. Games such as Cootie and Ants in the Pants are popular partly because these fears are common. An ant farm (or a cricket in a terrarium) allows her to interact with bugs while keeping them safely behind glass. Let her comfort level guide you throughout the process.

Parents can be an immense help by giving children ideas for working through the fears during play. One of my children was very afraid of ghosts. Instead of telling him that there aren't any ghosts, we told him that sometimes the ghosts were even more afraid of him than he was of them. When he said, "Boo!" the ghosts would run away—and they did! We joined him in his play and guided him to a way that worked for him to conquer his fears.

It's important to remember "that worked for him" is a key part of the process. Many pretend suggestions I've made have been corrected by my kids. They might tell me, "These monsters aren't afraid of words. These monsters are afraid of my flashlight!" Making suggestions is helpful, but listen eagerly to their corrections. This is our children's battle that they need to win in their own ways.

Children's literature is a great resource for this type of work. Try reading classic fairy tales that feature a child overcoming witches and monsters. (I like *Where the Wild Things Are* by Maurice Sendak.)

Frightening television shows and videos, on the other hand, tend to be overwhelming rather than healing. These vivid visual images anchor fears and remain seared into the memory. Visual processing of fears is a potent tool, but it needs to come in a form that the child can then partially forget.

It's no coincidence that nightmares are common during this season. If your child wakes up from a nightmare (not night terrors), assure her of your protection, and gently encourage her to tell you what happened in the dream. This will point you toward the themes (abandonment, loss, powerlessness) that are most important to work through.

Your child's artwork is a great resource for working through fears. Get her drawing pictures, finger-painting, making models, designing games around her fears—where the fears are met and overcome. Blocks, toy buildings, cars, dolls, puppets, crayons, and paper are basic ingredients to successful play.

In the same ways, stories that originate in your own family can be even more powerful than the classics of children's literature. Listen to the stories that your child tells while playing, and tell them back to her. Create your own tales on the same themes. If you feel stuck, you might like *Tell Me a Fairy Tale* by Bill Adler, a parent's guide to telling magical and mythical stories. Use these same tools to connect with your daughter about pleasant dreams as well.

This season of heightened imagination is a precious time. Dreaming of wonders and pretending great exploits are the seedbed where life's dreams are born. These times are fun. But the darker side of this imaginative growth, the working through fears, is even more valuable. Here you teach your child to recognize the fears that can hobble dreams, to acknowledge these fears, to face them, and to find her own way to break through to the other side. The courage she learns now will be the roots that determine how high she can grow. Far from ignoring her fears, treat them with tenderness and eager patience. They are an invaluable window into your daughter's inner life and the development of her soul.

GENDER ISSUES

No matter how adamant you are about your son not playing with toy guns, chances are he will make pretend guns out of a stick, or even a peanut butter and jelly sandwich! Toddlers are just becoming aware of their gender. Sometimes they seem to be doing so with a vengeance—boys want to shoot everything they see, girls want to spend hours dressing up their Barbies. Why is that? And is it OK for parents to let them do it? In this entry, we hear from the Eliums and Dr. Greene about how best to foster blossoming gender identities.

Is It OK for Girls to Play with Barbie?

Q: My daughter is two and her aunt wants to buy her a Barbie doll. I have mixed feelings about how this might affect my daughter's self-image and self-esteem. Should I let her have one or not?

   ~ *Parent Soup member Senorpepe1*

THE ELIUMS' POINT OF VIEW

A: Mattel's Barbie is actually modeled after a 1959 German-made risque gag gift for men, a streetwalker doll named Lilli (source: *Parade* magazine). If you don't believe it, just look at her closely, with her platinum blonde hair, feet designed for stiletto high heels, and body measurements that rarely reflect a girl's. All children use toys to deal with the uncomfortable realities

g

of their everyday world. Sticks become swords to ward off scary things in the night; animal figures assume the identities of playmates or siblings to work out conflicts; dolls become babies, confidantes, or best friends. Barbie's appeal, however, seems to be aimed at the materialistic— collecting, never having enough, overspending, and glitz—at younger and younger ages.

Ideally, toys reflect the child. We encourage you to take your daughter or son to the fabric store for simple materials to make a simple doll. That warm, cuddly creation will comfort and live in the memory forever. If you must buy a doll, find one of natural, soft materials with few features. If you wish to encourage collecting, buy a doll that is childlike with accessories. To become healthy women, young daughters need room for their own imagination and self-esteem to soar in a safe and childlike way, rather than being locked into an adult man's sexual fantasy.

What About Boys and Toy Guns?

Q: My almost four-year-old son loves to play war, fight, and shoot at things with anything—from his fingers to broom handles to baseball bats. I feel like I should get him a realistic-looking toy gun, since he is using everything else just like a gun. Then I read that some major toy stores were banning realistic-looking assault-weapon toys. What do you think?

~ *Doug G., New York, New York*

THE ELIUMS' POINT OF VIEW

A: Say it slowly, "Assault . . . weapon . . . toy." It's an absurd phrase. Boys will always be attracted to toys that they can use to challenge, fight, and hit. One father told us his story, about how he had no guns, no TV, and lived in the woods away from the towns in the wilds of Oregon. When his son was three, he chewed his breakfast toast into the shape of a gun and went "bang." A mother told us that her son wanted a Barbie doll like the neighborhood girl. She bought him one, and he held it by the head and used the legs as gun barrels. It's in their nature. A young boy's imagination is the key to facing life's problems with more than just brute force. Simple toys are better than a hard plastic AK-47 look-alike that they stop playing with one hour after they get it home. A simple toy allows room for our sons' imagination to create whatever their hearts desire. Simple toys that run off imagination instead of batteries give him the opportunity for his testosterone to thrust, his heart to open, and his spirit to soar.

Is It OK for Boys to Play with Dolls?

Q: Dr. Greene, my little boy likes playing with dolls. In fact, he wants a Barbie for his birthday. My husband is very upset about this. Is he OK? What should we do?

~ Talia, New York

DR. GREENE'S INSIGHT

A: It's easy to tell a boy baby from a girl baby—if he's naked, or if she's dressed in pink. But if you catch a baby wearing nothing but a diaper, you'll find that although the proud parents know that the gender is obvious, boys and girls look and act similar enough to fool even pediatricians. Whether we are conscious of it or not, we parents feel strongly about the gender of our babies. If someone calls our her a him, we get just a little defensive. We dress her in a way to remove doubt. We pierce her ears or put bows in her hair. Even though we might want to avoid stereotyped gender roles, we want the world (and our daughter) to know that she is a she.

Part of the defining change from being a baby to becoming a toddler is this dawning gender identity. By 18 months most children know their sex.

115

They don't look like babies any longer. They look and act and speak like little boys or little girls. Between 18 and 30 months most children learn that genders persist, that boys become men and that girls become women. The desire to imitate the same-sex parent becomes quite strong. But this imitation is by no means limited to the same-sex parent.

This explains why a little boy might enjoy clomping around the house in a pair of high heels, a necklace swaying with each step, bright red lipstick painted on his face. The first such moment is an adorable, comical scene, but what if he really likes it? What if he prefers dolls to trucks?

Almost all healthy toddlers will copy and enjoy behaviors of the other gender. This kind of play is expected and desirable. Often toddlers will imitate many activities of the opposite sex. For most children the best way to handle this is to not draw a lot of attention to it one way or the other. Certainly don't punish them. Be careful not to belittle or criticize them for what they like. By school age, this experimentation usually gives way to new interests.

When might a child's exploration into the other gender indicate a problem? Several warning signs can tip you off that gender issues bear looking into:

- a child who does not know his or her own sex by the third birthday

- a child who consistently says that he or she prefers to be the opposite sex

- a child who consistently speaks ill of or denies his or her own sexual anatomy

- a child who maintains that opposite anatomic structures will develop

In the absence of signs such as these, a boy playing with Barbies or a girl playing with toy guns doesn't concern me any more than a girl playing with Barbies or a boy playing with toy guns. Relax and appreciate the innocent play of your son, who is able for a time to explore the world without concern.

GRIEF

Hopefully, you won't need to refer to this chapter for personal reasons. But just as birth is an inevitable and necessary part of life, so is death. Explaining to kids that they'll never see someone again can be just as heartbreaking as experiencing the loss of someone close to you. Below, Dr. Greene has some ideas on talking to toddlers about death and helping them deal with their grief.

Saying Good-Bye to a Grandmother

Q: My four-year-old daughter, Patricia, refuses to go to school. She is a bright and bubbly child who attended preschool at three. However, this year she suddenly didn't want to go to school, and she has also fixated on the subject of dying. Patricia's grandmother died four months ago. They were quite close, and my daughter asks me with increasing frequency what she can do so she will not grow up. She says she does not want to grow up, as she does not want to grow old and die like her grandmother. Death bothers her a lot. Is this fear of death related to her refusal to go to school? How can we help Patricia? Does she need to see a child psychologist or psychiatrist?

~ *Bong*

THE ELIUMS' POINT OF VIEW

A: We think that your daughter is experiencing a combination of things that cause her to want to stay home from school. The trauma of losing someone close to her could be enough to make your daughter fearful of leaving you and leaving home. She may be afraid that you will die while she is gone. This fear is common in young children, whether or not they have lost someone to death. We advise that you keep your daughter home if she wants to be home during this grieving period. Only time heals the wounds of loss. However, invite her friends over to play and provide lots of ways for her to practice becoming strong and physically adept.

How Does Grief Manifest Itself in Children?

Q: My wonderful father recently passed away, and we will all miss him very much. I am especially concerned about how this will impact my three-year-old son. He is an outgoing little boy who adored his grandfather. What things should I be watching for, and what suggestions do you have to make this easier?

~ *Parent Soup member Anonymous*

DR. GREENE'S INSIGHT

A: The grieving process is a long and difficult one for adults and children alike. The first step in dealing with grief is to recognize the many forms of expression it may take. You may feel depressed, sad, lonely, lethargic, and experience a lack of appetite. These expressions are common and easy to link to grief, but there are many other expressions that are harder to identify as grief-related. They include anger, aggression, ravenous appetite, lack of direction, lack of motivation, inability to focus on a task, short attention span, and forgetfulness. One of the best things you can do to help your son cope with his pain is to give yourself the opportunity to grieve for your father and to allow him to observe your grieving process. It is important to accept now that you will be very fragile for the next year or more. During this time you will need to be very kind to yourself and to your family members.

In terms of helping your son through this process, start by paying careful attention to his physical needs. Make sure that he gets proper rest, nutrition, and exercise. If possible, give him the opportunity to play out of doors. A combination of sunshine and being in physical contact with nature has a strong positive effect on all our bodies as well as our emotions. Paying attention to the basics will give your son the opportunity to begin the process of grieving from a healthy position. Whether your child is feeling anger, sadness, depression, or aggression, he will probably express his pain through temper tantrums or bouts of uncontrollable crying. By nature, this will happen when you are in a public place or you have pressing obligations that are very important to you. This is not an accident. It is at these times that he will feel the depth of his loss most acutely. In general, you will want to handle these episodes much the way you normally would. However, it is important that you recognize what is going on and make extra space for his pain. Your son may not be able to associate what he is feeling with your father's death, and you do not need to bring it up every time he acts out. In point of fact, it is important that you do not allow him to get in the habit of using this as an excuse to act out. You can also expect your son to regress as a direct result of the stress of losing his grandfather. This may include waking up more frequently at night, excessive amounts of thumb-sucking, bed-wetting, daytime incontinence, returning to baby talk, and in severe cases refusing to talk all together.

These things are only temporary, and your son will undoubtedly regain the skills and maturity level that he was functioning at before your father's death if he is able to process his grief in a positive way. An excellent way to help him do this is creative play. This is accomplished by encouraging children to use puppets or action figures to act out what they are feeling. Children have the ability to project their feelings on inanimate objects much more easily than they can own them. After your son has begun to talk about how he is feeling, consider working together to compile a scrapbook of memories about his grandfather. Include lots of photos and memorabilia, but focus on getting your child's memories into tangible form. Ask him to draw pictures of the things he remembers about his grandfather, then ask him to tell you about the picture. Write down whatever your child says, and when he is finished, read it back to him. Give him the opportunity to add to or change what he says until it clearly expresses what he is feeling. In this way you will not only help your child capture memories of his grandfather that will be with him for the rest of his life, but you will help your son to clarify his current feelings. Another idea is to create a family video. Invite family members (and close family friends) to recount their memories of your father and tape them. Allow your son to be as involved in the process as he would like. This might include helping to tell stories about his grandfather, listening while others talk, or just playing in the room while it is going on.

In any case, it will help him bring his feelings to the surface. It also does not need to be a great artistic work to be therapeutic.

GROWING PAINS

The term *growing pains* is often used to describe the emotional turmoil that can go hand in hand with growing up. It also refers to a benign physical pain that some children experience as their muscles try to keep up with their growing bones. Dr. Greene explains the physical phenomenon in this entry.

Is This a Growing Pain?

Q: My three-year-old daughter is always complaining of pains in her legs during the night. Could these be growing pains?

~ *Shelly, West Kamiah, Indiana*

DR. GREENE'S INSIGHT

A: During childhood the human body goes through an amazing series of changes. When babies are born, their heads, hands, and feet are proportionally much larger in relation to their bodies than at any other time in life. It's one of the things that make babies distinct and adorable. Throughout the growing-up process, the human body changes proportions many, many times. Sometimes long, gangly arms and legs seem to shoot out overnight! During these spurts of growth, children often complain of nighttime leg pain, hence the common label growing pains.

When children are plagued by episodes of recurrent, brief leg pain, it is a good idea for them to be checked by a physician. If the physical examination is normal, with no redness, tenderness, swelling, or limitation of movement, and if the pain is not provoked by moving or associated with any abnormal gait, then this situation is what we often call growing pains. These pains typically occur at night with no resultant daytime disability. The actual source of the pain has never been proved, but experience has taught us that they are benign and self-limited.

If the physical examination is not normal, your doctor will be able to discuss other diagnoses with you, from chronic trauma to childhood arthritis. In children with benign growing pains, the muscles or tendons are still a little too tight for the growing long bones. Muscle spasms lasting from 1 to 15 minutes cause the pain. Many of these children are unable to touch their toes with their fingertips without bending their knees. During a pain episode, stretching the foot and toes upward will often resolve the muscle spasm. Gentle massage and moist heat over the painful spot can also help. In most cases the pain can be prevented with simple, daily stretching exercises. These exercises must be continued even after the pain subsides in order to keep the muscles and tendons relaxed and able to accommodate the next growth spurt. Some physicians recommend giving a glass of tonic water (quinine) before bed. I have never seen any studies evaluating this suggestion, but it might help and wouldn't hurt. Plenty of fluids should make cramping less likely. Although these painful occurrences of growing up are nothing to be worried about, like all of life's growing pains, they can be quite bothersome during an episode. It is precisely the reshaping of ourselves that causes physical and emotional growing pains—in both situations, the pain results in our becoming more mature people.

HEAD-BANGING

Children develop a range of habits that are bewildering to parents, and head-banging may just top the list. When your son drops what he's doing and starts banging his head against the wall, the floor, or the asphalt, he may be trying to say (in a most dramatic fashion), "I am frustrated" or "I am bored" or "I want you to pay attention to me." Whatever the reason may be—and following are some tips to help you find that out—know that your child is not some sort of deviant. The parents of Parent Soup say it happens all the time, and with a little thoughtful parenting, your little one's head-banging phase will surely come to an end.

Is This Normal?

Q: I have a 19-month-old who started slamming his head into things about six weeks ago. Three times I was sure he had knocked himself out cold. If he isn't hitting his head on the floor he's slamming it into walls, windows, and doors. He doesn't do this only when he's mad, either. I noticed the other day he was doing it in the family room and nobody was around him. He hasn't started talking yet, but I know he can hear because he will do simple tasks you tell him to do. I know that somehow the head banging and the not talking are connected, but I can't figure out why. Any ideas?

~ *Parent Soup member PawzNClawz*

h head-banging

It May Be Strange, but Yes, It Is Normal

A: He may be frustrated that he cannot communicate. You might try some sign language; it will actually help his speech. Or he may be doing it for the sensory input. If so, swinging or bouncing could help fill that need less painfully.

 ~ *Suzanne L., Pasadena, California*

A: Yup, it's normal. He is just frustrated and angry. At that age, he doesn't have any control of his emotions. My daughter did it too, and it only lasted three or four months.

 ~ *Parent Soup member KatCT97*

A: This seems to be very common. I have two boys, and the older one banged his head until he would get a bruise. The youngest is still in that phase, and he will even bang his head on the concrete! I've been told to ignore it, and with my older son, that did work, even though it was torture to watch. I think they do it for attention, so if you don't give it the attention they're seeking, it should die off. Sometimes it just helps to know your child isn't the only one who does this strange behavior!

 ~ *Parent Soup member GaPcho07*

DR. GREENE'S INSIGHT

A: It should come as a relief to you to know that up to 20 percent of healthy children are head-bangers for a time (*Journal of the American Academy of Child Psychiatry*, July 1983). Head-banging appears in the latter half of the first year of life and generally ends spontaneously by four years of age. Boys are three or four times more likely to be head-bangers than girls.

The child seems compelled to rhythmically move his head against a solid object such as a wall or the side of a crib. Often he rocks his entire body. For most children it occurs at sleepy times or when upset (often as part of tantrums). This behavior can last for minutes at a time—or sometimes for hours. It can even continue once the child has fallen asleep.

Parents of children who bang their heads often have an unspoken fear of autism. This concern makes sense, since head-banging, head-rolling, and body rocking are each far more common in autistic children. But these rhythmic motor activities are also normal behaviors in healthy infants and young children (and young monkeys for that matter!). This behavior is abnormal, though, if it persists beyond the early years. Any child who is still head-banging beyond three years of age deserves further evaluation.

How can one tell if the head-banging is a part of normal development or an early sign of autism? Researchers at Cambridge University have found an easy and early way to detect autism. Three hallmark behaviors are the key signs:

1. Lack of pointing—by 14 months of age most children will point at objects in order to get another person to look.

2. Lack of gaze-following—by 14 months, infants will often turn to look in the same direction an adult is looking.

3. Lack of pretend play—by 14 months children will begin to play using object substitution, e.g., pretending to comb the hair with a block.

All three behaviors are typically absent in children with autism. If a child begins even one of these three behaviors by 18 months, the chances of ever developing true autism are vanishingly small (*British Journal of Psychiatry*, February 1996).

Why Do Kids Without Autism Bang Their Heads?

Many theories have been put forward to explain this common behavior. Perhaps the rocking and even the head-banging provide a form of pleasure related to the movement. This joy in movement is called our kinesthetic drive. All infants are rocked by their mothers when they are carried about in utero. Later on, they enjoy being held and rocked in parents' arms. Movement activities continue as kids grow: the pleasure of jump rope, swings, slides, amusement park rides (bumper cars!), and dancing. These activities all engage the vestibular system of the brain. The amount and type of movement that provides pleasure varies from child to child.

Kids who are understimulated (those who are blind, deaf, bored, or lonely) head-bang for stimulation. But children who are overstimulated (in an overwhelming environment) find these rhythmic movements soothing.

For some children head-banging is a way to release tension and prepare for sleep. Some kids head-bang for relief when they are teething or have an ear infection (*Primary Pediatric Care*, Mosby 1992). Some kids bang the head out of frustration or anger, as in a temper tantrum. Head-banging is an effective attention-seeking maneuver. The more reaction children get from parents or other adults, the more likely they are to continue this habit. Generally, healthy children do not head-bang in order to injure themselves.

Will They Hurt Themselves?

Toddlers don't seriously injure themselves from this habit. Pain prevents them from banging too hard, but even if it didn't, children under three don't generate enough force to cause brain damage or neurologic problems. The front or front/side of the head is the most frequently struck. Toddler heads are built to take all of the minor head trauma that is a normal part of learning to walk and climb. Healthy infants and toddlers who are head-bangers grow up to be coordinated and completely normal children.

How Can You Get Head-Banging to Stop?
Most children will outgrow the habit on their own. You can speed up this process by reacting to it in a matter-of-fact way. Pretend not to notice. And if it is part of a tantrum, do not give her whatever she threw the tantrum to get. When you notice her head-banging, you might be able to get her to stop for the moment by distracting her or engaging her in a different activity. By decreasing the amount of time she spends in this habitual activity, she will outgrow it more quickly.

Will It Affect Intelligence?
Curiously, the one large study of this habit in 525 healthy children found head-bangers to be measurably advanced compared to their peers (*Developmental Medicine and Child Neurology*, August 1977). If anything, then, head-banging in healthy children is a sign of increased intelligence. So the very behavior that is frightening could be a sign of something positive.

MOTHER LOVE

There's nothing quite like hearing your child say "I love you" for the first time. Now that she's talking, there are moments when the things she says just make your heart melt. Savoring these little expressions of affection can carry you through even the worst tantrum-filled day. Here,

KIDS SAY THE DARNEDEST THINGS

When my son was a tad over three years, I had my second child (a beautiful daughter). I had gained several pounds during my pregnancy and was in the bathroom surveying the pot belly I was left with, with its deep crease down the center, when my son wandered in and laughed. "Look Mommy, you have two fannies." Needless to say the exercise program started the next morning. Ya gotta love 'em.
~ *Parent Soup member OHDIANA1*

127

m mother love

KIDS SAY THE DARNEDEST THINGS

We all know what pregnancy does to our bodies—I was drying off after a shower one day when my daughter (then four) walked in. She asked me why I had stripes on my belly. I told this to one of my friends and we were laughing about it when she told me her daughter said to her (after walking in on her shower!), "Mommy, when I grow up I want to have long boobies just like yours!"

~ Pam M., Bolingbrook, Illinois

some Parent Soup members share some of their most touching moments with their kids, instances when suddenly it becomes clear just how fulfilling being a parent can be.

A Bushel and a Peck and a Hug Around the Neck

I knew I was a great mom when my 15-month-old son stopped playing with his toys and came to me and gave me a hug and kiss. When I think about it I can still feel it!

~ Parent Soup member Ptmli

An Added Dimension

I knew I was a great mom when my almost three-year-old said, "Mama, you and me are friends." It made my year.

~ Parent Soup member MAMA ME794

The Eye of the Beholder

My three-year-old son walked into the bathroom when I was getting ready for work the other day and asked me what I was doing. I told him I was fixing my hair and getting ready to put on my makeup. He looked up at me and smiled his sleepy little smile (it was six in the morning) and said, "You no have to put on makeup or fix hair, Mommy." I said, "Why not, baby?" And he replied, "Cause you booiful, Mommy." I cried and went to work with no makeup on just for him. He made my millennium!

~ Parent Soup member BartenderG

Once my four-year-old heard me complaining about my weight to my husband. He told me, "Mom you are pretty just the way you are." I cried for an hour.

~ Parent Soup member Rkinney352

Role Reversal
The one thing I love about being a mom is when my three-year-old son teaches me things. Especially new songs that he learns in preschool. And when I do it right, he claps and says, "Good job, Mama, good job" and high-fives me.
  ~ *Parent Soup member KuteTay*

Now That's Saying Something!
I knew I was a great mom when my four-year-old told me she loved me more than cake and ice cream.
  ~ *Tia L., Wingdale, New York*

NO!

Chances are you've already heard this word from your toddler's mouth at least three times already today. So you know how exasperating it is when, no matter what question you ask, you are constantly being told "No." This exasperation is a good clue to what's going on in your toddler's mind—he is beginning to realize that he has the ability to make his own decisions, but you are still calling all the shots. Here, Dr. Greene explains why toddlers are compelled to say no all the time, and how to best deal with this behavior so that your child can learn to make decisions on his own with minimal exasperation (yes!).

n no!

~~~~~~

The Dreaded No Monster

Q: My two-year-old has switched personalities with a monster. He says no to everything I say or ask. He used to be such a sweet and loving boy—he still is, but only sometimes now. It seems as though he sets out to test me every step of the way, and I am afraid I am doing something wrong, or that one day I am going to lose control. Has anybody been through this, and what worked for you?

~ *Parent Soup member NrsnMom*

DR. GREENE'S INSIGHT

A: Children of perfect parents (if there were such a thing!) would still need to go through the developmental phase your son is going through. Ideal children do *not* always agree with their parents. Ideal parenting does not prevent the "Terrible Twos"—it helps children navigate them. Although children are each born with a unique personality, their early experiences are profoundly influenced by their physical states and by their environments (primarily their parents). Thus, early on, your son wanted things that made you happy, that engaged your attention. When you smiled, he smiled. When you became tense, he became emotionally agitated. Because his moods were usually in synch with yours, he seemed like a "good boy." Gradually, though, sometime after he had mastered walking, an irresistible urge to make his own choices began to well up inside him. This is an exciting development, but the difficulty with his making an independent choice is that he must disagree with you in order for the choice to be his own. Now, when you ask him to do something, he refuses. It is unpleasant to have anyone passionately disagree with you. When this opposition comes from your own child, the situation is decidedly disagreeable.

Many people call this important phase of development the "Terrible Twos." I prefer to call it the "First Adolescence." This period begins long before age two and actually continues long afterward, but in the majority of children, it is most intensely focused around the period from one and a half to three years of age. The hallmark of this stage is oppositional behavior. Our wonderful children instinctively want to do exactly the opposite of what we want. We have nice, reasonable expectations and they say, "No!" or they simply dissolve into tears. Suppose you have some place to get to in a hurry. Your son has been in a great mood all day . . . until you say, "I need you to get into the car right now." He will, of course, want to do anything except get into the car. As if this weren't enough, children in this phase of development have a great deal of difficulty making the choices they so desperately want to make. You ask your child what he would like for dinner, and he says macaroni. You lovingly prepare it for him, and then as soon as it's made he says, "I don't want that!" It is perfectly normal for him to reverse a decision as soon as he has made it, because at this stage, he even disagrees with himself. His task is to gain skill at making appropriate choices. To help him accomplish this, offer your son limited choices at every opportunity. He will be frustrated when he is given direct commands with no options. On the other hand, he will be frustrated if he has too many alternatives. So two or three options generally work best. Your son still needs the security of knowing that he's not calling all the shots. When it's time to eat, say something like, "Would you rather have a slice of apple or a banana?" He feels both the reassuring limits that you set and the freedom to exercise his power within those limits.

This phase is difficult for parents; it is also hard for children. When children take a stand that opposes their parents, they experience intense emotions. Although they are driven to become their own unique persons, they also long to please their parents. Even now, when I do something that my parents disagree with, I feel very conflicted. For a child who is tentatively learning to make choices, who is dependent on his parents for food, shelter, and emotional support, it's even more intense. Dissolving into tears is an appropriate expression of the inner turmoil that is so real for children who are in the midst of this process. I like to think of the process as similar to childbirth. Labor is a very intense experience. Pain after pain after pain eventually produces something beautiful—a child is born. The episodes of oppositional behavior in "First Adolescence" are psychological labor pains—one difficult situation, then another, and another, and as a result your son's own persona is being born psychologically. This is a beautiful (but difficult) time with a truly worthwhile result. Try to remember that these conflicts are not caused by something you are doing wrong, and it won't last forever.

Lessening the Impact

A: Typical two! My daughter has been the same way. Here are some ways I have dealt with it. Largely, I try not to let it get to me. I came to the conclusion that two-year-olds just like to use the word _no_ even when they don't mean it. I think it becomes habit. Second, I make her stick to her decisions. For instance, if I ask her if she wants some juice and she says no, I don't give her any. When she tries to change her mind, I stick to my guns and say, "I'm sorry, you told Mommy no. You'll just have to wait until later." It didn't take too many times of this happening for my daughter to really think about how she would answer my questions. Also, along the same line I realized I had to give her the right kind of choices. I no longer ask her, "Do you want to wear this?" or, "Do you want peas?" I try to find other choices, to let her make her own decision, like picking out what bow or barrette she wants to wear in her hair. That way, she feels like she gets the opportunity to make decisions, but they aren't vital decisions.

> ~ Lisa K., Tucker, Georgia

Humor Always Helps

A: Have the Tickle Monster pay a visit. When your child is refusing to do something (get in her booster chair or have her diaper changed), use humor to break the tension between the two of you. She may just forget what she was so adamantly against.

> ~ Monica H., Evanston, Illinois

NURSING

The two main concerns of Parent Soup moms who are nursing their toddlers are the negative reactions of other people ("You're *still* breastfeeding?") and how to gradually wean without losing the special feeling of closeness that breastfeeding provides. Here the experts— nursing mothers and La Leche League—share their tips.

Dealing with Flak

Q: Has anyone noticed that the hardest thing about toddler nursing is the attitudes of other people?

> ~ Christina E., San Lorenzo, California

n nursing

Short and Sweet Responses

A: I do get strange looks and comments, but I simply tell people that the World Health Organization states that worldwide the norm is to breastfeed into the third and sometimes the fourth year. Or sometimes I just tell strangers with questions, "Yeah, I'm weird and happy."
~ *Wendi H., Montreal, Quebec*

LA LECHE LEAGUE RESPONDS

A: If you truly don't want to nurse in public, you can try to make certain you've nursed your toddler before you go somewhere. You can nurse at home before you go out, in the car before you go into a store or establishment, or at a friend's house before going somewhere. You can keep drinks and snacks on hand to dissuade her as much as she'll allow. But if you have a toddler who really needs to nurse when you're out, even these tricks may not work. And this is when you'll have to decide how to handle it. You can wear clothes that make nursing easier (shirts that pull up, nursing tops, jumpers with long armholes and tops, and occasionally shirts that you can unbutton from the middle, for example). One nice thing about a toddler who really wants and needs to nurse, no matter where you are, is that they usually get right down to business and nurse. You can quickly and discreetly put your child to your breast and usually not attract much attention. But refusing or trying to put off a toddler who really can't understand "No" or "Wait," will attract more attention! Having a code word for nursing can make this even easier. Some babies will say "Na-na" or something that sounds similar to "nurse" to let Mom know they need to nurse. Also, there are some places in public that make it easier to nurse. If you're in a mall, dressing rooms are very convenient. Most restaurants are convenient, especially if you're not in the middle of the room. If anyone notices you, they'll probably just think your child is falling asleep in your arms. As far as any concerns you have about your right to nurse, you have every right to nurture and nourish your child by nursing her. Many, many women are nursing toddlers (and in public), and this is perfectly OK. One way to find more support for your decision to nurse your toddler might be to contact your local La Leche League leader and attend meetings. It can be very reassuring to see others making the same choices.

When It's Time to Start Weaning

We are starting to slowly cut back on how often we nurse. I say "we," I guess I mean "me." A couple months ago my daughter was nursing every 20 minutes. I was going nuts. I felt so attacked, and so resentful. I started sending her off with her daddy whenever possible, just so I wouldn't have to nurse, which any idiot (except this one) could've figured out only made her want to nurse all the more when we were together. I was afraid that if I just said no, she would go ballistic. Finally I was desperate enough to risk saying, "No, we're not going to 'nooni' right now, but I'll read you a book!" She didn't cry and seemed perfectly happy to read instead. All she wanted was attention, and we were both in the habit of nursing for interaction. I started by making my goal to nurse no more than once an hour, then every two hours. Now we're down to four or five times a day. She's been great about it. Sometimes I think she asks to breastfeed when she really wants to read. Another trick for a few days was "pretend nooni." She knew all about pretend eating her plastic food, so one time when I told her she'd have to wait and she seemed a bit upset, I told her she could pretend. She put her mouth up to my (clothed) breast and made smacking noises, and I sang a special song, "I Like to Hold My Maggie." I want to be clear that I do not think kids "ought" to be weaned

n nursing

Worldwide, what is the
average age for weaning
children from the
breast?

a. 6 months

b. 15 months

c. 2.3 years

d. 3 years

e. 4.2 years

Answer: e

at any age. I have no idea how long it will be until she is completely
weaned. I just felt very strongly that it was time to cut back, that both of
us were using it as the only way to snuggle, to reassure, to comfort after a
bump on the head, to break boredom. Now it is one of several things we
do together, or ways to solve problems.

~ *Eliza K., Waltham, Massachusetts*

Cut Down on the Nursing, Keep the Closeness

I just weaned my 32-month-old son. I had to do it very gradually. After
my second child was born, he tapered off on his own, but I started to
resent his nursing and had to take the lead in weaning him. He nursed
about seven minutes at a time, so I started with that number and allowed
three nursings per day of that length (morning, nap, night). We decreased
a minute each week and finally ended up at 15 seconds. Then I made a
big deal about what a big boy he is and he doesn't need "nummies," just
cuddling and real food or milk. He accepted it, and even though he still
asks to nurse sometimes (mainly because his sister is), he is OK. I make it
a point to pay lots of attention and to cuddle when we would normally
nurse, so he still gets the closeness.

~ *Parent Soup member Tmellon40*

Enlisting the Help of the Sun and the Moon

Several of my friends who are nursing children over age two have begun
to limit nursing to only daylight hours. The child is interested in knowing
what is going on in the world around him, and pointing out the sun and
the moon to him may be just enough to get him to understand the difference between night and day. Telling my 20-month-old that "We are only
nursing when the sun is out" is an explanation that is right on his level of

understanding. He may even not ask to nurse on a cloudy day! For us, it helps to keep really busy during the day. My son definitely nurses a lot less when we are out and about. He still has the security of my presence, but doesn't seem to need to reconnect at the breast quite so much.

~ *Lisa J., Wellington, Florida*

PACIFIER *(See also Thumb-Sucking)*

Pacifiers can be both friend and foe to toddlers: they are soothing, but children can become dependent on them. There is the school of thought that a child should be able to use the pacifier until he decides to give it up himself (see the poll results on page 138). But many parents feel that there is a definite time and place for the pacifier to go, perhaps because they fear future orthodontia, or think their child is overdependent on the binky. If you're ready to say "bye-bye, binky," here are some tips that have worked for other families. Keep in mind that taking away the pacifier is taking away a source of comfort (imagine if someone told you no more mashed potatoes, or sweatpants), so be extra-sensitive to your child's need to be soothed.

An Incentive Program
My oldest daughter was so attached to the pacifier that we thought she would never give it up. Finally, she gave it up a little after her third birthday. I used stickers as incentives: When she slept through the night without the pacifier she got a sticker. When she filled her sticker book she got a present of her choosing. It worked really well.

~ *Judy V., Kennet Square, Pennsylvania*

p pacifier

Enlisting Santa's Help

This Christmas, tell your child to give his pacifier to Santa Claus so that he can give the pacifier to a newborn baby for Christmas. It worked for my nephew, who was just over three years old.

~ *Sharon H., Berwyn, Pennsylvania*

PARENT POLL

When should a child stop using a pacifier?

Of 1,396 total votes

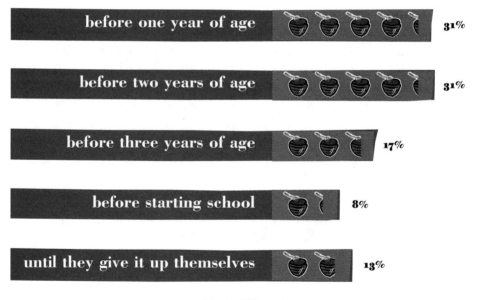

before one year of age	31%
before two years of age	31%
before three years of age	17%
before starting school	8%
until they give it up themselves	13%

1 bowl = 100 parents

Keep the Comfort Level High

I have read that sometimes you shouldn't use the "you're a big boy now" line on them because they don't want to be a big boy completely yet. So they might keep the habit because part of them still wants to be your little baby (especially if there is a younger sibling who is getting a lot of attention). If your son seems to need the pacifier for comfort, try substituting another comfort object, such as a stuffed animal or blanket. If you take away the pacifier sooner than he is ready, he may figure out about his thumb, and that is an even harder habit to break.

~ *Suzanne L., Pasadena, California*

Cold Turkey Works for Some

When my son was two and a half his speech therapist told us to get rid of the pacifier. She said the best way to do it was throw it out. It actually worked, we went cold turkey. He would wake up at night looking for it, but we told him it was lost, to go back to sleep. It didn't take him long to realize it was not going to be found. Once you stop giving it to him, be sure you don't break down and give it back if he's having a rough day— hang in there.

~ *Parent Soup member Debbwill*

"If It's Broke, Don't Fix It"

My two-year-old daughter kept her binky by her bed to have at bedtime. One day before her nap, I took her pacifier and cut off the nipple and laid both parts back where she kept them. She found her "broken" binky and we "tried" to fix it, to no avail. This way she could see the broken binky and not just be told that she couldn't have it anymore. Then she threw it away herself for better impact. She handled it quite well.

~ *Parent Soup member EricLive*

Don't Let the Naysayers Get You Down
If your child uses a pacifier as comforter for a long time, so what? I
never took away my children's special stuffed bunnies—they are still in
their rooms at ages 12 and 14. You don't have to let your three- or four-
year-old walk around with a pacifier all day. But, if it helps him separate
from the family at bedtime and provides nighttime comfort, so be it.
Don't let others make you feel bad about being sensitive to your little
one's needs.
   ~ Rebecca M., Richmond, Virginia

PICKY EATERS

You could go crazy with worry over how
much your child is (or isn't) eating. You
could constantly follow her around the
house with a plate of food, saying,
"Won't you eat for Mommy?" But that
would make you neurotic and her nervous.
And the only person who would end up
eating more would probably be you. How
can you make sure she eats enough of the
right stuff? First, remember that toddlers think differently about food than
adults do. Your daughter wants to graze as she moves from one activity
to another. She may love one food one day, hate it the next. You may not
be able to change (or understand) her relationship to food, but you can
accommodate it. Here are some tips that have worked for other parents
that have kept their kids healthy and themselves sane.

Compare Growth Records

It has been frustrating to get my daughter to eat throughout her entire toddlerhood. She fell off the growth chart a long time ago (she's 29 months, 24 pounds). I just compared my daughter's growth history to my sister's (she made my own mother a wreck when she was small) and my nephew's, and all three were almost identical. We were just always tiny and caught up as teenagers. It made me feel so much better!

~ *Mary K., Catonsville, Maryland*

Baby Fat Isn't Just Adorable

I'm convinced that this is why baby fat is so important! They live on all that fat they stored up during infancy.

~ *Lisa K., Tucker, Georgia*

Getting Them to Eat Their Veggies

Does your toddler say yuck to the green stuff? Try frozen peas. Most kids love them, and they are healthier than candy.

~ *Parent Soup member A Souper mom*

Both of my boys love pancakes, and I have started mincing veggies and blending them into the pancakes.

~ *Christine E., Norwich, Connecticut*

One thing I make for my two-year-old are potato pancakes with zucchini in them. He doesn't even realize it's there. Another trick I do is put peas in his toasted cheese. My son just doesn't realize you can have a toasted cheese any other way!

~ *Mary Jo W., Harrisburg, Pennsylvania*

We always offer vegetables. We always talk about how good the vegetables were that night at dinner. We never force veggies. We never say the kids have to eat them. We give a complete vitamin, so we don't worry. Our six-year-old is the first real graduate of this program. He lists his favorite foods as broccoli, green beans, and cauliflower. Our two-year-old grabs a carrot stick out of the fridge if he wants a snack. We have found that if we don't make a big deal out of veggies, then our kids don't know that it is a big deal.

~ *Parent Soup member Xccow*

The Magical Power of Grandparents
We just came back from vacation and found out something pretty funny: my son (27 months) ate all sorts of stuff at my mom's house that he normally doesn't eat when we were gone, such as steamed broccoli, cauliflower, and asparagus. She said she made little broccoli "trees" and then put them on a separate plate, out of his reach, and just put it near him on the table. He just looked at it for a while, then asked for the "trees." Of course, when we came home we tried this and it was nothing doing. But I am definitely going to try the out-of-reach idea and see if he will try some new things. I know that he is always interested in what's on our plates and will sometimes eat the food off of our plates, but ignore the same thing when it's on his.

~ *Amy A., Costa Mesa, California*

The one thing that encouraged a love of healthy food for our son (two and a half now) was the influence of my father-in-law. When my son started on table food full-time I happened to be staying with "Pop-pop" for a few months. Our son loved his Pop-pop, and he saw how Pop-pop liked his vegetables. He began to find that they weren't so bad. To tell you the truth, that was the same trick that worked with our daughter (six now). The only difference was that Pop-pop would talk with her on the phone. I'm not sure what it was about his touch, but it worked.

~ *Julie R., Millington, Tennessee*

Easy on the Liquids

I have been told by more than one doctor and nutritionist to watch how much fruit juice you give a small child, because it curbs their appetite by filling their stomachs up. If their cup is being filled all day long, they don't want much food, just a bite here and a bite there. If it makes any of you feel any better, I too feel like an automated snack machine.

~ *Jennifer G., Goose Creek, South Carolina*

Our toddler wasn't eating very much until we asked his doctor about it and she suggested we cut back on the amount of milk he drank during the day. As soon as we eliminated all-day milk drinking on demand, he suddenly became ravenous and even started eating vegetables.

~ *Ellen M., New York, New York*

Introducing New Foods

Whenever I was trying to get my son to eat a new food, I always kept one nearby that I knew he liked. We would rotate bites of the new food and the favorite. That way he wouldn't refuse to eat altogether.

~ *Parent Soup member Luvz49rz*

Fill his plate with things you know he'll eat and a little bit of something that is new. Don't make a big deal about tasting the new thing; in fact, don't even mention it's there. Sometimes they get on a roll and eat the new thing before they realize they've done it.

~ *Lisa K., Tucker, Georgia*

I read recently that you need to introduce a new food an average of 17 times before a toddler will accept it—most parents (I know I do) give up long before that!

~ *Holly W., Helena, Montana*

If you're enjoying what you eat, your child will get "jealous" and ask for some. Try to eat things that it would be OK to give to her, so you can offer a taste if she shows an interest.

~ *Anne W., Cranford, New Jersey*

When I feed my daughter new foods, I whistle. When I whistle she pays attention to me, and so I start sneaking in the food.

~ *Parent Soup member Joemagda*

Teaching Toddlers to Use Utensils

As far as the spoon goes, the only thing you can really do is keep giving it to her. Get two or three different kinds and give them all to her at every meal. Eat in front of her while she's in her chair so she can see you do it close-up. Help her hold it and scoop a spoonful a couple of times at each meal. And don't act tense or forceful about it, because kids can sense tension or fear better than a Doberman.

~ *Angela K., South Bound Brook, New Jersey*

Stop Obsessing

As much as it doesn't help to hear it, say it to yourself, chant it, or tattoo it on your forehead: You just have to relax about what your son eats and how he grows. I know how hard it is: my son has always been small. The bottom line is he's happy, smart, energetic, and a good kid. So if he skips meals, refuses fruit, rarely eats veggies, I've got a keeper and I might as well just learn to (sigh) grin and bear it. (One note: I put Ovaltine in his milk, as it adds lots of vitamins. He loves it, and I feel better.)

~ *Karen K., Concord, California*

Unless your child is losing weight, just let her eat what she wants and continue to offer different foods. She'll try them when you're not looking. I was really worried about my daughter's eating habits, and she didn't grow out of them until I quit making an issue out of it.

~ *Parent Soup member KyleFarrar*

Variety Is the Spice of Life

If your kids are picky eaters, offer them a variety of healthy foods—try the muffin-pan method. Put small amounts of finger food into the different sections of a muffin pan and leave the pan where they can help themselves. Another thing that helps ease my mind is I don't try to balance their daily intake. I shoot for a balanced week instead.

~ *Kristine S., Port Reading, New Jersey*

The Shape of Things to Come

Find out which design he likes and then cut his food to match—for example, cut his sandwich into a star shape. It helped with my son!

~ *Parent Soup member RAT253*

Have you discovered the joys of cookie cutters yet? My two-and-a-half-year-old insists that her lunch be in shapes. If it's possible to use a cookie cutter on it to make it something special, I do it. It really turns plain old sandwiches into something fun.

~ *Lisa K., Tucker, Georgia*

Top 10 Ways to Encourage a Healthy Appetite
Here are some activities that help enhance a child's interest in eating healthier foods:

1. Make "I tried it" badges for your child to wear (I actually have seen these at teacher supply stores recently).

2. Ask your child her favorite color and buy foods that color: orange for oranges or cantaloupe, green for kiwi, etc.

3. Have your children help plan menus and help with shopping. Plan a week of lunches out together. Tell your child that you need a fruit, vegetable, protein, and bread for each meal and give him the opportunity to pick which ones he wants. You can make a poster of choices if it is hard for him to remember which is which. Write it down and put it on the calendar. That way he can see that he is going to have grilled cheese, oranges, and carrots for lunch. Having a menu also makes it official—if you have it on the menu there won't be any whining. Even if your child isn't reading yet, you can tell him the menu says we are having this for lunch today, I am really sorry that you want something else, maybe you could choose it for our menu next week.

4. Let your child help with the meal preparation. Yes, it may take longer, but think of the time you will save not sitting at the table forever while she picks at supper.

5. Do art projects centered around food, place mats, puzzles, drawing, or making a collage of foods.

6. Prepare individual portions—miniloaves of bread or meat loaves

7. The easiest way to get a child to eat is to serve food with some sort of dip, dressing, or sauce.

8. Celebrate a theme: have a soup week, a color week, letter of the week (e.g., on Monday this week all foods will start with *A*).

9. Grow your own veggies—children will eat what they pick off a plant even if they won't eat it when you buy it at the store.

10. Don't serve foods that your child has a hard time eating—for example, soups are hard to spoon up. Get kid-sized metal eating utensils.
    ~ *Tarrant F., Gainesville, Florida*

When Picky Eaters Become Feisty Eaters
In our house, the rule is "If you throw it, you lose it." A few tummy grumblies might work wonders to break this habit! (Don't give in and give snacks until the next scheduled time to eat or the consequences won't be very effective.)
    ~ *Karen K., Appleton, Wisconsin*

TRIVIA QUESTION

Which vitamin—A, B, C, D, or E—promotes good eyesight and helps keep the skin resistant to infection?

Answer: A

Some of the best sources are sweet potatoes, fortified milk, carrots, kale, turnips, and liver.

From *Parent Soup: The Game*

147

PICKY EATERS' CARROT BROWNIES

¼ cup unsweetened
   cocoa powder
1 cup flour
1½ teaspoon baking
   powder
½ cup sugar
1 cup carrots (shredded)
¼ cup milk
2 tablespoons vegetable
   oil
2 eggs
1 teaspoon vanilla
   extract

Mix cocoa, flour, and baking powder. Mix in sugar and carrots. Lightly beat together the milk, oil, eggs, and vanilla. Then add to dry stuff. Mix until just blended. Bake in 350-degree oven for 20 minutes in a nine-inch square pan. Cool and cut into 16 squares.
   ~ *Karen K.,
   Concord,
   California*

My 13-month-old twins throw food, too. So now I ask them if they are finished (they don't really answer) and then clean up their tray. I hope that sometime in the future they will start to say "Done" and stop dropping their food on the floor to show me that they are finished.
   ~ *Lori F., Phoenix, Arizona*

My son, now 23 months, loves to throw food. After getting tired of cleaning up the mess off my walls and kitchen floor from his throwing food from his high chair, I got him a toddler table, which I put in the family room (right next to the kitchen). Even though I can't stop him from getting up and walking around during mealtime, he has totally stopped throwing food. I usually sit down and eat with him to help keep him sitting there longer, but he is actually eating more (probably because it stays on his plate, instead of landing on the floor). I try to prepare finger foods that he can take with him when he gets up to take a quick stroll around the room. Then he'll come back and sit down for a refill when his hands are empty.
   ~ *Parent Soup member Luvz49rz*

DR. GREENE'S INSIGHT on Kids and Vitamins

An ancient Greek definition of children is short humans who don't like vegetables. Vitamins are, by definition, compounds necessary in trace amounts for the normal functioning of the human body. We need vitamins in order to see the world around us, to grow, to make bones and connective tissue, to fight infections and cancer, to heal wounds, to stop from bleeding to death, and to keep our teeth from falling out. Vitamins cannot be manufactured in sufficient amounts by the body and must be taken in from the environment. They occur naturally in many foods and are also available as commercial nutritional supplements. By eating whole foods (such as fresh vegetables, fresh fruit, and whole grains), your child can get the necessary vitamins in the healthiest way. One of the challenges of parenting is to make eating these whole foods as pleasant an experience as possible. Even though many children have periods when they are quite picky eaters, most children get the minimum known requirements for vitamins from the foods they eat.

Nevertheless, we live in an age of highly processed foods. Even our fruits and vegetables are often grown using agricultural techniques that minimize the vitamin and mineral contents. Thus, I like giving children multivitamins as supplements to the vitamins they get in their food. For most children who began eating solid foods by six months old, I would begin adding a vitamin supplement at the first birthday. Often children in the toddler and preschool years are picky eaters. As children grow their tastes change, and over time they should begin to eat a more well-rounded diet. A vitamin "safety net" takes the pressure off of feeding issues during the early years. Without pressure or worry, you can be free to be creative about increasing whole foods in your child's diet knowing that vitamins are present to help your child grow strong and healthy.

A Possible Cause of a Seemingly Small Appetite

I was having a really hard time getting my son to eat anything other than junk. Because he was a preemie and still not talking (at almost two and a half), he was undergoing speech therapy. Part of the therapy was for the therapist to watch him eat. For some reason, he wasn't using all of the muscles in his mouth and tongue. What I never really noticed was that when he ate, he would only partially chew the food and swallow part of it whole. That was another reason he wasn't talking (not using the muscles). The therapist advised getting a certain toothbrush (Gerber NUK). The box comes with three different toothbrushes. One of the toothbrushes has an oval rubber tip with little bumbles all over it. If you rub this brush over the roof of his mouth, the inside of his cheeks, tongue, gums, and lips, it stimulates the muscles. It worked! From not eating anything, my son will now eat chicken, sandwiches, turkey, and even some fruit (we are still working on vegetables).

~ Parent Soup member Tio909

Making Food Preparation Easier

I cut up things like spaghetti or other types of pasta with a pizza cutter. It's easier than sitting and cutting with a fork and knife; you just roll it back and forth. Just be sure to keep it away from your child!

~ Parent Soup member Powerstrt

When Picky Eaters Get Constipated

Q: My son is an incredibly picky eater. He won't eat meat, peanut butter, peanuts, or beans of any kind. He only eats cheese, anything with cheese on it, spaghetti (plain), and drinks tons of milk. Consequently, he is forever constipated. I have talked to the doctor, and he has suggested giving him mineral oil. I tried that, and he spit it right out. Does anyone have any ideas?

~ Parent Soup member JRStrait

A: This may sound gross, but my daughter eats it: put prunes in a food processor, blender, or minichopper (my personal favorite), chop them up pretty fine, and then make a batch of muffins. Substitute prune juice for part of the milk in the recipe if you want to. They taste pretty good, and they do the trick.

~ Allison A., Hope Mills, South Carolina

What do you do if your toddler refuses to eat vegetables?

Of 811 total votes

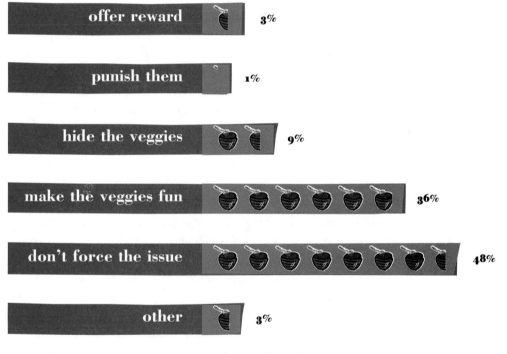

offer reward — 3%

punish them — 1%

hide the veggies — 9%

make the veggies fun — 36%

don't force the issue — 48%

other — 3%

1 bowl = 50 parents

p picky eaters

TRIVIA QUESTION

What vegetable has three times the vitamin C of an orange?
a. Cabbage
b. Peppers
c. Corn
d. Beets

Answer: b

A: Try mixing the mineral oil with pudding. It usually works for my little constipation king.

~ *Parent Soup member Mrich86*

Homemade Fruit-Flavored Yogurt

I'm sure Earth's Best makes a fabulous yogurt, but I also know that their jars of food can run up to 75 cents each. Why waste all that money? I always buy the large containers of plain yogurt (not fat free or low fat) and mix it with fruit I've pureed in my blender. Stephanie is 13 months old and eats it every day for lunch. I really love it because I can be creative with the flavors. I use bananas, peaches, pears, pineapples, prunes, and mandarin oranges, all packed in water or fruit juice (drained).

~ *Parent Soup member Imperamas*

Incorporating Tofu

I've recently added tofu to my 19-month-old daughter's diet. She actually really likes it. She would choose raisins or carrots over a cookie, too (strange child, huh?). Here are some things we've tried:

1. Stir-fry firm tofu with veggies and stir-fry sauce. Serve alone or with rice.

2. Tofu with mushrooms: Sauté some chopped onions in a little butter, add mushrooms (sliced, halved, or whole) and cubed tofu. Cook until mushrooms are done. Season with a little sugar, salt, and soy sauce.

3. Spinach lasagna with tofu: add the tofu (crumbled finely or mashed) to the ricotta. You can also add it directly to the sauce (mashed also) for either spaghetti or lasagna.

From *Parent Soup: The Game*

152

4. You can buy "tofu burger" mixes, or you can make your own tofu burgers by mixing sautéed veggies (shredded is best) with mashed tofu and some eggs to hold it together. Form into patties and panfry.

Good luck!

~ *Phoebe L., Plainfield, New Hampshire*

Getting Them to Eat Fruit

Slice a banana in half lengthwise, spread with peanut butter, and put it back together like a sandwich. Provide whole strawberries, grapes, and banana slices with dip selections like powdered sugar, cool whip, and plain yogurt. Some people like to eat grapes and watermelon frozen. There are also lots of recipes out for smoothies made with fruit, yogurt, and milk or ice-cream.

~ *Lisa K., Tucker, Georgia*

One way I found to get my son to eat fruit was to puree it and freeze it in cups. It's like having a slushee, except it's healthy, and he eats it up.

~ *Linda L., Morrison, New York*

POTTY TRAINING

It's easy for adults to forget just how strange it is to go from using diapers to sitting on the toilet. It can be so hard, in fact, that you begin to envision your child as the only person at the senior prom in diapers. This is one issue that can quickly escalate into a battle of wills between you and your child, so it's best to have an arsenal of strategies handy to avoid getting stuck in any one routine. So here is that arsenal. But remember, just as with all parenting issues, there is no one best way to potty train your child. Be prepared to try a few different tactics before you find one that will let you say "So long" to diapers.

Getting Started

Pick a week that you can devote to full-time potty teaching. Tell your daughter that D day is coming. ("Starting Monday, you aren't going to wear diapers anymore.") Don't buy any more diapers or pull-ups. Get her up on D day and take her to the bathroom. (Don't ask, "Honey, do you need to go potty?" the answer will be no.) Take her and sit with her. After she goes or after a reasonable amount of time on the potty (five minutes) have her put her panties on and dress her in something easy to get on and off, perhaps a cotton dress or T-shirt. Set the timer for 30 minutes if she didn't go, an hour if she did. Show her what you are doing. Say that when the timer rings it will be time to sit on the potty again. That way potty time isn't some bizarre mommy-just-has-nothing-to-do-but-torture-me thing. Make sure you give her plenty to drink between potty visits. If she has an accident, don't fuss about it, have her change her panties and clean it up. After the first day you can space out the time between successful visits. It may be effective for you to give something like a piece of candy or a sticker after some successful visits.

   ~ *Tarrant F., Gainesville, Florida*

Maybe you should ask her if she wants to wear a diaper or pants—we did that every day for two months with my daughter. She picked the diaper all the time first and then gradually switched to the pants.

   ~ *Parent Soup member Ckurkowski*

Take your child to play with children who've already mastered using the
toilet. Learning by example works wonders!
  ~ *Parent Soup member A Souper Mom*

DR. GREENE'S INSIGHT

A: Most children are ready to tackle the challenge of potty use somewhere
  between age two and shortly after their third birthday, with boys generally at
  the latter end of this range. Letting you know when their diapers are dirty is
  an early sign of readiness. When they start to let you know just before they
  need to go, it is time to begin. By understanding the underlying forces that
  surround this issue, you will be able to identify which of the many
  suggestions out there are most likely to work for your child.

  The first force is the intrinsic powerful urge in children to grow and
  develop. Closely coupled with this is the strong desire to imitate those they
  care about and admire. You can capitalize on this by reading aloud together
  as a family one of the outstanding books that describe potty use as a part of
  growing up. My favorite is *Toilet Learning* by Alison Mack. Illustrations of
  firefighters, doctors, babysitters, and parents all going to the bathroom will
  delight and educate your son. Watching the same-sex parent or older sibling
  in the bathroom reinforces this process. Buying him fun new underwear can
  further encourage him. If these were the only forces affecting potty training,
  there would be no problem. Fear often plays a major role: fear of failure,
  fear of disappointing one's parents, or fear of the potty can derail the
  process. Potty training tends to come at an age when children's fears are
  most intense. Depressurize the situation: if your child seems to be afraid of
  the toilet itself, then gradually acclimatize him to the potty. Have him sit on
  one of the little potties fully clothed for a few minutes each day while you
  read to him or tell him a story. When that becomes old hat, take his diaper

155

off so he can sit on it just like Dad and Mom. Eventually this will become old hat, too. Begin putting his dirty diapers in the pot so he can see what happens. Then give him the opportunity to run around bare-bottomed so he can try to go on the pot if he wants. If your child is afraid of failure, it is paramount that when he does make a mistake your response is not an exasperated or a punishing one. Instead say something like, "Oops, there it went. Someday soon they're all going to land in the potty. We'll try again." Reassure him that accidents are OK, and that he will ultimately succeed.

The desire for approval is another strong motivating force that impacts potty training. When he does get something in the potty, leave it there for him to admire. Congratulate him warmly, but don't get too excited or he will feel more pressure. Sometimes the desire for approval can work against potty training, particularly when a younger sibling is enchanting parents. The child may think that the best way to gain approval is to act like a baby again. Simple physical comfort can be a helpful force. Usually, going in the potty is considerably more comfortable than the alternatives. If children begin holding their stool in, however, the stool can become hard. It will be important to soften the stool using either diet or a gentle medicine from your doctor. During the toilet training process, it can be comfortable and convenient for children to wear pull-ups, but for some, this can slow the process by minimizing comfort as a motivating force. Physical readiness for potty training often occurs around the time that children develop strong oppositional behavior—you say "yes," they say "no!"; you say "red," they say "blue!" This underlying negativity is the final powerful force affecting potty training. Thankfully, this begins to fade at about age three. Still, if you tell him, "This is what you've got to do," his natural, healthy response is "no," because he is in the process of developing his unique independent personality. Potty training is not an area to enter into any kind of battle—everyone involved will lose. Instead, minimize the issue. Help teach him how to do it, but don't push and don't punish. Our role as parents is to help and to teach, but this will be his achievement.

Why Bowel Movements Are Harder to Learn

Many children are unable to have a bowel movement while sitting down until well into their fourth year. They have used the pressure on the bottom of their feet for the last three or so years to aid the process and are just physically unable to let their muscles relax without it. If you suspect that this is the case with your child (and it might be if you're hearing "I want a diaper, Mom/Dad"), you could try putting a footstool under your children's feet while on the potty. This obviously won't be effective if they are already using a child's potty chair, but if they are on a potty ring on the adult toilet, it might be just what is needed. Second, now is a great time to throw in an extra dose of affection at this time of great challenge in your child's (and your) life.

~ *Parent Soup member PSWendy*

Making Bowel Movements Easier

I had the hardest time getting my daughter to go number two in the toilet. Until I got an idea one morning as I was making coffee: I put some decaf in a mug her size, with lots of cream and sugar, and we went into the bathroom. I sat her on the toilet and we drank our coffee, stopping occasionally to make a toast, "To poop!" Eventually the coffee did its thing, and she pooped for the first time in the potty. Well, what an event

p potty training

When my son was smaller, he went through a phase where he had to look at every bathroom in town. We had gone to a nice restaurant for Father's Day that year, and as soon as we entered the door, he had to see the bathroom. I took him to the bathroom and he didn't have to do anything, so we got a table. About halfway through our meal, he tells us he has to go potty. I thought he was just saying this because he wanted to go see the bathroom again, so I told him to sit down and hush. He proceeds

that was! The light bulb went off in her little brain and she finally realized what I'd been trying to teach her. We had a couple more coffee club mornings to make sure she got the idea. The only thing was, when we went out to a restaurant shortly after that, I ordered coffee, and my daughter picked up her water glass when I picked up my mug, clicked her glass on mine, and shouted, "To poop!" That was fun to explain to my husband and the waitress!

~ Andrea L., Temecula, California

A hint that I just heard from someone whose child had a fear of the potty is to get one of the padded toilet seats. Apparently the softness of it helped a great deal in making the child comfortable to do a bowel movement on the potty.

~ Tarrant F., Gainesville, Florida

When Progress Stalls

Q: I have a three-year-old daughter who is not potty trained. She wears pull-ups, enjoys sitting on the toilet, and gets very excited when she urinates. The problem is she has been doing this for months. She has not made the transition to going to the toilet and using it when she has to go. How do I help her to make the transition from an occasional fun thing to do to using the toilet every time she has to go? I have been very relaxed about the whole potty training situation. I am beginning to think I have been too relaxed and need to give her a little more guidance and direction, and I am not sure how to do this without being too pushy.

~ Parent Soup member Anonymous

DR. GREENE'S INSIGHT

A: When toilet training progress comes to a halt, take time to consider the constellation of forces that work together to motivate a child to complete toilet training, and those that oppose completion. Altering the balance of forces will generally get the process rolling again. I commend you for not being pushy. Pushiness creates and complicates toileting problems. Trust your instinct, though, that your daughter needs "a little more guidance and direction." For a child to successfully master toilet training, there are two core concepts that must be assimilated.

First, a child needs to learn how to use the potty. This includes recognizing the urge to go, voluntarily using her muscles to hold it in, walking to the potty, and using different muscles to move the waste out. The second core concept is learning to use the potty consistently. This includes overcoming any reason for resistance and assuming responsibility for her own toileting. Explain to your daughter that every day her body is making pee and poop, and that pee and poop belong in the potty. Explain that since she has already done such a good job peeing in the potty, it's time for her to move to wearing panties throughout the day, instead of diapers or pull-ups. Tell her that when she feels the need to go, she should hold it in just long enough to walk to the potty, sit down, and let it go. It's OK if she has accidents—they're part of learning. At first she may need a little help recognizing the urge. When you notice behavior such as tugging at her clothes or shifting from foot to foot, point it out to her, and suggest that this might be a good time for the potty. Every time she comes to you and says she needs to go, smile. If she has already pooped in her pants, help her take it the rest of the way, and put the poop in the potty. Be excited with her when she gets it right! Be matter-of-fact about accidents. Say something

to stand up on his chair, grab both butt cheeks, and scream at the top of his lungs, "It's coming out!" Needless to say, his dad took him to the potty.

~ Parent Soup member M681CST

159

encouraging like, "Soon you'll get it in the potty every time!" Have her take off her dirty clothes and put them in the laundry. Avoid putting her back in pull-ups during the day, unless she seems truly overwhelmed (in which case offer reassurance, use pull-ups for the rest of that day only, and try underpants again in the morning).

Although this time can be a frustrating and messy one, it's a great opportunity for you to model for your daughter how to approach many of life's challenges:

- Facing new challenges, even scary ones, is the way we learn.

- Poop happens.

- Accidents are part of learning to do it right.

- Don't beat yourself up over mistakes.

- Overcoming a challenge is a process.

- Sometimes you just need to do it.

- Celebrate successes!

Yellow and Blue Make Green

Try putting a few drops of a different color food coloring in her potty dish every day. Tell her that when she makes pee-pee, she'll see a different color every time. This will encourage her as well as be entertaining and fun. After all, going to the bathroom is not very exciting, you need to make her excited about the experience, and she'll be excited to make that pee-pee in the potty.

~ *Parent Soup member Mabdf*

If Advertisements Work So Well for Toys, Why Not Toilets?
Here are some ideas to make potty learning more attractive to your little one. Make like a Madison Avenue advertising agency: make posters to hang around the house showing what life is like after toilet training. Come up with a jingle that you hum all the time, especially when you are using the toilet. Videotape a commercial for using the potty and then tape an episode of her favorite TV show to follow it; in the middle of the episode put another commercial for using the potty, and then again at the end. Round up children, friends, and relatives to "act" in the commercial. Use your daughter's stuffed animals using the potty in the commercial. Play potty-song tapes. Make a place mat of happy children using the potty for under her plate. Casually remark on how her bagels and Cheerios look like potty seats. Mention to your husband at supper that some "New statistics you read in the newspaper say that diaper changes take four times as long as using the toilet." He can reply, "Oh, I am so glad I use the potty." Overhearing something tends to sink in faster than lecturing. Don't say anything to her about her using the potty—just fill her life with these positive images of using the potty.

~ *Tarrant F., Gainesville, Florida*

Hi-Ho Cheerio
Try putting Cheerios in the potty to see if your son can sink them. My son loves it.

~ *Jeannie M., Phoenix, Arizona*

KIDS SAY THE
DARNEDEST
THINGS

My sister exaggerated quite a bit about her husband's inability to "hit the toilet" when he was urinating. When my nephew was being potty trained, he started crying one day when he had to go pee-pee. When my sister asked him what was wrong, he said, "If Daddy can't hit the potty with his great big pee-pee, how do you expect me to do it?" We still laugh about it today.

~ *Parent Soup member Ckhunter2*

161

p potty training

KIDS SAY THE DARNEDEST THINGS

My three-year-old son recently discovered hitting the bottom of a jar to make something come out—like a ketchup bottle. One day he was sitting on the toilet when I saw him hit himself on the top of the head. I asked why he was doing that, and he replied "It won't come out!"

~ *Judy D., Wolcott, Connecticut*

Getting Her to Sit Still on the Potty

My daughter sits very still when I do her nails. So, I put her on the potty and let her pick out a color. As I did her nails, I asked, "Did you go yet?" and she got the idea.

~ *Parent Soup member A Souper Mom*

Bed-Wetting

Do you notice whether or not your daughter is a heavy sleeper? When my son was three and a half, he was completely potty trained during the day, but at night he would continue to wet the bed. It wasn't that he didn't care that he was wet, it was just that he slept so soundly he didn't even know that he was, and when you woke him up he was a little upset about it. He couldn't feel the sensation of having to use the bathroom. It was really tough, but the only way we broke him of it was to set our alarm clock for around 2 A.M. and get up, wake him up, and have him go to the bathroom. Going potty was already a natural thing for him during the day, so there wasn't much fuss over going when we woke him. If you find that 2 A.M. is too late for your daughter, keep setting your clock back in half-hour increments until you catch her before she wets. We only had to keep it up for two weeks before he started waking up at that time on his own to go to the bathroom.

~ *Parent Soup member JustTeeezn*

Let Your Child Lead the Way

My advice—from experience—is that if your child wants a diaper, or asks for one, give it to her/him. It will make your life a lot easier, and he'll grow out of it when he's ready. Forcing them to go in their pants is unpleasant for the child and for the parent. However, there are a couple

162

of things I would do under these circumstances. If the child goes off and makes a mess in his diaper, wait a few minutes to change him. Don't be in such a rush. By age three and a half or four, many kids go to the bathroom in their diapers or pants, but then they want to be changed right away. This is the perfect opportunity to show them that they'd be more comfortable going in the toilet. Tell them, "Daddy is busy and I'll be with you in a few minutes." Remember that five minutes to a kid seems like an hour or so. Then, sit them down and take the opportunity to discuss what transpired. Let him or her explain the situation to you from their perspective. It may give you some insight into how the child is thinking or what concerns or fears they have. Ask them how they feel. Then, have the child help in some way with the cleanup. The bottom line is, don't scold them or punish them, but don't make it easy for them either. A delicate balance is needed. We've all been there! Someday, you'll have nothing more than faint memories.

~ *Brian F., East Meadow, New Jersey*

Trust me, with four of my own (and a three-year-old who is just now becoming cooperative at potty learning) I know from experience that you are beating your head against a wall to try to push a child into going in a potty before they are ready. You will end up fighting this until he is physiologically ready anyway. It's my opinion that you are way better off to wait and try again in several months. I mean, put the potty chair out in the garage and forget about it for that amount of time. Maybe then your son will be ready. If not, put it away again for another few months. This method of "working with the child" has been very successful for me and many of my friends' little ones.

~ *Parent Soup member PSWendy*

I think the best thing to do is to wait until your child lets you know when they are ready to potty train. I know it is easier said than done.

~ *Parent Soup member Never30*

Book Recommendation

The Parent's Book of Toilet Teaching is a great resource on the methods of toilet teaching a toddler. It goes through everything from the cues for readiness to how to teach them to wipe when they are done.

~ *Tarrant F., Gainesville, Florida*

PRESCHOOL

The subject of preschool causes some spirited discussions pro and con on the Parent Soup message boards. There are many reasons why you might decide to send your daughter to preschool—you need to go back to work, she longs to socialize, or you both could use a little time outside of the house. Ultimately, it's a decision only you can make. Here are some ideas to help you make your decision work for you and your daughter.

The Benefits of Preschool—for Mother and Child

The mother is not the only thing in a toddler's life now. They need to interact with other people, adults and children. When I went back to work, it was out of pure necessity and my son was two and a half. We were both ready for a social life. I was working part-time, which meant I was able to finally be around adults and he was able to have a lot of fun with other kids, do activities, and learn to play in a group. It was very good for both of us. I have two-year-old twins and am going to put them in some kind of a part-time program just to give me a break and let them have a change of pace. This doesn't mean I'm turning my children over to a stranger to raise.

~ *Parent Soup member Dickip*

I just put my toddlers in preschool twice a week, and have mornings free to do part-time work at home from the computer. It's worked miracles in my life. I'm still stressed all the time, but this is a good stress. I actually feel brain waves moving up there in my head. I realize I'm not so boring or unworthy or unattractive or unappealing after all. And it sure feels good to get that paycheck in hand. And the kids have a happier mom.

~ *Tracy R., Englewood, Ohio*

Setting the Stage
When it came time to go to preschool I talked to my daughter about it for weeks, telling her what a big girl she was and how much fun she would have at school. I took the time to visit a couple of times for anywhere from one to three hours with my daughter during the two weeks before she started. That way she sees that the place is OK because you are there with her and you have more time in between visits to talk about it with her; you're not just "leaving her there." I believe that talking it over with them makes all the difference. Remember, they are very intuitive, so skirting the issue will only be confusing to her.

~ *Parent Soup member CMReed32*

p preschool

Easing the First-Day Jitters

Q: My daughter will be starting preschool at two and a half. The only caregivers she has ever known are her parents and grandparents. What should I do on the first day of school? Do I just say goodbye and leave? That seems harsh. Should I stay with her in class for the first day or week? I would love to hear how others handled this transition.

~ *Michelle M., Morris Plains, New Jersey*

A: My son is starting preschool in a few weeks, too. We all went together to visit his school. The teacher was great. Even though the room was a mess since school was out, she talked about all the areas and activities, the kids that would be in the class, where the bathroom was, etc. Colin now talks about his school, his new friends at school (who he knows only by name), and especially the handyman (the teacher pointed out everything he would fix!). He talks like he's been going there already. Try to meet other classmates, so maybe when he starts, he already has a friend. Also, I know I'm more nervous about it than my son. But I know it's best that he has some time away from me. My husband may be the one to drop him off at the beginning, so my anxiety isn't transferred to my son.

~ *Julie D., Queensbury, New York*

A: I sat down with my two-year-old and drew a frame-by-frame story of exactly what was going to happen when I took him to his new school. When he went to school, he said, "Now you are going to go away, but you will come back like in the story, right Mom?"

~ *Parent Soup member Judi J.*

Find Out if You Can Stay the First Day

I would check with the school to see if you're able to stay with your child on the first day. I was allowed to stay the first day, but not after that. They told me they would call me if there was a problem. You know I was sitting by that phone for almost two weeks!

~ *Lynn S., Bellmore, New York*

The First-Day Blues—Yours

Q: Have you ever found yourself crying at drop-off, lingering too long, watching the clock until it's time to pick up your child? What do you do when you've decided to send your child to preschool and you are the one who's having a hard time with the separation?

~ *Parent Soup member AZ Michele*

A: I was very teary-eyed on my daughter's first day, but she just bounced right in. For the first week or so I watched the clock and really didn't accomplish anything while she was at school. Now it's getting better. I just matter of factly take her and go get her. I really don't think about it. Some days I accomplish a lot while she's in school and others I decide to be lazy. She is just doing great and loves every minute of it. I have accepted that she is a schoolgirl now and growing up, but I'm still sad when I think of her as a newborn and know that is never going to come back. I am so proud of her and all her accomplishments that I feel like my heart will burst, but

KIDS SAY THE DARNEDEST THINGS

My son started preschool yesterday not knowing any of the children in his class. It was his first day at preschool ever, so of course it was the highlight of the family's conversation last night. My son burst out, "Daddy, guess what, there were some of my friends in class today." My husband and I were both shocked—we had been to the open house the night before and no one we knew was there. So my husband said, "Really? What were their names?" My son said, "I don't know what their names are yet!" Now I thought this was funny at first, but when my husband and I were reflecting on it, we realized that he has the most wonderful view of life. Imagine how different your life would be if you went into a strange situation and viewed it not as a situation where you encounter strangers, but as a situation where you meet friends whose names you don't know yet.

~ *Tarrant F., Gainesville, Florida*

p preschool

KIDS SAY THE DARNEDEST THINGS

On my daughter's first day of preschool, I was so excited to pick her up and ask her how she liked it. I was surprised when she said, "Mommy, I didn't like it. My teacher doesn't know anything!" When I asked why, she replied, "She always asks, 'What color is this?' Mommy, she doesn't know her colors. I always have to tell her."

~ *Parent Soup member Rsevi10094*

at the same time I would love nothing better than to keep her little and helpless and home with me. According to my mom that feeling never goes away, so I guess it's pretty good that I am able to drop her off without bursting into tears.

~ *Angela K., South Bound Brook, New Jersey*

Getting Ready to Go

Have your preschooler choose clothes the night before for the following day. This eliminates some of the morning scramble and helps her remember everything from underpants to hair ties.

~ *Christina M., Galion, Ohio*

Send a Loving Lunch

As a preschool teacher of over 17 years, I can attest that the following ideas for lunch boxes help both the parent and the child feel more comfortable in their new setting. Put a picture of your family taped inside the lunch box as a way for the child to be having "lunch" with you, leave notes of encouragement on their napkin, and include some stickers so they can decorate the outside of their lunch box. Some good lunch ideas are the following: make "ants on a log" by cutting a celery stick in half, spreading on cream cheese or peanut butter, and then putting raisins on top; cut their sandwiches with cookie-cutter shapes; pack some dip and cut-up veggies for your child.

~ *Janice D., Austin, Texas*

How about slipping a special treat into your child's lunch box every now and then, something he doesn't normally get to eat? Sometimes I would even put a treat in my daughter's lunch that she could share with everyone. It made her feel so special to give a bit of her lunch to her friends. You can also draw little pictures on his napkin or decorate the plastic sandwich bags with stickers. And craft stores sell plain white lunch bags—you can use one of these occasionally and decorate the outside with stickers, magic markers, and glitter. He might even enjoy decorating his own lunch bag from time to time.

~ *Lisa K., Tucker, Georgia*

If Preschool Isn't a Viable Option

Preschool is not free in most places. If you can't afford preschool, there are many things you can do that give you the same result for far less cost. Library story times, classes with the local Department of Recreation, play groups, and similar activities introduce your child to socialization and structured learning. You can also buy inexpensive materials at any teacher's supply store or through educational catalogs to help you teach your child letters and their sounds, numbers, colors, and shapes.

~ *Isadora P., Rockville, Maryland*

Homeschooling

I really struggled when my son turned three and a half and all of his friends were going off to preschool. I started homeschooling my son with this kit from Learning Adventures, and it's great. It only costs $12, and we just love it. Every morning after breakfast we say the Pledge of Allegiance. Then we pray for God to open up his little mind and help make learning fun. Then we do two activities out of the workbook, which teaches everything from shapes, the alphabet, and simple math to writing, counting, and more. Afterward, we either do some music or an art activity. He just loves it, and his baby brother is learning too. I don't think that a preschool would care as much about my son as I do, and I don't think that anything can take the place of a mother's love. Oh, and for social interaction we do something every week with his friends in the neighborhood, such as going to the zoo, nature centers, or museums. So don't let others make you feel bad about keeping your kids home.

~ *Parent Soup member Mneeley933*

Homeschool Activity Ideas

Go to your local teacher supply store and get or just look at a book that covers activities for preschoolers. There are many good ones that cover everything: how to set up a room so that the child gets the most out of it, the best toys for the child's age (which are not expensive and usually can be found at yard sales or even in your home), different activities for your child, etc. A good basic one is *Every Day in Every Way*. There are some little books called *Teaching Home* and *Teaching Town* that go over different activities you can do in your home and how they teach while the children are having fun.

~ *Tarrant F., Gainesville, Florida*

How to Tell if Your Child Is Sick Enough to Stay Home from Preschool

My daughter's school has these guidelines. Maybe they will help. You should keep your child at home if they have one or more of these symptoms:

● a very sore throat or difficulty swallowing

● temperature of 100 degrees Fahrenheit or more

- a headache plus another symptom, such as vomiting

- an earache

- a severe cough

- diarrhea or vomiting

- a rash
  ~ Angela K., South Bound Brook, New Jersey

RESOURCES

For more specialized information on a variety of parenting topics, from allergies to dealing with divorce to special-needs children, please contact any of the following parenting organizations. Also included here are the best Web sites for parents, provided by such experts as the American Medical Association, the U.S. Department of Health and Human Services, and the American Academy of Pediatrics.

ASTHMA/ALLERGIES—The Asthma and Allergy Foundation of America
The Asthma and Allergy Foundation of America, 1125 Fifteenth Street NW, Suite 502, Washington, DC 20005; (800) 7-ASTHMA or (202) 466-7643.

r resources

ONLINE RESOURCES

ADVICE

www.parentsoup.com
Parent Soup
How could we not include
ourselves here? If you need
the advice of another parent
or a parenting expert, this is
your place. Just come to
Parent Soup and look
around—you'll find a unique
combination of information,
support, usefulness, and
conversation. Parent Soup
also has great interactive
tools, such as the Baby
Name Finder, and fun
games, such as the Baby
Name Jumble. No matter
where you're from or how old
your kids are, there's
something for you in the
Soup.

If your child is suffering from asthma or any other kind of allergy, this is
the place to call. A 24-hour toll-free hotline, (800) 7-ASTHMA handles
patient inquiries, such as how to find a doctor in your area. They also
have a helpful publication list, which includes booklets like "Sniffles
& Sneezes: A Parent's Guide to Managing Kids' Allergies"; call
(202) 466-7643, extension 226, to get one.

BREASTFEEDING—La Leche League
La Leche League International, P.O. Box 4079, Schaumburg, IL 60168-
4079; (800) LA-LECHE (9 A.M. to 3 P.M. CT, Monday through Friday).
Web site: www.lalecheleague.org

If you're breastfeeding, La Leche League can offer you education,
encouragement, and support. Their local support groups help you
connect with other mothers who are breastfeeding and give you a forum
to get answers to all your breastfeeding questions. La Leche also
publishes a comprehensive catalog that offers books, pamphlets,
accessories, gift packs, and videos on everything from birth to
adolescence. La Leche Leaders also answer questions and lead chats
on Parent Soup, so you can access all their good information via your
computer (www.parentsoup.com or AOL Keyword: ParentSoup). Call
their 800 number for a free catalog and information on support groups
near you.

CHILD ABUSE—Parents Anonymous
Parents Anonymous, 675 West Foothill Boulevard, Suite 220, Claremont,
CA 91711; (909) 621-6184 (for information on local chapters) and
(800) 352-0528 (24-hour crisis hotline).

Do you sometimes feel frustrated and angry with your children, overwhelmed by the responsibilities of being a parent, or afraid that you might hurt your children? Being a parent isn't always easy, but you can always get help from Parents Anonymous. Parents Anonymous is a child abuse prevention organization. Their Help Line provides 24-hour confidential support from trained volunteers who really understand. They can offer advice, suggest resources, answer questions, and give referrals. Local chapters of Parents Anonymous hold Parent Support Groups to provide help for parents from parents with the assistance of trained facilitators. Local chapters also offer the Nurturing Program—a series of parenting classes (with a class for parents with kids under age four) that work with parents and children to increase communication and self-esteem.

CHILD CARE—Child Care Aware

Child Care Aware, 2116 Campus Drive SE, Rochester, MN 55904; (800) 424-2246 (toll-free parent information line, 8:30 A.M. to 4:30 P.M., CT). E-mail: HN6125@handsnet.org. Web site: http://www.childcarerr.org/childcareaware/index.htm

Child Care Aware is a nonprofit association whose mission is to ensure that every parent has access to good information about finding quality child care and resources in their community. A partnership with the National Association of Child Care Resource and Referral Agencies (NACCRRA), the Child Care Action Campaign (CCAC), and the National Association for Family Child Care (NAFCC), Child Care Aware can help you find child-care solutions. Their Web site has articles with topics such as "What to Do When There's Not Enough Good, Affordable Care" and "Five

BEDTIME STORIES

http://www.bedtime-story. com/bedtime-story

This Web site is the stuff pleasant dreams are made of. With hundreds of bedtime stories organized by practical categories, you'll never run out of bedtime ideas. It's especially perfect for parents who have to be away from their kids—just print out a story and read it over the phone, and you can still have that special time together.

BREASTFEEDING

http://www.lalecheleague.org La Leche League

Since breastfeeding isn't always intuitive, La Leche provides worldwide encouragement and mother-to-mother support via articles, chats, and reference materials.

r resources

CHILD CARE

http://nccic.org

National Child Care Information Center

This isn't the best-looking site in the world, but it's a great way to find the best care for your kids. The site also has information on the latest research and White House initiatives concerning child care.

Steps to Choosing Care." Or you can call their 800 number to order tip sheets on choosing child care, to get the phone number for your local Child Care Resource and Referral Agency, or to ask a child-care professional any of your child-care questions. You are not alone in your child-care search!

DEVELOPMENT—Zero to Three

Zero to Three: National Center for Clinical Infant Programs, 734 Fifteenth Street NW, Suite 1000, Washington, DC 20005; (202) 638-1144. Web site: www.zerotothree.org.

Like most parents, you probably have questions about your child's development. Or you may just want to know what you can do to ensure your child's happy and healthy growth. Zero to Three, a nonprofit organization dedicated solely to advancing the healthy development of babies and young children, can help you navigate this critical period. Zero to Three enlists top developmental experts to produce articles such as "Helping Toddlers with Peer Group Entry Skills" and "Helping Your Child Channel Their Aggressive Energies." They also have a series of handy reference materials for parents, such as wall charts that define and explain the key stages in development (the toddlers and two-year-olds chart is $4) and New Visions for Parents materials for parents who are concerned about their child's development. All materials are available through the organization's Web site or by calling (202) 638-1144.

DIVORCED PARENTS—The Children's Rights Council

The Children's Rights Council, 300 I Street NE, Suite 401, Washington, DC 20002-4362; (202) 547-6227.

The Children's Rights Council is dedicated to the rights of children who are members of divorced families. The CRC maintains that ensuring a child's access to both parents is the healthiest option following a divorce. They have developed a resource catalog of more than 75 books, written reports, audio/video cassettes, legal briefs, and children's materials, available to parents at little cost. The CRC also holds national conferences that bring together prominent professionals from around the country to educate the public as well as policy makers about the importance of strong families. A one-year membership is $35 and includes the newsletters *Speak Out for Children* and *Action Alerts*, discounts on materials and conferences, a The Best Parent Is Both Parents bumper sticker, and a 16-page catalog with discounts on books and reports. The CRC can also provide parents referrals for counseling and support during any access or visitation problems.

FATHERS—The National Fatherhood Initiative
National Fatherhood Initiative, 1 Bank Street, Suite 160, Gaithersburg, MD 20878; (301) 948-0599, fax (301) 948-4325.
E-mail: NFI1995@aol.com. Web site: http://www.fatherhood.org.

The National Fatherhood Initiative (NFI) is a national nonprofit that strives to make responsible fatherhood a national priority. In addition to organizing national conferences and increasing awareness of fatherhood issues, the Initiative publishes a Fatherhood Resource Catalog of books, tapes, and other fatherhood products. The catalog offers brochures such as "10 Ways to Be a Better Dad," which contains easy, helpful suggestions to help any dad become a more effective father. The cost is only 10¢ per brochure, and brochures are also available in Spanish. The

http://www.nannynetwork. com/
A NaniNet—Nanny Employment Placement and Referral Connection
A NaniNet features a searchable database of nanny placement agencies and nanny referral services, directories of firms offering nanny tax services, nanny health and workman's compensation insurance, nanny background verification, and a reading room with articles of interest to nannies and nanny employers.

DEVELOPMENT

http://iamyourchild.org/start.
   html

Here's a guide to
understanding how the first
three years of your child's life
will affect her lifelong
development. The information
here covers research on brain
development, what you can
expect your child to be doing
when, and professional
advice from top child
development experts.

EMERGENCIES AND FIRST AID

http://www.ama-assn.org/
   insight/h_focus/nemours/

KidsHealth at the American
Medical Association

This site covers all topics
relating to kids' health, but it
highlights safety and accident
prevention as well as first aid.
A great reference for things
like poison control centers in
your area and emergency
numbers to keep by the
phone.

catalog is broken down into categories such as Fathering Skills,
Inspiration, and Humor. To order a free copy of the Resource Catalog,
call (301) 948-0599. NFI membership is $35 a year. As an NFI member,
you will receive their quarterly newsletter, an NFI information/media kit, a
community impact brochure, their Fatherhood Warehouse Catalog, and
advance notice of meetings and events.

INJURIES—The Injury Prevention Program
The American Academy of Pediatrics, P.O. Box 927, Elk Grove Village, IL
60009-0927; (847) 228-5005.

The Injury Prevention Program (TIPP), an arm of the American Academy
of Pediatrics, is an educational program for parents of children newborn
through age 12 to help prevent common injuries. TIPP publishes "safety
surveys" to help parents identify at-risk situations in their homes. TIPP
also offers a series of books (such as *Guide to Your Child's Symptoms:
Birth Through Adolescence*, for $19.95) and videos (such as *Infant and
Toddler Emergency First Aid*, a two-video set for $49.95). For a free
catalog of their publications, call (847) 228-5005. For more general
information about the program, ask your doctor.

INSURANCE—The Insurance Information Institute
The Insurance Information Institute, 110 William Street, New York, NY
10038; (212) 669-9200 or (800) 942-4242. Web site: www.iii.org.

The mission of the Insurance Information Institute is to improve the
public's understanding of insurance—what it does, how it works, and
how to make it work for you. Funded by insurance providers in the
United States, the Insurance Information Institute is a valuable source of

information for parents who need many types of insurance. The Institute runs a consumer hotline to answer consumer questions about all types of insurance, covering such topics as how to file a claim or what to do if a natural disaster strikes. They also publish several informative pamphlets, including "How to Get Your Money's Worth in Home and Auto Insurance" and "Twelve Ways to Lower Your Homeowner's Insurance Cost." For more information, including a catalog of publications and videos, call the National Insurance Consumer Helpline (NICH) at (800) 942-4242 from 8:00 A.M. to 8:00 P.M., EST, Monday through Friday.

MULTIPLES—The National Organization of Mothers of Twins Clubs
The National Organization of Mothers of Twins Clubs, Inc., P.O. Box 23188, Albuquerque, NM 87192-1188; (505) 275-0955 or (800) 243-2276. Web site: www.nomotc.org. E-mail: nomotc@aol.com.

If you're the parent, grandparent, or foster parent of twins, your local chapters of the Mothers of Twins Clubs are a great place to share information and discuss the physical, emotional, and financial problems that often accompany multiple births. The groups offer a Support Services program to help you keep up with your large immediate family, a pen-pal program for mothers who have children with disabilities or illnesses, bereavement support outreach to help parents who have experienced the loss of one or more of the multiple-birth children, and single parent outreach offering solo parents the opportunity to share information with others. By joining the NOMOTC, you'll receive *Notebook*, a quarterly magazine full of multiple-birth families' stories, scientific research, and referrals to experts in the field. For information on membership in your area, or to order NOMOTC publications, call them at (800) 243-2276.

FAMILY RELATIONSHIPS
http://www.parentsplace.com
ParentsPlace
ParentsPlace has loads of information on a range of subjects—from health to activity ideas. But what really makes it stand out from other parenting sites is its attention to family relationships. With articles on such important topics as communication, sex, and stress, ParentsPlace talks to you as if you were a person, in addition to being a mom or wife. Come ask Dr. Gayle, their certified family therapist, about how to keep you and your family sane, strong, and healthy. ParentsPlace also has an extensive recipe swap, so the next time dinnertime causes you heart palpitations, you can come find a parent-tested, quick and easy recipe at the click of a mouse.

r resources

FATHERS

http://www.fathersforum.com

This site is "committed to helping educate men about the psychological and emotional changes they experience when they become fathers." With a great guide to how having a child changes men and their relationships, this site eases the transition from man to dad.

HEALTH

http://ericps.crc.uiuc.edu/
npin/repar/textx/teens/
ch-healt.html

The United States Department of Health and Human Services

This site helps parents "put prevention into practice" with information on everything from what to expect at each checkup to printable forms that help you keep a day-to-

NATURAL REMEDIES—Homeopathic Educational Services

Homeopathic Educational Services, 2124 Kitteridge Street, Berkeley, CA 94704; (510) 649-0294. Store: 2036 Blake Street, Berkeley, CA.

If you're worried about the large amount of antibiotics being prescribed to your child or just have an interest in natural medicine, Homeopathic Educational Services is a great place to start. They can provide you with access to a comprehensive assortment of information, about products that blend natural medicine and traditional science. Homeopathic Educational Services has a catalog of books, tapes, and other products, such as the book *Your Healthy Child: A Guide to Natural Health Care for Children*. For more information, call them at (510) 649-0294.

POSTPARTUM DEPRESSION—Depression After Delivery

Depression After Delivery, P.O. Box 1282, Morrisville, PA 19067; (800) 944-4773 or (212) 295-3994.

Because postpartum depression is a very real phenomenon, and because it doesn't always remedy itself or go away as quickly as you'd like, there are support groups such as Depression After Delivery (DAD). DAD is a national self-help organization founded to provide information and support for women and families suffering from postpartum distress. You can call their 800 number for a referral to a local support group. The groups meet twice a month to share their personal experiences, discuss medical resources, and lend a friendly, supportive ear. The national organization also functions as a clearinghouse of information and publishes a quarterly newsletter. Yearly membership is $30.

PRODUCT SAFETY—U.S. Consumer Product Safety Commission
Office of Information and Public Affairs, Washington, DC 20207;
(301) 504-0580. Web site: www.cpsc.gov.

To receive a publications list, send a postcard to: U.S. Consumer Product
Safety Commission, Washington, DC 20207. To request specific
publications or to report a faulty product, call the hotline at (800) 638-
2772 or (800) 638-8270 (for the hearing impaired) or E-mail: Info@cpsc.gov.
The U.S. Consumer Product Safety Commission is an independent
federal regulatory agency founded to protect the public against
unreasonable risks of injuries and deaths associated with consumer
products. If you're getting ready to make a purchase and want safety
information about a particular brand, or if you're wondering about the
latest product recalls, call the hotline at (800) 638-2772. The CPSC sets
mandatory consumer product standards and requires manufacturers to
report defects in products that could create substantial hazards to the
public. They have jurisdiction over 15,000 products, from automatic-drip
coffeemakers to toys to lawn mowers, so if you have a question about any
consumer product, chances are they can help.

SINGLE PARENTS—Parents Without Partners
Parents Without Partners International, Inc., 401 North Michigan Avenue,
Chicago, IL 60611-4267; (312) 644-6610.
Web site: http://www.parentswithoutpartners.org. E-mail: pwp@sba.com.

If you're a single parent dealing with the struggles of raising a child
alone, Parents Without Partners can help. PwP provides real assistance

day log of your child's health. You'd have to be a little obsessive to use everything on this site, but that just means there's something here for everyone.

NUTRITION
http://vm.cfsan.fda.gov/~dms/
wh-infnt.html
The United States Food and Drug Administration Center for Food Safety and Applied Nutrition
Here's where to go if you're concerned about making sure your child is well-nourished with food that is safe to eat. There's a special section on women's health, including women with toddlers and preschoolers.

r resources

PARENTING NEWS

http://www.raisinnet.com/

Raisin

Raisin bills the information it offers as "Currents for parents raisin' children." What that means is news tidbits on a range of parenting topics, such as Family Matters, Kidstuff, Education, Health & Safety, Entertainment, Byte to Byte, What's in Print, and Travel.

PEDIATRICS

http://www.DrGreene.com

Dr. Greene's House Calls

Dr. Greene gives his pediatric advice for the information age on this well-maintained site. It's a terrific resource for in-depth, thoughtful answers to a range of pediatric questions. Many of Dr. Greene's Insights in this book were originally found on Dr. Greene's House Calls Web site.

by offering three basic types of activities through its local chapters: educational, family-oriented, and adult social functions. Educational activities may be group discussions; lectures by psychologists, lawyers, and other professionals; study groups; training seminars; and leadership and personal growth opportunities. Family activities include holiday activities, potluck suppers, fun and educational outings, picnics, hikes, camping, and bowling. The adult social functions help single parents learn to relate again with other adults as single persons. In addition to these opportunities, membership in Parents Without Partners gives you access to group insurance programs and discounts to certain national businesses such as Hertz Rent-a-Car. For more information about membership, call them or visit their Web site.

SPECIAL-NEEDS CHILDREN—Parents Helping Parents

Parents Helping Parents; The Family Resource Center; 3041 Olcott Street; Santa Clara, CA 95054-3222; (408) 727-5775

Parents Helping Parents (PHP) is dedicated to helping parents of special-needs children. If your child has special needs due to illness, accidents, birth defects, allergies, learning problems, family problems or family stress, PHP is for you. A United Way agency and a Presidential Point of Light organization, PHP offers its members the chance to research your child's specific disability, financial relief information to help cope with added medical expenses, advocacy skills to protect the rights of your child, as well as counseling and support for both you and your children. The PHP support group system matches experienced special-needs parents with new parents, so that new parents always have someone to turn to, whether they need advice, or just someone to listen. PHP also has therapeutic fun programs for the siblings of special-needs children. Members (and even non-members, although membership is encouraged) can also check out books and videos on a variety of topics (such as autism, ADD, and allergies) from the PHP library. An annual membership is $35 (professionals, $60).

STAY-AT-HOME MOTHERS—FEMALE
Formerly Employed Mothers at the Leading Edge,
P.O. Box 31, Elmhurst, IL 60126; (630) 941-3553.
Web site: http://www.FEMALEhome.org.
E-mail: femaleofc@aol.com.

FEMALE (Formerly Employed Mothers at the Leading Edge) is a national nonprofit organization that supports women taking time out from full-time paid employment to raise their children at home. For moms who need to talk to someone over three feet tall, this is your place! Yes, there is intelligent life outside of the parenting world. FEMALE also lives on Parent Soup, where their message boards and chats are a personal network for mothers to meet one another and talk about their lives. In the real world, they have more than 150 chapters and more than 6,000 members across the world—maybe one is near you. Call them or stop by their Web site for more information about membership.

WORKING MOTHERS—9 to 5
9 to 5 National Association of Working Women, 238 West Wisconsin Avenue, Suite 700, Milwaukee, WI 53203-2308; (414) 274-0925 or (800) 522-0925. Web site: members.aol.com/naw925.
E-mail: namww9to5@execpc.com.

PRODUCT RECALL INFORMATION
http://www.notice.com/recalls.html
Wondering if that car seat is still safe? Check here for information from the United States Consumer Product Safety Commission on all the children's products that have been recalled, past and present. The site can be a little scary to read, but the information is vital to parents and children alike.

A membership organization for working women, 9 to 5 combines grassroots activism with cutting-edge research and sophisticated media work to win real changes in the workplace. The organization provides a toll-free job problem hotline with free counseling on legal rights for working women on issues such as sexual harassment or discrimination in the workplace. In addition, 9 to 5 helps women to learn how to balance work and family—the book *The Job/Family Challenge,* by 9 to 5 director Ellen Bravo, is available for $9. They also have informative booklets on issues important to working mothers, such as the Family and Medical Leave Act. To order publications or to receive a list of publications, call them at (414) 274-0925. Members receive the 9 to 5 newsletter, which contains job advice, charts trends in office work, and other useful information. (The film *9 to 5,* starring Dolly Parton, Lily Tomlin, and Jane Fonda, was based on stories told to 9 to 5 problem counselors.) Annual dues are $25.

SANITY SAVERS

Everyone has a bad day now and again. Maybe your son had a temper tantrum in the grocery store. Maybe you're just a little blue. Here are some perspectives to help you cope with the emotional roller coaster that parenting can be and help you realize that without bad days, you wouldn't be able to fully appreciate the good days.

The Two Magic Times of Day
I live for 8:00 when my son goes to bed. Of course, I can't wait to hear him call me the next morning.
     ~ *Parent Soup member ABUCK22*

That reminds me of something my mom told me about children that I never understood until ours hit the two-year stage. She said, "The two best times of the day for moms are when they first get up and when they go to sleep." Boy, isn't that true!

~ *Parent Soup member Susan2638*

The World According to a Toddler

My brother-in-law sent this to me this morning, I thought it was pretty cute:

"Toddler's Creed"

If I want it, it's mine.

If I give it to you and change my mind later, it's mine.

If I can take it away from you, it's mine.

If I had it a little while ago, it's mine.

If it's mine, it will never belong to anyone else, no matter what.

If we are building something together, all the pieces are mine.

If it looks like mine, it's mine.

If it's broken, it's yours.

I thought this was a pretty accurate representation of what runs through a toddler's mind.

~ *Maureen M., Framingham, Massachusetts*

The Silver Lining of Behavior Problems

I know how low I feel about myself when I can't seem to control my daughter, and when I find a solution that works, how great I feel, and how much closer it brings me to my daughter.

~ *Dayna M., Santa Rosa, California*

Consolation for Parents of Kids Who Are into Everything
The child that you can tell once not to touch something and they listen is
rare. My friend has one of those kids, and believe me it is pretty
annoying. Most of us aren't that lucky. But just think—20 years from
now you'll be wishing you had that rambunctious 18-month-old back.
   ~ Parent Soup member JAZEN101

Dealing with "Super Parents"
Nothing is more demoralizing to hear while trying to cope with an extra-
intense child than another mother saying, "Well, my child doesn't do
that. I wouldn't stand for it," as if to say, "You aren't a good enough
parent." If you see me or someone like me dealing with a high-strung
child in public, try not to judge us until you have walked in our shoes.
Chances are we've already tried the technique that worked for your
child, and not to say you are wrong, but not every idea is right for every
child. A little sympathy and understanding rather than raised eyebrows
and judging can really help a mom who is dealing with an extra-intense
child. One day my pediatrician complimented me by saying that I was the
most natural parent she knows. A compliment like that can keep one
going for months. Basically, I listen to other people's ideas and
techniques, do nothing about it for a few days, and then my subconscious
seems to percolate all this and I suddenly know what to try next. This is
called listening to your instincts and not relying on experts for
everything, I guess. No one knows your child better than you do. As my
La Leche leader says, take what sounds good and leave the rest.
   ~ Alison V., Louisa, Virginia

You'll Like This Even if You're not a Billy Ray Cyrus Fan
The following is a parody I made one day that could best be described as
the "parenting mantra" for two-year-olds. I know a couple of parents
who sing this two or three times a day.

"The Two-Year-Old's Theme Song"
(to the tune of "Achy Breaky Heart")

I'm telling you, ever since I turned two,
I've really tried hard to communicate.
While I'm sometimes more sweet, than any kid you'd meet
Some days you're better off to stay away.
It comes from the heart, right when a new day starts
I try to run around naked all day.
I won't ever stop and eat, I'm always on my feet,
But folks sometimes just won't do what I say.
Here comes a fit, I'm gonna throw a fit
I'll tantrum 'bout most anything I see.
And when I throw a fit, you just cannot do spit,
Except pray it gets better when I'm three.
Hey, you can't sit there, my teddy's on that chair,
You cannot move one single toy away.
If the plan at bedtime's just slightly out of line
I'll make your life miserable the next day.
Don't think I'll be fine, till every toy is mine,
The laws of physics really bug me, too.
Now maybe if you wait, we can negotiate

But I'll just make you talk until you're blue.
Here comes a fit, I'm gonna throw a fit
I will not put up with your saying "No."
I will never go to bed, or let you shampoo my head,
No matter what, what I want's gonna go.
Here comes a fit, I'm gonna throw a fit
I will say "No" to anything you say.
And when I throw a fit, you just cannot do spit,
Except pray by age three it goes away.

~ *Douglas F., Canton, Ohio*

SEPARATION ANXIETY

Almost every child will go through phases when he will become very
upset if you aren't in the immediate vicinity. This can make it very hard
to get anything done (including going to the bathroom). You may be sick
of hearing this, but it's a phase. His clingyness is an expression of his
need to know that you're there for him. Here are some tips for fulfilling
his needs while maintaining your mental health.

When She Won't Let You Out of Her Sight
Q: I have a question regarding my daughter, who is soon to be three
    years old. In just the last three or four months she won't let my
    husband or me get out of her sight. She just screams or has a fit. I'm
    going crazy because I'm with her 24 hours a day. And there is no way
    for me to have time to myself. If it makes any difference, she also has

a 20-month-old brother. Help, I can't even go to the bathroom
by myself.

> ~ *Rebecca M., Bloomington, Illinois*

When She Only Wants Her Mommy

A: Have you ever tried leaving her alone with Daddy for a day? My 18-
month-old used to be the same way until I started taking Sundays off.
I leave her with her daddy while I go shopping or visiting friends.
With me gone, she has no choice but to let Daddy feed her and change
her diaper. Not only has this really improved their relationship, it's
also helped me regain my sanity! Now she's just as happy and
comfortable with Daddy as she is with me. Sometimes she even
prefers his help over mine (he's more fun).

> ~ *Ranelle D., Hurt, Virginia*

Build up Their Tolerance

A: My daughter is 24 months, and has just recently been OK with sitters.
A few months ago, I had the sitter come and play with her while I was
there, then I left for an hour, then gradually longer. Now I always tell
her if I am going to leave. She seems to understand, and hugs and
kisses me goodbye. And when I return I talk about how I went away
and came back. This seems to help my daughter deal with my
absence. It is really hard to leave a crying child, but they usually stop
crying shortly after you leave. But if you come right back if they are
crying, they learn that if they cry hard enough you may return, which
only makes it harder the next time. I would try just going on a short
errand, then longer as she gets more comfortable with the sitter. I was
eventually able to leave my daughter overnight with the sitter (who is

a 21-year-old cousin). I never thought I would be able to do this, but she did great, and I enjoyed a lovely wedding four hours from home.

~ *Parent Soup member MumToMaddi*

Yet Another Use for the Baby Blanket

A: One thing that helped my daughter's separation anxiety was when I gave her a "mommy blanket." When she needed extra attention, I'd wrap it around her and set her where she could watch me work. Another thing that helped was getting her to help me. I'd give her a stack of clothes, and she put them in the washer while I'd hang up what just came out.

~ *Parent Soup member Rroden1*

THE ELIUMS' POINT OF VIEW

A: From birth to about four or five years of age, parents often have to do what we call "wearing the baby." This means that our little ones are constantly with us and literally take all of our physical, emotional, and psychic energy. Another way of saying it is that they "nurse" from us even after they have stopped breastfeeding! When we have a superdependent child, we can become exhausted, unless we have a supportive and active parenting partner and do things that nurture ourselves. Three years of age is a time when some children have separation or abandonment worries, so be considerate of your child's fears. Do your best to make safe places for her to be in, do not leave her for a very long period of time (we know this is hard, because you are tired), and give her time with you and her daddy alone. Most importantly, find those little moments when you can do something that pleases and nurtures you. Most of the time, we do not have the time, space, money, or energy to do things for ourselves when our children are young, but even if it means getting up a half an hour before everyone else does to watch the sun rise and give thanks for another day, this little act can feed your soul and mean the difference between a cranky mommy and a present, loving one.

Separation Anxiety in Reverse
(When Your Child Wants to Talk to Anyone but You)

Q: When I go out with my friends, or other family members, my three-and-a-half-year-old boy does not want to hold my hand or listen to anything I have to say. If I go for his hand, he says, "Not yours Mommy, I want so-and-so's hand" (whoever I happen to be with). This also goes for just talking in general. If he is asking a question out loud, not really specifying who he is talking to, and I answer it, he says the same thing, "Not you Mommy." I don't know how to handle this kind of thing, and I can't help feeling a little jealous.

~ *Jill C., Auburn, Washington*

A: I also have a three-and-a-half-year-old son who does the same thing. Whenever Papa or Nana is around, it's them he wants. It's disheartening sometimes when I answer something he asks and he says "Not you Mommy, I'm talking to Papa" or whoever is there at the time. As hard as it is at times, the best thing is not to take it to heart. It just means that your son is secure in you and your love and is not afraid to walk with someone else or hold someone else's hand. He knows that you aren't going anywhere and aren't going to leave him, so he's enjoying the stimulation of being with and talking to someone who he isn't around on a regular basis. Just let him be at those times. He's just exploring the stuff that these other people can teach him and the companionship they give him. When you go home, all the

189

hugs and kisses are for you, he gets his reassurance that you love him
once again, and you build more confidence in him to grow up a
happy, healthy, and social person.

~ *Parent Soup member JustTeeezn*

SEX *(See also Talking to Kids About Sex)*

It is one of the great ironies of life that sex
can cause you to have children, and having
children can cause you to not have sex. If
your sex life has changed, or dwindled, or
just about died since having kids, consider
yourself in good company. The parents of
Parent Soup can tell you that you are by no
means alone. But there are folks out there
who've found ways to regain—even
better—the intimacy they once had with their partner. They are here to
tell you that yes, you will have sex again. Hallelujah!

Take Time for Yourself

Try making yourself feel good about yourself again. I used to wear only
sweats, T-shirts, and a ponytail—it wasn't until I took an interest in
myself again that I felt sexy again. Try getting a sitter, go get your hair
done, get some clothes that accent your new figure, polish your

nails. Once you feel better about your new body, you will feel better
about sex.

~ *Parent Soup member Newschu*

Get to the Root of the Problem

I think part of the problem is fatigue, and some of the fatigue is mental,
not just physical. Taking care of small children is very draining
physically. I think a second issue is that for women sexuality starts with
the need to be touched, and if you have kids you are getting touched
plenty. You simply don't have that physical hunger that you used to have
for someone to touch you. My kids are four and seven, and they hug me
too much! One day in my old age I am sure that I will be starved for
human touch, but it sure isn't now. I don't want anyone to touch me, and
I don't want any more human interaction by the end of the day. I have
been touched and interacted with to death!

~ *Isadora P., Rockville, Maryland*

Food for Thought

Realize that like any beautiful garden your relationship must be tended
to before it can be enjoyed. We went through some very rough years, but
thankfully the kids are a little older and my husband and I can now
remember that it was just us before the kids came along. If we admire,
cherish, and respect each other, our children will see that and model
themselves after us. Show your kids what they need to see to help them
become happy, secure, loving, compassionate adults. If it's not working,
visualize, give it some time, and seriously meditate and visualize about

the perfect union. You'll see it when you believe it, and not the other way around.

~ *Parent Soup member TehaniK*

Appointment with Love
Set your alarm clock! Wake him up in the middle of the night doing naughty things to him. It's too late for him to resist.

~ *Parent Soup member Gottamnte*

Did You Hear Something, Dear?
My dear husband and I have been together for 22 years now, 14 of which have been spent in marriage and reproducing. Being the parents of four children, we have mastered the fine art of sneaking off. We thought that we had this mastered in our youth when parents, morals, and the police were looking out for our virginities, but nothing compares to finding the time and the privacy to commit the loving act with the kids in the house. I am forever amazed by my children's ability to seek and destroy. No matter the time of day, the dark of night, the lock on the door, they will, and do, find us. People come over and remark on our impressive collection of Disney movies and ask how we came to acquire such a mass of videos. We just wink at each other with the knowledge that once those folks reproduce they too will know that a new movie, one that's never been seen before by the little darlings, ensures a good hour or so of sexual contact for us, the elders. Still, all in all, no matter how wonderful or elaborate the plan for our union, you can be guaranteed that one of the little boogers will seek us out and demand to know what it is we are doing without them. I joke with my husband that the word *orgasm* is synonymous with a little hand banging on the bedroom door and loudly insisting to know why

they cannot come in and why the door is locked. Yes, I joke about this but fear that when they all move out, my sex life will be over. Kind of on the idea of Pavlov's dogs, I am conditioned to that height of awareness that enables me to hear the creaking of the third step from our bedroom door while whispering in my husband's ear about how great he is and managing to stifle several animal sounds from escaping from my throat. Yes, sex and marriage go hand in hand, but throw a couple of kids into the scenario and you have something akin to a strange mixture of 007, *Mission Impossible*, and *The Brady Bunch*. Before I end, I just want to say that the old adage stands true: Where there is a will, there is a way. And where there is a way, we will!

~ *Mare M., West Long Branch, New Jersey*

The Voices of Experience Say "Be Patient"

It seems to be pretty common with many that I have talked to that sex after kids takes a backseat, but only for a temporary time. There is not the time, the energy, or the drive . . . *but*, it is not due a lack of love or a lost-forever desire. I was told by many parents in Parent Soup that they had gone through this "sex lag" after kids, but years later they can look back and be glad that it was just another stage of being a couple raising young children. Once the energy is no longer needed for very dependent little ones, the sex does return, and it is better and more meaningful than anyone ever expects. Be patient with each other, and know that "this too shall pass." In the meantime, communicate, understand, and be supportive, knowing it will be rewarded in the long run. Everything I was told by those parents last year has been finally panning out to be a truth for us two here, with a three-year-old and five-year-old who are not as demanding as the one- and three-year-olds they once were.

~ *Parent Soup member PSValerie*

A Little Affection Goes a Long Way

Tell him all the wonderful things he does for you (name at least five things). Tell him and watch his face light up. P.S.—a long kiss every day works too!

~ *Parent Soup member Contessa63*

Don't Focus on Frequency

My husband and I do it when we can, which is maybe once every two or three months. We both know that when the kids are gone, we will do it anytime we want, and it doesn't get rusty from lack of use! Instead, we cuddle a lot when the kids are in bed, and when we are watching TV together at night. Keep in mind that you can try to have time with each other, even if it is in bed and cuddling for a half hour.

~ *Parent Soup member CareCare7*

Grab a Hug Where You Can

We have five kids. I know what it feels like to be extremely tired and to never have the opportunity for sex with my hubby. We have been married almost nine years, and I would say that in about the last year and a half things have gotten a lot better for us. We have found that you just have to grab a hug here, a kiss there. We sneak in the kitchen for a few minutes of foreplay while the kids are in another room. We sneak in the bathroom with each other, he follows me downstairs to "help" do laundry. That way we can at least sneak in some playtime during the day, and then when the kids are in bed and we both are awake we can have a long romantic night.

~ *Parent Soup member MomBw5kids*

SIBLINGS

The sibling relationship is full of intensity and mystery—one day your toddler may be content to play with his baby sister, the next he may throw a fit of jealousy over the attention you're giving her. No one can guarantee that your children will get along all the time, but you can take steps to minimize any bad blood between them. Here are those steps. And practically speaking, you'll also find the Parent Soup parents' picks for the best double strollers.

Getting a Toddler Ready for a New Baby

Q: We have a wonderful 21-month-old son and are expecting our second child this month. What can we do to prepare our son for the arrival of the new baby? What developmental regressions should we watch for?
~ *Robin K., Hillsborough, California*

DR. GREENE'S INSIGHT

A: There is so much we don't know about the little one that is going to be entering our lives. Will he or she be healthy, will he look like his father, or will she look like her grandmother, will he have colic, or will she "sleep like a baby"? For each of our questions, older siblings have at least 10. Will he or she take my place, will he like to play with my toys, will Mom and Dad let him play with my toys, will Mom like her more than me, will I still be Daddy's boy? In each of these areas, older siblings feel out of control. It is only natural that they express their fears through regression, acts that express anger such as temper tantrums, and by putting time demands on Mom and Dad. The best preparation is to reenforce your son's

195

role in the family—especially his role as older brother. At 21 months he is most likely ready to move into the responsibilities of an older brother, as long as he views this as a move up the family ladder.

Talk to your son about the new baby by calling him "your little brother or sister" instead of "Mommy's new baby" or even "the new baby." Try to use language that uses your son as the point of reference. In everything that you do, try to put yourself in your son's shoes and think about this new arrival the way he would. The first introduction of the two is very important. Have your son pick out a present to give to his new sibling and purchase a really cool present for your son's new baby sibling to give to *him* the first time they meet. When your son meets his new sibling for the first time, plan for his new little brother or sister to be in the bassinet and not in Mommy's or Daddy's arms. If your son is interested in holding his new baby sibling, then by all means, help him do that. If he wants to exchange presents first, let him do that instead. As the older brother, let him set the pace with whatever makes him feel most comfortable.

In the days and weeks to come, you will not be able, nor would it be best, to let your older son rule the household. Some things that will make the transition easier are to establish special one-on-one times each day with Dad and the big brother and Mom and the big brother. During these times, let him set the agenda. Not only will he feel that he has some control in life, but you will discover important things about your son.

Even if you do all that, some children will regress after a younger sibling is born. The most common areas affected are eating, toileting, crying, and sleeping. The best way to deal with this is to give your son more attention for his positive big brother acts than for his baby acts. Even negative attention can be motivation for acting "like a baby," so make sure you reward only the behaviors you want to continue. Many children, even

sweet-natured ones, express anger toward their younger siblings. Your son
may say that he hates his little brother or sister. If this happens, don't say,
"Now you know you are not supposed to hate anyone!" The reality is he is
experiencing intense emotions and he needs your help to work his way
through them. Help him grieve over losing his place as the only child in the
family by saying something like, "It sounds to me like you wish things were
the way they were before your baby brother or sister was born." Often this
will be enough to soften an older sibling—"Mommy, I wish you would hold
me instead of him." At that point the two of you can come up with positive
ways to love his new baby sibling that won't leave him feeling left out.

Defusing Any Aggression
Until recently, my two-and-a-half-year-old daughter pretty much ignored
her 18-month-old brother. Now that my son is a mobile creature,
however, with very definite needs and opinions, there is a turf war
waging. I've tried yelling, screaming, time-outs, explaining—all to no
avail. I've found a few things that have worked, though. First, the art of
distraction. I try to give my daughter plenty to do (painting, coloring,
whatever) while my son is wandering around the room. I also use a
reward system. "Here's a gold star for every day you're nice to your
brother, and at the end of the week there'll be a surprise." Sure, it's
bribery, but I figure that cause and effect is a good thing for a two-year-
old to learn anyway. Another thing that's proved to be helpful is keeping
my daughter's favorite toys out of my son's reach. That way the
territorial instincts aren't so strong. Finally, when all else fails, I go to
the mall. That way they're both in a stroller and simply have to tolerate
each other's company. Problem solved!
    ~ *Parent Soup member A1editor*

When my daughter was born, my son (then three years old) was thrilled. From the very first, we allowed him a position of "teacher" and "big brother" so that competition was limited. It has worked very well so far. Many times, when a younger sibling starts becoming mobile (walking, crawling) they are perceived as a threat, and teaching the older child to handle things with a positive approach ("Look, the baby wants to hug you") is a great tool.

~ *Patti F., Columbus, Ohio*

Who Gets the Crib?

Our son turned two four days after our daughter was born. I would highly suggest borrowing another crib for your newborn, if possible. If your first child wants to stay in the crib, let her stay in there—it will give you added rest in the morning and at night with a newborn, plus it makes naps stay a bit longer. Just be sure to move your older child in plenty of time before the new baby arrives and make a big deal out his new room. I had my son show it to everybody who came to visit, so he had a sense of ownership of it long before the new baby arrived.

~ *Laurie L., Novelty, Ohio*

A Second Shower?

Q: I'm expecting my second son in about eight weeks (my first is 18 months old). My friends are starting to ask when my shower is. But I have some questions: Is it appropriate to have a second shower? Also, since we really only need the essentials like diapers and wipes, how can I suggest gift certificates, cash, or these items? Does anyone have any creative, fun shower ideas? The only one I have heard of is everyone bringing a frozen casserole or something so you don't have to cook. Should I have it before the baby or should I wait until after and have a "meet Matthew's little brother party"?

~ *Debra G., Tuscon, Arizona*

A: I think it is very appropriate to have a shower for your second! After all, the shower is for the baby really, not the mom. (That is why it is called a baby shower, not a mom shower!) This is a new baby, and he or she deserves to be welcomed, as was the first.

~ *JoEllyn M., San Diego, California*

A: I recently had a shower for a mom who was expecting her second. She registered at Toys R Us (a great idea, because even if you don't want or need anything, you get a gift certificate just for registering and they send you coupons based on your child's age after your due date). You can register for diapers, shampoo, baby Tylenol, and whatever it is that you really need. Something else that is nice is that anyone in the country pretty much has access to Toys R Us and the registry is all on computer. (Oh no, I am sounding like a commercial for the Tantrum Palace.) Anyhow, for the shower I invited a list of friends that she supplied. Most of those friends had children, so I decided to have a big-sister shower at the same time for her daughter. I had my husband and a teenager from our church entertain the children in the playroom. They had their own party food and a pin-the-bundle-on-the-stork game (bought from the party store). Other showers I have been to have been fill-the-freezer showers (boy, did I wish someone had had one of those for me) and a diapers party where everyone is told to bring diapers. I have also been to a pamper-the-mom shower where everything was something for the mom—nice soaps, bubble bath, a nursing nightie, whatever.

~ *Tarrant F., Gainesville, Florida*

A Vote for Closely Spaced Siblings

My girls are 20 months apart. Although I was stressed to find out I was pregnant before my first was even one year old, now I would do it the same way again. You will not have the jealousy issue; neither will remember life without the other. As they grow older they will probably play together very well. Your memory is still intact regarding baby issues, so you don't have to reread all the books and constantly re-refer to them. I highly recommend letting your oldest "hold" the baby with you from day one (fetching, burping, diapers, and such), and try not to stress about the oldest one touching the baby at all. I believe this helped us tremendously.

~ *Melinda G., San Jose, California*

When Nap Time Becomes a Problem

Q: I have a newborn baby girl, and my two-year-old son has adjusted really well to her. My problem is that all of a sudden my son has decided to fight me at nap time. Here I am lying in bed with my newborn at the breast, and my two-year-old is fighting me. I get so frustrated, sometimes I find myself being rough with him just to get him to lie down, and I feel really guilty but right now I need for him to take that nap so that I can regroup. Am I doing something wrong? Please help!

~ *Parent Soup member NrsnMom*

Try a Special Nap Toy

A: My daughter was 14 months old when her brother came along. At nap time I put her in her bed (I used to have to lie down with her also) and give her a toy that her brother is not allowed to have. This is a special toy that only comes out at nap time (I took her shopping to pick out the toy). I put my son down for his nap, and then I put her in her bed with her toy and leave the room. She plays and sooner or later she falls asleep. It does take some time for them to adjust to this.

   ~ Parent Soup member Theresay

Changing Nap Time to Quiet Time

A: I could have written that note two years ago—I also had a newborn daughter and a two-year-old son. I had always loved our nap time—a respite in our busy day on the go-go-go to just cuddle, read, talk quietly, and nurse. Part of the anger I realized I had at my son when nap time with my daughter was so chaotic was the loss of this special time with my son and the realization that I didn't have it with my daughter. After many many days of yelling and feeling furious inside, I knew I had to make a change. So, I changed the sleeping cues for my son. Right after a carbo-filled lunch, all three of us would go to his room (he had previously always napped, and slept, in our bed) and read the same book every day and then lay down quietly together. If he didn't feel like sleeping, I would get him something to munch on and (now this is key) I would put on a story tape on his tape player. He understood that he needed to stay in his room until the story tape ended. This gave me plenty of time to nurse the baby to sleep. Well, my son didn't always sleep, but we all felt much better without the daily struggle.

~ *Patty K., Glastonbury, Connecticut*

A Birthday Tradition for Siblings
For each of our children's birthdays, the birthday child picks out a small gift (usually a paperback book or other low-cost item) to say thank you to the other. The fact that there is only the two of them keeps costs down, but it helps to even out just how important we all are to each other.

~ *Judy K., Valley Glen, California*

Could a New Baby Cause Your Toddler to Act Out?
Q: My three-year-old daughter is mean to babysitters. She does not want to be left with one (other than her nanny of three years), so she makes their lives hell (they ultimately quit). She won't do things with them, and she even makes herself throw up sometimes when they arrive. We hired a new 15-year-old mother's helper this past weekend, and she was close to tears by the end of the day because my daughter wouldn't let her into the car so we could drop her at the train station. I'm dreading having to leave her at all with a babysitter. I know that if I stay with her every moment she'll be happy; if I leave her with a strange babysitter she will be miserable, and I don't know if that's fair. I am at a loss what to do. Morgan has a baby brother named Jack, who is 14 months old. He's much nicer to babysitters.

~ *Mallory W., New York, New York*

THE ELIUMS' POINT OF VIEW
A: Part of Morgan's difficulty with babysitters may have to do with her brother, Jack. Having a younger brother can make it difficult for first children to be

away from Mom, and it can cause a lot of anger in the older child. This is a hunch, but Morgan may be taking her anger out on a babysitter because it is easy and safe to get away with that kind of behavior. Making a short-term babysitter go away means nothing. Making Mommy or Nanny so hurt or angry that she goes away is too dangerous, so Morgan reserves her angry behavior for babysitters. This is a pretty simple explanation and the problem probably won't be resolved quickly, but we wonder if providing other outlets for your daughter's anger might ease the babysitting situation. We suggest that you spend lots of time with your daughter without her baby brother around—do things that you both love to do. Continue to hold, hug, and rock her, just like you do for Jack. Offer lots of physical activities to work off that anger—kicking balls, hitting a punching bag, yelling, running, dancing, singing. Also, make lots of family time with plenty of Daddy-Mommy-Morgan-Jack interaction. For now, we suggest that you keep sitters to a minimum and when you must have one, coach them about Morgan's behavior and how to handle it. Best wishes.

Getting Around with Siblings

Q: I need advice on double strollers. I am about to have my second child, and I already have a 20-month-old.

> ~ *Debra G., Tuscon, Arizona*

A: We have the Graco Duo double stroller. It's seen some heavy usage (daily trips over bumpy sidewalks every day in summer) over the last 15 months and it's still in great shape. I highly recommend it. Also, it comes in primary colors, which we liked (every other one we saw had hot pink all over it, and I didn't like the way that looked for two boys).

> ~ *Parent Soup member Jonahzach*

A: Don't get the Graco 849ND double stroller! We bought it right before leaving for Disney World, and it squeaked so badly that it drove complete strangers nuts, not to mention us! The one we had prior to that was the Graco Duo Ltd., and it was great.

~ *Lisa L., Jacksonville, Florida*

A: If you are planning to get a double stroller, I'd recommend a tandem rather than a side by side—the side by side doesn't fit through aisles at the stores. We have a Perego that we use for walking; it has really big rubber wheels and works great on gravel parking lots, etc. We also have a Graco tandem that we use when we go to the mall or store.

~ *Parent Soup member Kybo818*

A: My boys are 13 months apart, and while my double stroller was handy at times in the early months, I found it most convenient to use a front pack for the baby and a plain, simple $15 umbrella stroller for the older one. This was much less cumbersome and kept the older boy from messing with the newborn. As soon as the little one turned six months, I switched him to a backpack, where he remains today at age two. Backpacks are also good for the kids who wiggle out of stroller seat belts. My back strength has grown with the child, so nowadays I can carry 30 pounds on my back half the day and hardly notice.

~ *Parent Soup member Pammola*

A: If the 20-month-old is old enough to sit on the back, I would recommend the Sit-n-Stand. I got one when my second was born (my oldest was 26 months), and we love it! It is much more compact than most double strollers and is strong enough to handle uneven terrain.

Plus, the older child isn't as confined. My daughter (now almost four) loves to ride between stores then hop off inside and look around. She can either sit on the back or stand and look over the baby's head, and she likes to do both.

~ *Angela K., South Bound Brook, New Jersey*

PARENT POLL

Should parents use a leash on their toddlers in public spaces?

Of 728 total votes

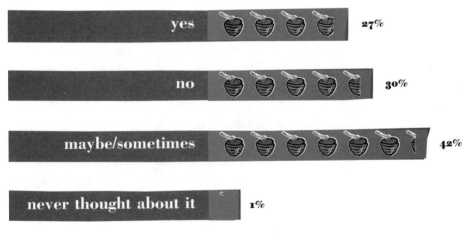

yes 27%

no 30%

maybe/sometimes 42%

never thought about it 1%

1 bowl = 50 parents

A: This is what I find easiest (I have an almost two-year-old girl and a two-month-old boy). Whenever I go out, I put my daughter in an umbrella stroller and I wear my son in a front carrier. This way I have my hands free to push the stroller, and the constant movement of my walking lulls my son to sleep.
 ~ *Victoria M., Hinsdale, Illinois*

SLEEP *(See also Crib to Bed and Fears)*

The word *bedtime* conjures up images of children hopping into pj's, snuggling into the covers, and sweetly calling out "Nighty-night." Reality is often different: kids don't want to go to bed. Once you get them in bed (finally), they get right back out. Here are suggestions for soothing your children and sending them off to the land of sweet dreams without tears, tantrums, or tugs-of-war. The best part of these suggestions is that they can be modified to fit your own family. So get ready to actually look forward to bedtime.

What Causes Sudden Sleeplessness?
Q: My two-year-old son will not sleep in his own bed. I attempt to put him to bed one hour after the other kids (9:00 P.M.), but all he does is scream so much that it almost gags him. I have tried going and comforting him every 10 minutes or so, and that didn't work. There have even been a few times I have let him scream, figuring that he would just eventually stop. I was wrong—he screamed 35 minutes. Not only will he not go to sleep, but he wants to stay up all

night long, and it is frightening because he has gotten up after everyone else has fallen asleep and wandered from room to room. What if he gets hurt? Any suggestions will be greatly appreciated—please, I am at a loss.

~ *Parent Soup member BABIES03*

A: He is going through a phase of needing you more. Fulfill it now or it will leave a hole to be filled up later. There is nothing wrong with this behavior, and you are a kind mother to be willing to help him rather than force him to be independent when he's not ready for it at this moment. I'll bet this will last only a short period of time.

~ *Alisa B., Amherst, Massachusetts*

DR. GREENE'S INSIGHT

A: For most of us, adult and child alike, there are many reasons for occasional sleeplessness. In children it is usually associated with physical illness, physical discomfort (such as teething), or entering a new developmental stage. Often when a child is learning a new skill, such as sitting, standing, walking, or language, he or she has a great deal of difficulty sleeping through the night. At each of those landmarks you can expect to have your child wake up frequently during the night to "try out" what he is learning. It is not at all unusual to have a child who is sleeping through the night without any problem, and then, when he learns one of these new skills, your nights of blissful rest are over. In the transition period it is helpful to give him a children's cassette tape player with a tape of his favorite stories being read by Mom and Dad. Often when children can turn the tape on and listen as long as they want, they will fall asleep very rapidly. This is particularly true when you tell them that you'll come back in and check on them in a while.

Bedtime Rituals

Every night I tell my two-year-old son a story called "The Little Boy Named Aaron." It's a story of his day from the time he wakes up until I put him in bed. We always end it, "And the mommy picked up her little boy named Aaron, like this. Then she gave him a big kiss, like this. And then she carried him to his bed like this." It has been a great way to ease into bed rather than just "The end. Go to bed." The wonderful thing is that now he has started to add his own comments about what he did, and I think it will be a good foundation for an evening chat when he gets older and may not want to talk to me as much in the daytime. I have also found that after I turn his radio on, if I do a few things quietly in his room (such as put laundry away, or get out the next day's things), any last-minute request can be dealt with quickly and quietly rather that having him yell down to me. I've noticed fewer requests since I've been doing this.

~ *Parent Soup member Catwright2*

Getting a Few Precious Minutes of Sleep

Some things that have worked with my 21-month-old are: I bring him out and place him in his playpen and let him watch television while I lie on the couch and go back to sleep. I don't get great sleep, since I wake up every few minutes to check on him, but I am surprised at how much this helps me. Also, we play some soft music while we are putting him to bed, so if he wakes up he can concentrate on the music and maybe go back to sleep (it works about half the time).

~ *Patti S., Lebanon, Ohio*

Keeping Them in Their Room

I would suggest that you buy a baby gate to put across the doorway so that your child can't roam the house at night. Make sure that your toddler's room is as childproof as possible.

~ *Parent Soup member Donnajean6*

I have seen a "tent" for putting over a crib to keep kids from climbing out. It was either in the Right Start or One Step Ahead catalog. The tent is made of mesh so there is no danger of suffocating, and you can still see into the crib clearly with it on.

~ *Karen D., Wilbraham, Massachusetts*

A friend of ours suggested a screen door on the child's room. It's the best of all worlds because you can see in and your child can see out, but he is not free to roam the house.

~ *J. O., Edmond, Oklahoma*

Believe in Magic

My four-year-old hates to sleep in her bed every now and then. What sometimes works is if we put "magic dream powder" (baby powder) on her pillow and in her bed (of course, a very light dusting, or even fake it, so that she doesn't inhale it).

~ *Parent Soup member Mrek2807*

Gradually Withdraw Your Presence

You might consider sitting in a chair beside her bed while your daughter goes to sleep, holding her hand or stroking her at first and then moving the chair farther and farther from the bed until you are out of the door.

Don't be tempted to leave the room until she is completely asleep. Repeat this pattern if she wakes in the middle of the night. This should let her know that you are there for her, but also give her the message that she needs to sleep in her own bed without you.

~ *Kristin H., Portland, Oregon*

When my son was two and didn't want to sleep in his bed, my husband and I took turns sleeping with him in his room. We first started sleeping in the bed with him. Then after a week or so, we slept on the floor and Eric slept in his bed. After a few days of this, we started leaving the room after he fell asleep. Pretty soon, he was going to bed all by himself.

~ *Parent Soup member Bsuzie*

Things That Go Lump in the Night

Have you checked to see if there are any lumps in her mattress that might be uncomfortable for her, or maybe a stray spring? Maybe the mattress isn't firm enough and she prefers something with a little less give. Another idea might be to rearrange her furniture. There might just be something about where the bed is placed that she has decided she doesn't like. Toddlers are quirky little people.

~ *Lisa K., Tucker, Georgia*

Dress for Success

My 15-month-old was still waking up to nurse several times a night, and I was beginning to get a little annoyed. My mother (who was a La Leche League leader for 15 years) suggested that my daughter may simply be cold. I hadn't thought of that! Since she sleeps with us, I always just dressed her the same way I dress at night, in just a lightweight T-shirt. I thought about it and realized that although I sleep with the covers pulled

up to my neck, she hates covers and constantly kicks them off. Last week
I started dressing her warmly at night as if she were sleeping in a crib
without covers. It worked! This past week she's been sleeping six- to
eight-hour stretches before waking up. I'm thrilled.

~ *Laura H., Cockeysville, Maryland*

A Little White Noise Goes a Long Way
Have you tried a radio tuned in softly to a classical station, or a favorite
cassette turned down softly? We leave the television on in the room next
to our two-year-old's—as long as he hears the TV, he thinks we are right
there.

~ *Eleanor M., Wendell, North Carolina*

A Room with a View
I thought changing the "scene" in my son's room might get him to sleep
better, so for his birthday last week, we bought those glow-in-the-dark
stars and put them on the walls. Knock on wood, there have been no cries
from his room.

~ *Parent Soup member Monica3107*

Sweet-Smelling Dreams
Put a dab of vanilla on the back of your daughter's hand and tell her to
keep sniffing it until the smell is gone. The deep breathing may relax her
enough to help her fall asleep.

~ *Monica H., Evanston, Illinois*

In Support of the Family Bed
Since we brought her home from the hospital our daughter (now 15
months) has slept with us. It has worked out great for us, with all of us

sleeping better. I love it because I do not have to get out of bed to nurse her at night, much less climb in her crib. And there she is in the morning cuddling with me and we both slowly wake up. We have taken down one side of her crib and put it up next to the bed in a "sidecar" arrangement, and this gives us all more room. Not for everyone, but we love it.

~ *Michelle C., Round Lake Beach, Illinois*

When my three-year-old daughter suddenly started coming into our bed at night, we got worried and determined to break her "bad habit." When we'd put her back in her bed in the middle of the night she would cry like her heart was broken, and it was loud. Then I thought, why should she be expected to stay in there all night with nobody when we get to sleep together every night and have that human contact? She is just a little girl who wants her mommy and daddy at night, and why is that such a bad thing? I am quite sure she will stop it on her own someday. If what I hear about teenagers is true, in a few years she will probably not want to be in the same room with me when we're awake, so I'm going to forget about making her stay out of our bed and enjoy her visits instead. I have actually come to look forward to it some nights. The 19-month-old is still in her crib, so if she starts the same thing when we put her in her toddler bed we may have a full bed, but we'll cross that bridge when we come to it.

~ *Angela K., South Bound Brook, New Jersey*

Our bed is the family bed when our little one needs it to be. My husband at first didn't like the thought of the kids being in bed with us, but I truly believe that he is so close to our last child because he's spent so much more time with him in bed. I nursed him for 10 months, not one night of which he slept through, so we were snuggle buddies for a while. Now, whenever he really wants to, we let him hop in with us. Years ago, with our daughter, my husband would grumble, but now he just laughs and makes room.

~ *Jennifer G., Goose Creek, South Carolina*

I just want to say that for us, the family bed has been wonderful. All three of our children have been in the bed with us, and I will probably be very sad the day my baby wants to go in her own. In 20 years I will be so glad I got the chance to be so close to them when they were little. They grow up so fast and will be out of the house before you know it. To me, all the extra time I've spent with them is worth all the kicks in the face.

~ *Sandy M., Napa, California*

Setting up a Schedule

We used to have a lot of trouble getting our daughter in bed at night. I put a schedule on the wall, and we would read what it said and then do it. She had so much fun that soon she was reminding us it was bedtime! Now I catch her looking at the schedule and telling herself what needs to be done. If we leave even one thing out she refuses to go to bed.

~ *Parent Soup member Rroden1*

I have a 28-month-old who also started not staying in bed around the age of two. My husband and I have found that we need to keep to a schedule with him. We still have nights where we put him back in bed many times, but they are now fewer. We allow at least a half hour of bedtime preparation, involving brushing teeth and playing with the water, putting on jammies, picking out a book to read, turning on the night-light, turning off the regular light, winding up the lullaby toy, tucking in, and hugs and kisses. It's quite a routine we've built. But it is reassuring to him, and I think it gives his mind preparation for sleep as well.

~ *Sharon G., Port Monmouth, New Jersey*

Let the Timer Be the Bad Guy

Approximately 10 minutes before bath time, I tell our almost three-year-old daughter that I'm setting the timer. When the timer goes "ding" she must take a bath, put her jammies on, get into bed, read a story, and give hugs and kisses. Then I leave the room. The timer idea was excellent for us—she used to squabble when I told her it was time for bed, but now she knows she can't argue with the alarm.

~ *Jennifer L., Covington, Georgia*

Maintaining Flexibility

I think that children do best with a routine, but I have developed a variation that I call the "tolerance" schedule. It seems to help my kids be flexible for when something comes up to disrupt our schedules. Basically, we have a half-hour window for nap and bedtime. Some days it's earlier, some days it's later. Our kids are quite tolerant of nap- and bedtime delays caused by disrupted schedules. This makes them much easier to travel with. My sister-in-law was commenting that she wished her kids were less frantic under similar circumstances. I shared my system, and she tried it. Now she has better luck with the kids.

~ *Parent Soup member AnCapo*

Monsters Be Gone

Q: I have a 27-month-old daughter with quite the imagination. I have no idea where she picked this up, but she thinks "Scary monsters are in the carpet" or "Scary monsters are in the window." The big problem is she won't sleep alone. Yes (gasp), she's in Mommy and Daddy's bed, almost every night. She will sleep in her crib only as long as someone is in the room with her. The problem is that after we leave we awaken at 3 A.M. to her horrible screaming of "scary monsters." Does anyone have any insight on this?

~ *Parent Soup member USSTEW*

A: We found that a spray bottle, filled with something sweet-smelling, really helped my daughter with monster control. Lavender water was our favorite monster-dispenser, and I bought her a small, bright-colored plant mister she could operate herself. We made a ritual of going through the house and spraying any area where a monster might be hiding, including the entire basement, every closet, and under every bed. She also decided to spray the doorknobs and windowsills. We let her keep the spray bottle on her nightstand, and we told her she could spray any time she felt the need. My husband and I would be sitting in the living room after putting her to bed, and occasionally we would hear "ssssssssss" as she dispatched one spookie or another. This method seemed to lend her a sense of control over an otherwise uncontrollable fear. I believe our house smelled like lavender for about five months before she was sure she had chased away all the things that go bump in the night.

~ *Parent Soup member Liarn*

S sleep

I gave birth to two very
different children. The
oldest, Brandon, has
always been a light
sleeper, a morning dove,
and up at the crack of
dawn. The younger,
Daniel, is very much like
his mother; he is a very
sound sleeper and would
sleep quite late if you let
him. One weekday, when
Daniel was three, I had
a particularly trying
time in waking him to get
dressed and ready to
take to the sitter's
house. I said, "Daniel,
it's time to get up and
get dressed." His
response was, "But I did
that yesterday!"

~ *Parent Soup
member SeussSMG*

Making Bedtime Non-Negotiable

If my son is unwilling to go to bed, I remind him, "There is a time for
everything, and now it is time to go to sleep. Mommies and Daddies get
tired, too." That's all I say, and then I carry him to his crib. I then give
him a quick drink of water, and he says his prayers and I tuck him in,
and we tell him we love him and give him kisses. If during all this the
child is having a tantrum, I just go on as if all is normal. As long as we
tell them we love them and have attended to all their needs, beyond that I
feel it becomes undue attention. Soon the tantrums stop because they
realize Mom and Dad are firm about bedtime.

~ *Parent Soup member Skiinaz*

Making Wake-Up Time Non-Negotiable

Try giving your early-rising preschooler a digital alarm clock. Tell her
that when the clock reads a certain hour, it's time to get up. Until then,
she can stay in bed.

~ *Christina M., Galion, Ohio*

Are These Night Terrors?

Q: What are "night terrors," and why do children get them?

~ *Grace M., Fremont, California*

DR. GREENE'S INSIGHT

A: Children get their deepest sleep of the night within the first 15 minutes.
This period of slow-wave sleep, or deep non-REM sleep, will typically last
from 45 to 75 minutes. At this time, most children will transition to a lighter
sleep stage or will wake briefly before returning to sleep. Some children,
however, get stuck—unable to completely emerge from slow-wave sleep.

Caught between stages, these children experience a period of partial
arousal. Partial arousal states are classified in three categories:

1. sleepwalking

2. confusional arousal

3. true sleep terrors

These are closely related phenomena that are all part of the same
spectrum of behavior. When most people (including the popular press and
popular parenting literature) speak of sleep terrors, they are generally
referring to what are called confusional arousals by most pediatric sleep
experts (*Principles and Practice of Sleep Medicine in the Child*, by Ferber
and Kryger). Confusional arousals are quite common, taking place in as
many as 15 percent of toddlers and preschool children. They typically occur
in the first third of the night on nights when the child is overtired or when
the sleep/wake schedule has been irregular for several days. A confusional
arousal begins with the child moaning and moving about. It progresses
quickly to the child crying out and thrashing wildly. The eyes may be open
or closed, and perspiration is common. The child will look confused, upset,
or even "possessed" (a description volunteered by many parents). Even if
the child does call out her parents' names, she will not recognize them. She
will appear to look right through them, unable to see them. Parental
attempts to comfort the child by holding or cuddling tend to prolong the
situation. Typically a confusional arousal will last for about 10 minutes,
although it may be as short as 1 minute and it is not unusual for an episode
to last for a seemingly eternal 40 minutes. During these frightening

episodes, the child is not dreaming and typically will have no memory of the event afterward (unlike a nightmare). If any memory persists, it will be a vague feeling of being chased or of being trapped. The event itself seems to be a storm of neural emissions in which the child experiences an intense flight-or-fight sensation. Once over, a child usually settles back to quiet sleep without difficulty.

Confusional arousal is very different from nightmares. You won't become aware of your child's nightmares until after she awakens and tells you about them. They are scary dreams that usually occur during the second half of the night, when dreaming is most concentrated. A child may be fearful following a nightmare, but will recognize you and be reassured by your presence. She may have trouble falling back asleep, though, because of her vivid memory of the scary dream. True sleep terrors are a more intense form of partial arousal. They are considerably less common than confusional arousals, and are seldom described in popular parenting literature. True sleep terrors are primarily a phenomenon of adolescence. They occur in less than 1 percent of the population. These bizarre episodes begin with the child suddenly sitting bolt upright with the eyes bulging wide open and emitting a bloodcurdling scream. The child is drenched in sweat with a look of abject terror on his or her face. The child will leap out of bed, heart pounding, and run blindly from an unseen threat, breaking windows and furniture that block the way. Thus true sleep terrors can be quite dangerous, in that injury during these episodes is not unusual. Thankfully, they are much shorter in duration than the more common confusional arousals of the preschool period.

The tendency toward sleepwalking, confusional arousals, and true sleep terrors often runs in families. The events are often triggered by sleep deprivation or by the sleep schedule shifting irregularly over the preceding few days. A coincidentally timed external stimulus, such as moving a

How do you feel about an infant or toddler sleeping in her parents' bed,
and how often do you do it in your household?

Of 1,733 total votes

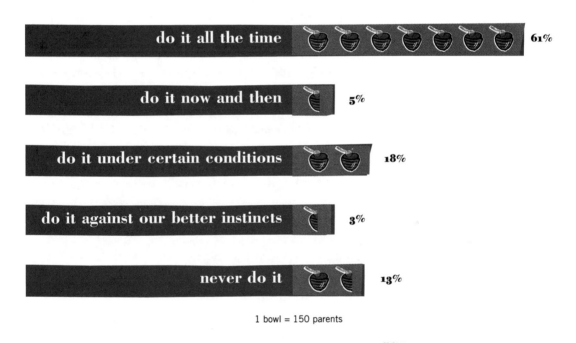

do it all the time	61%
do it now and then	5%
do it under certain conditions	18%
do it against our better instincts	3%
never do it	13%

1 bowl = 150 parents

blanket or making a loud noise, can also trigger a partial arousal (which again shows that the event is a sudden neural storm rather than a result of a complicated dream). Treatment usually involves trying to avoid letting the child get overtired and trying to keep the wake/sleep schedule as regular as possible. When an event does occur, do not try to wake the child—not because it is dangerous, but because it will tend to prolong the event. It is generally best not to hold or restrain the child, since her subjective experience is one of being held or restrained; she would likely arch her back and struggle all the more. Instead, try to relax and to verbally comfort the child if possible. Speak slowly, soothingly, and repetitively. Turning on the lights may also be calming. Protect your child from injury by moving furniture and standing between him or her and windows. In most cases the event will be over in a matter of minutes. True night terrors, or bothersome confusional arousals, can also be treated with medications, hypnotherapy, or with other types of relaxation training. I have sat with my children through confusional arousals and know how powerfully these episodes tug at a parent's heart. Just understanding what they are (normal childhood sleep phenomena that children outgrow—not a sign of maladjustment or the result of bad parenting) helps tremendously.

A Possible Cause for Confusional Arousals

Our son would partially wake up disoriented and highly agitated. It was more frightening to me than to him, as he seemed to be sleeping through them. All I can say is comforting and waiting out the screaming is about all you can do. I also cut out overstimulating television before bed (I think *The Lion King* was a big problem with our son's dreams), and it did get better.

~ *Parent Soup member Kytykatt*

TALKING

Walking, talking, and potty training are probably the biggest developmental milestones in a young child's life. Which means that they are three issues that parents can become obsessed with as they are waiting for them to happen. When children learn to talk, it's especially exciting, because now you can begin to find out what's going on behind those adorable eyes. Learning to talk also gives kids an outlet for their emotions and can help to lessen all those behaviors (such as biting, hitting, and head-banging) that make parents cringe. If your child isn't talking yet, here are some guidelines for what to expect from Dr. Greene and parents who've been there.

The Waiting Game

Waiting for those first words can seem like an eternity, and you are so relieved when that day comes. Remember it's not a reflection on you that your child may not be talking. I always liked to think that my kids knew how to speak but just didn't care to yet and would speak a great deal when ready. That turned out to be the case with my daughter (she's a five-year-old chatterbox now).

~ *Parent Soup member AnCapo*

I think sometimes it's just the child's personality to talk or not to talk, and if there is no physical problem, don't worry too much, even if your child is constantly sucking their thumb or a pacifier. When they have something they want to say badly enough and you make it clear that you can't understand them with something in their mouth, they'll take it out. I think sometimes if you make too big a deal of it, you only make it worse and make them cling to their little vice all the more.

~ *Angela K., South Bound Brook, New Jersey*

Is My Child Talking Enough for Her Age?

Q: Dr. Greene, my daughter is two years and eight months young and she does not speak very well. Actually, she only knows how to say some easy words such as *up, come, go,* and *mama.* I am concerned because she does not even make an effort to say more. I make her repeat words after me and we learn the alphabet together. She will repeat some easy words, but will not use them until I make her. She explains everything in sign language, but she does understand almost everything you tell her. Should I be concerned? Is it time for her to start talking? Is she a late bloomer?

~ *Irina, San Mateo, California*

DR. GREENE'S INSIGHT

A: The pace of language development varies wildly from child to child, but the pattern is often the same. There are two sides of the language coin: understanding and speech. The two develop in tandem, but understanding, or receptive language, leads the way at each stage. Receptive language begins to develop even before birth, as babies begin to respond to, and to remember, words and voices and music—as well as the steady sound of their mothers' hearts. Since spoken language is easier to observe than this silent, steady growth in understanding, I will focus here on expressive language, or speech.

Babies begin by making cooing sounds—beautiful, soft vowel sounds—unbroken by syllables. As the weeks go by, they begin to experiment with varying the volume of their cooing. Within several months they practice varying the pitch. (Note: all of this happens even in children who are completely deaf.) Sometime in the second half of the first year, babbling begins to emerge. This is the sweet sound of consonants and vowels mixed together. The amount and quality of babbling vary, depending on how well babies hear and how much people speak to them. The dadada sound is easier to say than the mama sound. My guess is that, in ages past, moms heard this sound and told the dads that this sound meant "father" (to get the dads involved and make them feel better).

Babbling gives way to jargon, kids imitating the sounds and tones of adult speech. They jabber on and on, and if you didn't know better, you would swear it must be some real language. Around this time, kids begin to point at objects around them (pointing is a key step in language development). Kids' jargon begins to coalesce into a few words, using the same sound for the same object over and over again. This might be "ba" for ball, or "dah" for dog. The first words are usually nouns—names of people, animals, or objects that are important to them. Symbolic gestures begin during this period. A child will pick up an object, say a remote controller, pointing it at the television, to indicate that she knows its use. The time period for gaining the first 50 or so words is often very slow.

These early words are usually very simple and useful for getting the children's needs met. Most kids at this stage either overgeneralize (all men are Daddy, all animals are doggy) or over-restrict (only my cat is kitty). Words appear and disappear in kids' vocabularies. This slow ebb and flow causes many parents to worry—especially if they know other kids of the same age who are talking up a storm. During this slow gain in single words, a rich, complex comprehension is developing almost unseen. An explosion of language follows, when children rapidly learn to use hundreds of words and begin combining them in unique ways ("spoon comb" for fork, or "me puter TV now" for wanting her turn at the computer monitor). Most kids come out with delightful, original utterances during this stage—great fodder for baby book memoirs. Verbs, adjectives, and pronouns are incorporated into their repertoires.

After another plateau, most kids go through another language explosion, this time of sentence complexity. At first, all past tenses end with *ed* ("boy falled down") and all plurals end in *s* ("I like mouses and gooses"). Rules of grammar begin to find their places, and at the same time intelligibility improves greatly. Others outside the family can understand whatever the child is saying. Now, before you know it, language becomes sophisticated enough to give rise to wordplay. Puns, jokes, and poetry mark the flowering of this remarkable growth. ("Daddy, you can't take a shower, Mom already took it!" followed by giggles.) Several warning signs along the way suggest that this powerful process may need some extra help. There may be no problem at all, but a child should definitely get a hearing and speech evaluation if any of the following applies (*Nelson Textbook of Pediatrics*, Saunders, 1996):

- at 12 months: no babbling or jargon

- 18 months: no single words

- 24 months: vocabulary of 10 words or less

- 30 months: vocabulary of less than 100 words or no 2-word phrases

- 36 months: vocabulary of less than 200 words, no sentences, clarity less than 50 percent

- 48 months: vocabulary of less than 600 words, no complete sentences, clarity less than 80 percent

Children who point at objects in the first year and who use symbolic gestures at 13 months are likely to have completely normal language, even if they are late bloomers. I don't know if your daughter is a late bloomer who is on the perfect course for her, or if there is some obstacle (such as fluid in the ears) hindering her development. Either way, a hearing test is the next step. Even if your daughter should turn out to need some extra help, most speech problems can be successfully dealt with when discovered at this age.

Getting an Evaluation

I work for a preschool program and see many preschoolers who have articulation and language delays. The best thing to do if you are concerned is to have a speech and language evaluation done to assess the delay. If the evaluation shows areas of concern, look into preschool for language stimulation. You would be surprised at the difference this will make. Also, when your child asks "What's that?" say, "I don't know, can you tell me what that is?"

~ *Parent Soup member CLCCRAFT*

Our 23-month-old daughter is speech-delayed. Our pediatrician recommended speech therapy, which we go to once per week. The program is through our school district, so it's free (!). Check with your school district and see if they have an Early Intervention or Birth to Three Program. Although I have not always been happy with the individual sessions, the overall result has been reassuring. They recommended that we teach our daughter sign language, and now she has at least 100 signed words. This means that she has the right number of words for her age, and she's still learning them. Her spoken words have increased and improved also. Also, they keep reminding me that many toddlers don't talk until they are two and a half years old. It's really hard and frustrating when we have play-group friends who verbalize freely and I have to interpret my daughter's waving arms and hands. Another thought from the therapist we use: at this tender age, if a toddler thinks she is not performing a task up to the level that is expected or wanted by the parent(s), she may not even try for fear of failing to meet the expectation. So we've started mimicking her silly sounds back, to help her gain confidence in her voice and speaking ability.

~ *Dorothy P., O'Fallon, Missouri*

Ask the doctor about the Early Intervention Program (EIP), funded by the government for at-risk babies and toddlers until age three, after which the school district takes over, but supposedly it doesn't work nearly as well as EIP. In many states, evaluation and therapy is at no cost to you, even if you have a nice income. They may try to bill your insurance, but if they don't pay, the government does. Some states do charge clients, but it is usually less than private therapy. Ask your pediatrician for the phone number to the EIP, look in the phone book in the government pages, or call the social worker at a hospital with a large neonatal intensive care unit (NICU). Some children respond to fun words well. With my son we used a See-n-Say that makes animal sounds and had him repeat them: Baa, Moo, Meow, etc. He picked them up quickly, and it seemed to spark his interest in using real words.

~ *Suzanne L., Pasadena, California*

How Talking Influences Behavior

My son was driving me nuts until about the end of October, then what a change! His birthday was September 10, and at the end of October he started talking up a storm out of nowhere. Throwing, hitting, and other behaviors have all but come to a screeching halt. So there is hope. Mine was such a terror, I swear this one woman in our play group started praying we would quit after my son whacked her child in the head very hard over a toy struggle! I thought I'd die of embarrassment. If it got better for us, then it can for anyone!

~ *Terri I., Stamford, Connecticut*

My experience with my kids (ages two and five), and what I've heard from other moms, is that as the children's verbal abilities advance, the tantrums and "Terrible Twos" lessen. Even if you are really in tune with your child, sometimes they cannot communicate what they want, so you cannot give them what they want. I've noticed just in the last couple months that my two-and-a-half-year-old will no longer pitch a fit when, for example, I deny her ice cream right before dinner; she will understand when I say, "Dinner first, then ice cream," and tell me "OK!" And when she does get upset, it calms her to be able to explain her anger ("Brother hit me") and I can more effectively deal with the problem

KIDS SAY THE DARNEDEST THINGS

Preserve the adorable things your child says in a quote book you can give him years later.

~ *Christina M., Galion, Ohio*

t talking

TRIVIA QUESTION

It's good to do all of the following as your baby learns to speak, except:

a. Insist on proper diction
b. Explain colors
c. Talk like a grown-up
d. Explain cause and effect
e. Introduce pronouns

Answer: c.

Encourage your baby to speak by soliciting responses, but never punish if words are mispronounced.

From *Parent Soup: The Game*

rather than just quieting the tears. So all you moms of Terrible Twos, hang in there, relief is in sight!

~ *Parent Soup member Turcoal*

Hand Signals

We started teaching hand signs when my daughter was seven months old. It does help out with frustration in the early months of trying to speak—signs are so much easier for children to do because it takes less muscle control and coordination.

~ *Shannah B., Carmichael, California*

We have been working with hand signs and our toddler to help him communicate before he has the ability to speak. We've achieved great results, with fewer frustrations for him and us. He expresses great joy when we understand his sign. If he starts whining I ask him to show me a sign, and he tries to use his visual vocabulary. He seems to benefit greatly from this boost to his ability to show us what he wants.

~ *Parent Soup member Cpumph1021*

Helpful Tactics

For toddlers who are having trouble with their language development, try to model two-word phrases, such as "go car" and "Mommy eat." Also, try to encourage him to verbalize to ask for things. When he points to an object, name it for him. Play little games where you lay out three familiar objects, and ask him to get them one at a time as you name them. Eventually ask him to go to another room in the house to retrieve a familiar object, one that is easily accessible, like a familiar toy laying on the floor.

~ *Brenda N., Burlington, Kentucky*

Is Stuttering Normal?

Q: We have an extremely verbal 26-month-old son. We have noticed he is beginning to stutter. Is this a normal speech pattern? Will it pass? Is this something we should be concerned about?

~ *Robin K., Hillsborough, California*

DR. GREENE'S INSIGHT

A: When a child stutters, parents are often told to relax, that the stuttering is a phase that will soon be outgrown, and that nothing need be done. This advice can be unfortunate. Treatment of stuttering is more effective the earlier it is begun. By needlessly delaying evaluation, parents can miss an important window of time when their child's stuttering is most treatable. On the other hand, many children go through a developmental stage of speech disfluency that is often confused with true stuttering. This normal disfluency does disappear over time without need for treatment. If a two-year-old begins to repeat syllables, short words, or phrases (*su-su-such as this*, or *such as . . . such as such as this*) about once every 10 sentences, and begins to use more filler words (*um*, with *uh* pauses or *er* hesitations), is this normal disfluency or stuttering? Children with true stuttering tend to repeat syllables four or more times (*a-a-a-a* as opposed to once or twice for normal disfluency). They *mmmmmay* also occasionally prolong sounds. Children with stuttering show signs of reacting to their stuttering—blinking the eyes, looking to the side, raising the pitch of the voice. True stuttering is frequent—at least 3 percent of the child's speech. While normal disfluency is especially noticeable when the child is tired, anxious, or excited, true stuttering is noticeable most of the time. Children with true stuttering are usually concerned, frustrated, or embarrassed by the difficulty. About 4 percent of all children will have true stuttering for at least 6 months, most commonly between the ages of two and five. Most of these will recover by late childhood, but about a quarter of them will develop severe, chronic stuttering. Whenever parents suspect that their child has true stuttering, it is important to bring it to their pediatrician's attention—it is easily treatable, unless you miss the window of time when treatment is so effective.

TALKING TO KIDS ABOUT SEX

"Mommy, what's a penis?" When your son starts asking questions about sex, will you be ready? What about when you see him touching his penis? Toddlers are curious creatures, and their inquiring minds want to know what genitals are and what purpose they serve. Here are some tips on dealing with the potentially sensitive subjects so that you can foster a healthy sexuality in your child.

Just the Facts, Ma'am
My then three-year-old son was asking me questions about the female anatomy when I was pregnant with my daughter. I taught him the correct names for his body parts, which, I might add, he uses very appropriately (albeit at inappropriate times). I simply told him that mommies have a special opening for the babies to come out of and actually pointed to where it was located. That seemed to sate his curiosity. The main thing, I think, is to keep it simple. Kids aren't really looking for a long and involved explanation with all the correct terms—tell him as much as he asks about, be direct and honest, but keep it simple.
~ *Patti F., Columbus, Ohio*

At what age should your children stop seeing you naked?

Of 1,286 total votes

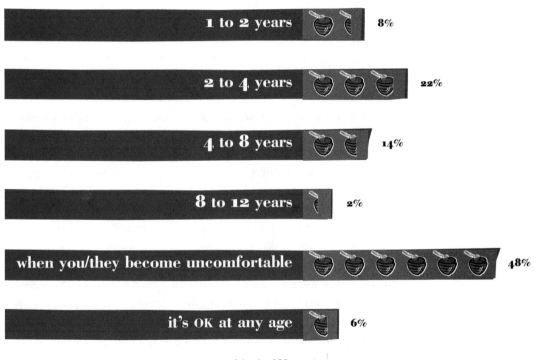

1 to 2 years	8%
2 to 4 years	22%
4 to 8 years	14%
8 to 12 years	2%
when you/they become uncomfortable	48%
it's OK at any age	6%

1 bowl = 100 parents

KIDS SAY THE
DARNEDEST
THINGS

My three-year-old niece
walked in on her
grandfather while he was
in the bathroom. She
looked around to the
front of him and asked
him, "You got a PoPo
(penis)?" He said, "Uh,
yes," and she said, "Us
girls, we just got butts!"
~ *Debbie C.,*
Maryville,
Tennessee

Is It Masturbation?

Q: I need to know about a two-year-old's masturbating. What brings it
on, and how concerned should I be about a sudden constant desire to
engage in the behavior?
~ *L. D., Ramona, California*

DR. GREENE'S INSIGHT

A: Most children begin to explore their genitals at about the same time they
begin to look more like little boys and girls than like babies. Just when we
are beginning to adjust to their not being babies anymore, we are
confronted with the sight of our little boy fondling his erection or our little
girl moving her hips up and down on top of her pillow with a glazed look in
her eyes. How jarring!

A glimpse of our little ones as sexually mature adolescents is
superimposed on our image of them as innocent babies—and all of this
resonates with our complicated feelings about our own sexuality and
innocence. No wonder this can elicit such concern. If we take a step back,
though, we can see that it makes sense that kids would want to explore
their own bodies. When toilet learning becomes a focus of interest, we
might anticipate that kids would also be curious about those parts of the
body that have in the past been largely hidden under the diapers. Boys will
play with their penises. Girls will finger their vaginas, and even insert
objects. Many kids will reach down every chance they get. This exploration
produces pleasurable feelings, as we are well aware.

Most, if not all, two-year-olds will engage in some degree of this
behavior. Although many parenting books refer to this as childhood
masturbation, I believe the term is misleading and unfortunate. Save the
term *masturbation* for genital stimulation accompanied by sexual fantasy—

another challenge to face years down the road. Toddlers just do it because it feels good. Babies will often tug on the genitals in much the same way they tug on the ears or toes. Toddlers, though, begin to recognize that the genitals are special. They are far more interesting and more fun than toes. For some children, playing with the genitals becomes a self-comforting behavior not unlike thumb-sucking. For a few, this settles into a time-consuming habit that takes them away from other important play and development.

What is the wisest way for parents to approach genital play in their toddlers? First, remember that one of our important responsibilities as parents is to teach our children about healthy sexuality. Of course, the many parents reading this will have wildly different ideas as to what constitutes healthy sexuality. Whatever your values, you will want to communicate them to your children. You will want to teach them that healthy sexuality is not dirty, nor is it cheap. The key to passing on your values effectively is keeping the lines of respect and communication open. My advice is not to try to stop this normal part of development. If the genital play becomes and remains a consuming passion, I would look for and address underlying reasons, rather than trying to stop the behavior. Is the child tense and in extra need of self-comforting? Are people overreacting and thus reinforcing the habit? Is there a chronic, low-grade urinary tract infection or yeast infection? Is the child overstimulated and needing to soothe himself to withdraw? Is she understimulated and bored? Dealing with the cause will bring the behavior back to a level of enthusiasm that doesn't take away from other interests.

If you feel that the genital play should be reigned in a bit, then I recommend that when you see it happening you pretend to ignore what he is doing. Try to distract him with some new, engaging activity. Be as

My nephew was a very verbal, precocious two-year-old when he discovered that boys and girls are not equipped alike. At Thanksgiving dinner, after the blessing, he asked each person at the table whether or not they had a penis. My poor sister was beet red, and trying very hard to shush him, but he insisted on continuing until he had polled every person present. He certainly livened up the gathering, and we still joke about Robbie's Thanksgiving "penis poll."

> ~ *Parent Soup*
> *member*
> *SpcDlphn62*

nonchalant as you can manage to be. (Rushing over out of breath is not subtle!) You want to communicate by your actions that he and his body are OK, but that there is also a whole world out there to discover and enjoy.

Directly trying to get toddlers to stop touching themselves is a battle you cannot win. You can't just put the objects of their attention up on a high shelf out of their reach. If you actively discourage kids from self-exploration, or if you punish them for "masturbating," then genital play becomes a forbidden fruit.

Two things happen when something becomes a forbidden fruit. The fruit will be tasted when the opportunity arises, and people will hide what it is they have done. They will feel the need to be "semianonymous." This shameful hiding is the one outcome you don't want to produce. All too quickly, our little ones will launch out on the turbulent seas of true adolescence. Only if we have maintained open communication and mutual respect can we offer any effective guidance during those critical years.

TANTRUMS *(See also Behavior, No!, Time-Out)*

Two-year-olds and tantrums go together like teens and bad attitudes. Not every toddler will become a raging tantrum monster, but many will, and it's absolutely frustrating for parents. The thing is, tantrums are also absolutely frustrating for toddlers. Dr. Greene has some wonderful insights into the mind of a toddler that can help you react more effectively to tantrums—even episodes that happen for all the world to see in the grocery store. The key to surviving tantrums is to see them as an opportunity to teach your toddler how to deal with his emotions and life's frustrations. Such an important lesson is bound to be hard to teach and harder to learn. But with a combination of patience and empathy, this inevitable phase of development can give you and your child a wonderful reward.

The Dreaded Tantrum in Public

Q: My 25-month-old son throws temper tantrums at the worst possible times, like in the grocery store (which happened to me yesterday). What do I do? I'm so embarrassed!

~ Amber H., Savannah, Georgia

DR. GREENE'S INSIGHT

A: You are not alone! Temper tantrums are very common at this age, and when viewed in context, they can be an extremely constructive part of the development of a healthy child. Newborns and infants are quite happy as long as their basic physical needs are met. Children in the developmental stage known as the "Terrible Twos," or "First Adolescence," become aware of the choices available to them and as a result become angry or frustrated when they are powerless over those choices. The result is often temper tantrums, or what I like to call "emotional storms."

Let's look at the example you mentioned of the grocery store—as an adult, you can choose whether or not you want to go to the grocery store, when to go, what products you are going to buy, and which products you will not purchase. When you are in the middle of shopping in the grocery store, your child will see things he wants. To make the supermarket situation worse, there are cleverly designed packages up and down the aisles that scream, "Buy me!" For a small child who is just learning to make choices, it's like going to a rock concert. Visually they are overwhelmed.

They want multiple attractive items. When they can't have what they want, they dissolve into tears and worse—deafening screams. Of course, everybody in the store turns and looks at your child and (shudder) at you!

Surveys have shown that there are two common reactions of parents in this situation. The first is to spank or discipline the child in some way. Our role during this phase is to teach our children to make choices, to teach them to grow up as independent, highly functioning people. If you discipline a child for a temper tantrum in a store, you are teaching a powerful unconscious lesson: down the road, when he or she is in second adolescence, and is confused, hurting, scared, and doesn't know what choices to make—don't talk to Mom or Dad, because they will not understand and it will hurt. The second major way that people deal with temper tantrums in stores is to give the children whatever they had the temper tantrums to get. Basically, this teaches kids that if they cry hard enough, or act out sufficiently, they will get whatever they want. We don't want to teach our children that either.

So, what does one do about temper tantrums? Try to avoid emotional storms whenever possible. Children are most susceptible to storms when they are tired, hungry, uncomfortable, or bored. When possible, plan shopping for times when your child is rested, fed, and healthy. Interact with your son throughout shopping and/or bring along stimulating toys or books. It's often helpful to let your child pick out one or two things when at the store. A good way to do this is when a child asks for something, instead of saying, "No," (which will immediately make him or her say, "Yes!") say, "Let's write that down." Then write it down. When your child asks for something else, write that down, too. Then when you are all done, read back a few of the things on the list that you think would be good choices,

and let him pick one or two of the things on the list. If children can make
some choices, they will both learn more and feel better. Another thing that
is really worthwhile is for you to make a list before you go to the store. That
way it won't look so arbitrary when you pick what you want off the shelf,
and your child doesn't get his choice. As you shop, whenever you put
something in your basket, check it off your list (even if it is not on your list,
check it off. The list is to teach that each item has a purpose, not that you
had thought of it previously).

These strategies can greatly reduce the number of emotional storms, but
their appearance is inevitable. What then? First, take a deep breath. You
probably have a normal child and are a good parent. It is not a defect in
parenting that your child is acting this way. People who don't have kids may
not understand, yet. That is their problem, though. Try to be patient with
them. Next, while you are taking a deep breath, consciously relax. Kids
really play off your emotions. It's so hard to relax in this situation, but just
let your muscles go. The more uptight you are, the more energy is available
for their tantrums. Kids thrive on attention, even negative attention. Where
you go from here depends on your child. Some children will calm down if
you pick them up and hold them. My first son was like that. His storm would
dissolve if you just gave him a big hug and told him it would be all right. If
you picked up my second son during a storm, he would hit you. Each child
is unique. One thing that often works very well is to try to voice to the child
what he is going through. "You must really want to get this, don't you?"
Then he may melt and say, "Uh huh." You will have to experiment with your
son to see what it is that can help him understand that everything is OK,
these bad feelings will pass, and that it's all a normal part of growing up.
Whatever you do, if your child has a temper tantrum to try to get something,

don't give it to him, even if you would have ordinarily done so. Giving in to tantrums is what spoils a child. Giving in is the easiest, quickest solution in the short run, but it damages your child, prolongs this phase, and ultimately creates far more discomfort for you. Choosing your son's long-term gain over such dramatic short-term relief is part of what makes properly handling temper tantrums so heroic. Instead you might say, "Sorry, I would love to give you what you want, but because you had a temper tantrum, I can't right now. Next time, let's do that." Stand by your child during this difficult time for both of you. When you feel yourself getting tense, again say to yourself: temper tantrums are a beautiful, albeit painful, part of growing up.

Avoiding a Grocery Store Outburst

A: To cut down on frustration in the grocery store, it helps to prepare your child ahead of time. Preview the trip with your child, tell her she will be allowed to pick out two items, and if she has a tantrum, you will just have to leave. Tell her if the trip goes well, you can have popsicles together when you get home.

~ Susan H., Syracuse, New York

Tantrum Remedies

When your son starts screaming, take him outside and tell him to scream his head off. Encourage him to scream or yell the entire time he is out there. You might even do it yourself (neighbors will think you're nuts, but what the heck). When you are ready to go back in, start to use your quiet voice and explain, "It's fun to scream and yell outside *only*! Now it's time to go in and use our quiet voices." If you are ready to go into a store, you might even try letting him scream in the parking lot to get it out of his system before you walk in. I have often found with my kids that when one of their behaviors goes from being irritating to something that I allow and even encourage, it ceases to be as much fun and they soon stop it altogether.

~ *Lisa K., Tucker, Georgia*

When my kids are in a bratty stage, I:

1. Make clear in my own mind what behavior I will accept or not accept. I'm not wishy washy! Kids really need consistency at times like this.

2. I take away privileges when they misbehave, or send them to their rooms, whatever seems best at the time. And I stick with whatever punishment I assign.

3. When the storm has passed, we do something fun that we both enjoy. Then we can start getting the closeness back, and both I and the child feel like she is OK, not out of control anymore.

4. Don't panic. I frequently tell myself I have 15 or so more years to produce a competent, decent adult—it doesn't have to all come together by the time they're five.

~ *Parent Soup member Juli Kauf*

The Art of Distraction
I have also noticed that if you keep them talking through anything you're doing, it takes their mind off the situation. This tactic has been my saving

grace with my soon-to-be-three-years-old boy. As soon as I see there maybe a tantrum on the horizon or he's going to whack his sister, I simply get him on to something else.

~ *Lisa W., Hudson, New Hampshire*

Keeping Yourself in Control

What a child who's throwing a tantrum really needs is for you not to get angry and lose it, which can be really hard when you're looking at that distorted little face and wondering what demon is possessing your child. Try getting down to her level physically, looking at her calmly and firmly, and saying, "Honey, you need to stop crying or we will have to leave the mall. Do you want me to pick you up to help you stop crying?" You have to be ready to leave if you're going to do this, of course. Just stay calm. Your daughter's crying isn't a reflection on you, but your own behavior is. Remember, she's only two. Look how hard it is for us to control our anger. Sometimes I ask myself when I am screaming like a shrew at my children, "How I can expect them to control themselves, when I, an adult, can't do it myself?"

~ *Parent Soup member mahopac*

Change Their Behavior by Changing Yours

My four-year-old son started getting really out of control. I always used time-outs, and recently he started refusing them, screaming at me "No!" and even running away from me when I tried putting him in the time-out spot. I next resorted to spankings, which I was hesitant about, but didn't know what else to do. Every time I yelled at him he would yell right back at me "You're getting a spanking," and "Go in time-out now." I didn't know if I should laugh or cry! It got me so incredibly mad that I would end up screaming at him and even saying things such as, "How did you end up being such a brat?" Then, of course, I felt really badly and we'd hug and I'd lose the battle. So, I decided it was time for a new approach: When he was acting like a maniac and I got to the point where I was ready to break, I stopped and said, "Josh, can we have a talk?" and to my surprise he said, "Sure, Mom" and sat right down. We talked about his behavior and how it was inappropriate and what type of behavior would be appropriate at that time. I've been doing this for a few weeks now, and it works! I learned that yelling and hitting and screaming is a waste of time. Kids like to be treated with respect as much as parents do.

~ *Jody W., Plainview, New York*

PARENT POLL

Does the possibility of public reaction (criticism from strangers) make you hesitant to discipline your kids in public?

Of 962 total votes

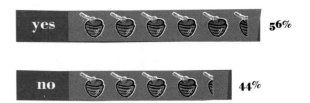

yes 56%

no 44%

1 bowl = 100 parents

I too was very guilty of yelling and the occasional swatting of a little rear end. The stress of the day would build as my three-and-a-half-year-old was trying to exert his independence. It was a explosive combination. Two things have happened, and they have been blessings. I learned how to take time-outs for myself: when I'm stressed or angry about something, I pop in a short video for my son or have someone keep an eye on him for about 30 minutes, and I take a walk, or go pull weeds, or just go somewhere where it's quiet and I can regroup. The other thing is that

KIDS SAY THE DARNEDEST THINGS

My husband always makes deals with our three-and-a-half-year-old daughter, such as, "I'll make you a deal— you finish eating your dinner, and we'll go to the playground. Deal?" So our daughter came to me one day, and said, "Mommy, I'll make you a deal—you let me play a game on the computer, and I won't scream." I just had to laugh while I explained to her that that was not a fair deal.

~ *Parent Soup member MIKMICH93*

I've started to sit down and explain things to my son rather than just saying "Because I said" or "Because I don't want you to." I try to validate his feeling of not understanding or not wanting to do something, but explain what he needs to do (for example nap time) and all the things he can do when we get done. I have noticed a remarkable difference in his behavior—he's much more calm and we have very little tantrum throwing. It's the combination of a few different changes in my behavior that has helped me curb the undesirable behavior in him.

~ *Parent Soup member JustTeeezn*

Give Them an Outlet for Their Anger
Try to give your daughter something to take her frustration out on, such as a pillow or couch cushion. If you are out of the house, try carrying along some tissues for her to tear. It might make a mess, but it is better than her hurting herself. I know it is hard, but the less attention you give the behavior, the sooner she will stop doing it.

~ *Parent Soup member JulJimEvKy*

Create a "feelings" box for the times when your child does not get her own way. Props can include a noisemaker to express anger, a mirror for practicing making angry faces, and paper and crayons to draw how she is feeling.

~ *Christina M., Galion, Ohio*

A Completely Different Approach to Discipline
I learned something yesterday about my three-year-old. We left the babysitter's house in tears because he wanted to stay and play a game. His frustration and anger continued when we arrived home and he realized he had painted a picture and left it behind. I attempted to get him side-

tracked by asking him to help with dinner, but this just seemed to make
the situation worse. Here I was attempting to fix dinner, diffuse a three-
year-old, as well as deal with my own frustration. I turned off the kitchen
light, sat down on the floor, and announced that it was a good time for a
hug. He came over, sat on my lap, and we just sat there for a few minutes
hugging each other. And you know what, it helped both of us get a grip.

~ *Caroline I., Glendale, Arizona*

Sometimes when my daughter is acting up I feel like saying, "Cut it out!"
or "Be quiet!" to her. I have found it to be completely ineffective. All she
does is scream louder. I have discovered that when she is acting her
worst, she might suddenly say, " I want you Mommy!" or "Hold me
Mommy!" as if to let me know that she is scared of her own emotions. She
seems to really need the comforting, stable arms of a parent. Even if it is
a parent who won't let her do what she thought she should be able to do.
She calms more easily if I hold and hug her and talk quietly to her.
Please remember that "this too, shall pass."

~ *Rebecca M., Richmond, Virginia*

I read a great quote a few months before my daughter was born: "The
times that you really don't want to hug your child are the times when
they need it the most."

~ *Susan B., Ridgefield, Connecticut*

When my son was in the two- and three-year-old tantrum phase, I
realized that the tantrums scared him even as they were happening. I
would take him in my arms and hold him until the fury passed,
"containing" the rage for him, as it were. I also made sure that his
tantrums were never effective, that is, I never gave in or changed my

position due to the tantrum. Eventually, he was able to control his anger a little better. I considered it real progress when he would just yell, "I am mad, Mom!" instead of hurling himself on the floor. And he realized tantrums were not an effective way of changing my mind. I hope this helps someone; I realize each kid is different and we are all out there trying whatever works for our own child.

~ *Parent Soup member CharJannay*

THUMB-SUCKING *(See also Pacifiers)*

Just like pacifiers, thumb-sucking is a way for kids to calm themselves. Unlike a pacifier, the thumb is always within reach. So thumb-sucking can be a harder habit to break (should you decide that it's necessary to do so). But being able to soothe herself is a good skill for your daughter to have. If you and she decide that it is time for the thumb-sucking to go, substituting another way for her to calm herself will make the transition easier and more likely to stick.

How Old Is Too Old?

Q: Does anyone have a child who sucks his thumb? My son is at day care, and he is two and a half years old and the only one there who

sucks his thumb. His caretakers have implied that I should be working with him on this. He is very content and has always been a good
baby and toddler as far as being able to calm himself with his thumb.

~ *Parent Soup member SharPon*

Get Your Child Involved in the Weaning Process

A: My daughter sucked her thumb until she was four and a half years
old. The pediatrician said to try the awful tasting stuff you put on
their thumbs. I wasn't really happy with that, but if that's what it
took, I was willing to try. Before trying it though, I sat down with her
and told her that that's what we might have to do. I was very careful
to stress that it wouldn't hurt her, just taste yucky and act as a
reminder not to suck. I asked her if we should do that or if she
wanted to try on her own first, and she chose to try it on her own. It
took about three weeks, but we broke the habit. I think putting the
responsibility in her hands helped a lot.

~ *Luanne K., Granger, Indiana*

A Vote for Letting Him Quit on His Own

A: My daughter is 26 months old, sucks her thumb and holds her
"blankey," and I have no plans to break her from this. If that is the
only way your son has to comfort himself, I say leave him alone. Our
pediatrician jokingly said, "Let her suck her thumb all she wants, the
orthodontics will be far more inexpensive than the years of
counseling."

~ *Lisa L., Jacksonville, Florida*

TIME FOR YOURSELF *(See also Sanity Savers)*

When you spend all day feeding, clothing, playing with, and chasing a toddler (not to mention any other children you might have), the time you once spent taking care of yourself seems to evaporate before your very eyes. You may have to ask yourself on a regular basis, "When was the last time I showered?" Of course you love your kids. Of course you wouldn't have it any other way. But what you wouldn't do for a little "me time!" Fear not, for help is at hand. Below, the Parent Soup moms share their secrets for reserving some time that is all their own to soak in the tub, or read, or just sit and stare at the wall. Here's to many rejuvenating "me moments."

The Problem
Time for me? What is that? When I am not being Elizabeth and Katherine's mommy and Jim's wife, I sometimes wonder who I am. I know I should not complain too much. I really prefer this life over the one I had before I had a husband and kids. At least I know that in this profession I am getting a regular salary (hugs and kisses go a long way).
~ *Marilyn R., East Brunswick, New Jersey*

I can't tell you the last time I had time to do my nails. I haven't had a haircut in months. I finally told my husband, I'm going to get it cut tomorrow or I'm going to buy myself a collar. I feel like such a complainer sometimes. I love my kids dearly, and I am so happy they have graced my life. I never knew I could love like this. It's just that everybody needs a break and a little time to love themselves, too. Would it be incredibly silly to actually rent a hotel room just for an afternoon of pay-per-view movies and cross-stitch in peace and quiet? Don't say, go into the bedroom and shut the door for the afternoon. That would never work. I can't even go into the bathroom long enough for a shower!

~ *Angela K., South Bound Brook, New Jersey*

Nap Time = Mommy Time

I do exactly as I please when my son goes down for his nap. No cleaning, only what I enjoy. It took a while to get used to, but now I won't have it any other way.

~ *Patty D., Las Vegas, Nevada*

Put Down That Laundry Basket

The mess can wait, it isn't impatient and it won't get up and walk away (unfortunately). I personally get my time when my little one sleeps— everything stops then, as long as I do. You have to just take the time whenever you see a few minutes. Take them, they belong to you. If the house looks a wreck and you can't bear to look, close your eyes for 10 minutes. The kids won't remember having a messy house, but they will remember a stressed out mom.

~ *Parent Soup member CozmikPerl*

Calgon, Take Me Away

I have begun to take a nice, hot bath in the evening and spend time alone either just soaking or reading. It gives me time to relax and just be alone. Being able to shave my legs slowly is a pleasant thing. These little things make me happy because I know that these times are precious and few. It relieves some tension that has built up during the day from being at home raising a baby, cooking, and cleaning.

~ *Kathy L., Indianapolis, Indiana*

Enlisting Help

We've made Sundays Daddy-Daughter Day. I either get out of the house for a while or my husband takes our two-year-old to Grandma's while I stay home and read and sleep. It helps a lot. Whenever I start getting stressed I just think about Sunday.

~ *Rannelle D., Altavista, Virginia*

When I really need time to myself, I end up asking my in-laws to take her for a few hours so I can get the house cleaning done. And I seem to remember that last time I did that I got nothing accomplished except a nice, long hot bath. When I went and picked her up, I was like a new person!

~ *Parent Soup member Blueeyed*

Time Away from Each Other Can Help

My three-year-old didn't start Terrible Twos until three and a half, and then her little brother started them early at 18 months, so I am stuck with two at the same time, and if one isn't in a time-out, the other one is, or both. I recently enrolled the younger one in a toddler program the same hours his older sister is in preschool. It's only two days a week of morning freedom, but that's a lifetime of needed vacation for me! I then take the time to run errands, do some work from home, do housework, or take a walk at the park. Working a part-time week from home has also added to my self-esteem.

~ *Tracy R., Englewood, Ohio*

Value Yourself
Never feel guilty about doing things for yourself—your kids learn by your actions too, and showing them that you value yourself goes a long way toward teaching them to enjoy life and to pursue their own personal goals.

~ *Patti F., Columbus, Ohio*

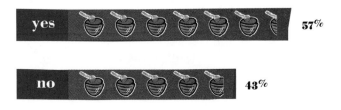

PARENT POLL

Would you turn down the most amazing job in the world if it meant spending less time with your kids?

Of 1,104 total votes

yes — 57%

no — 43%

1 bowl = 100 parents

When you are stressed out and depressed, your child can feel that, and the more upset you become, the worse it is for your child. I suggest that you start to work on you—you need to be healthy and happy first. If you are feeling at all depressed and incapable of coping with things, please contact your doctor. I remember the first time I was able to cope with a difficult situation after I got help with postpartum depression. I actually laughed instead of cried. And what a difference it made with my two-year-old. Once I was happy, he was much more responsive and I was much more patient. You are important. Take care of yourself!

~ *Parent Soup member AxisPM*

t time for yourself

Getting You and the Kids out of the House
(and Each Other's Hair)

The hardest part of being a stay-at-home mom is that it is so constant and
leaves very little break time. I still sometimes feel like I'm going nuts, but
I am glad I made this choice. My survival and happiness have come
through getting out and meeting other moms and by having some time to
myself. I work out a few days a week where there is babysitting. I trade
babysitting once a week with a friend with similar-age children. I get
together with friends at a park. I was in a play group for a while where
moms could talk while kids played. I joined MOPS (Mothers of
Preschoolers), a Christian organization with chapters in 50 states. We
meet twice a month. Mothers have discussions, do crafts, and hear
speakers while children are watched in another area. I am enrolling my
younger daughter in a "Mother's Morning Out" program at our church. I
am definitely not a natural at this, but I have worked hard at making it
manageable.

~ *Parent Soup member ROBINBRU*

Finding Time to Take a Shower

I've found something that works: I let my daughter sit in the tub while I
take a shower. I aim the spray so she doesn't have soap falling on her,
and she enjoys the "rain." I know she's safe, and I don't have to rush,
worrying what she might be doing unsupervised.

~ *Anne W., Cranford, New Jersey*

Getting out of the House

My son and I have very busy mornings: Tuesdays and Thursdays we have
school, Wednesday is reading time at the library, Monday is Gymboree,
and Friday is shopping. I found that if I had a day plan in my head and

250

did not stress about the housework, I was better with my toddler and he
was better with me.

~ *Gigi T., Providence, Rhode Island*

I am a stay-at-home mom of a two-year-old and a baby who is eight
months old. My husband generally leaves around 7 A.M. and gets home
around 7 P.M. Believe me, we are all at the window watching for Daddy in
the evening. Play groups are a great way for getting out of the house and
give both you and your child a chance to socialize. There are ways to get
out of the house and give your child some time with other children as well
as giving you a break if you look for them.

~ *Lisa K., Tucker, Georgia*

Create "Break Nights"
My husband and I have started "break nights." He gets one a week and I
get one. When it's my night, he does everything. Tonight he made dinner
(tuna sandwiches, but who's complaining?), picked up the kitchen, made
his lunch, made our daughter's snack, laid out her clothes, packed her
backpack, picked up all the toys, brushed her teeth, brushed her hair,
read her stories, and put her to bed. I sat on the couch and cross-
stitched!

~ *Angela K., South Bound Brook, New Jersey*

TIME-OUT *(See also Anger, Behavior, Tantrums)*

Time-out is a method of defusing tantrums. It can take many forms, but
the main idea is to remove your child from whatever situation instigated
the tantrum and give him a set amount of time to calm down. It's a lot

like going to the penalty box in hockey games. The beauty of time-out lies in its simplicity, and it has become a popular form of gentle discipline (as opposed to say, spanking). In fact, many parents take time-outs themselves to alleviate potentially eruptive situations with their kids (see the Anger entry for more information). Below are some suggestions for incorporating this effective tactic into your parenting toolbox.

Put a Timer to Work for You

I started time-out with my daughter when she was almost two. We use a time-out timer. It's great because I don't have to watch the clock constantly and she knows she must wait to until the bell rings. The other day, she was in time-out and I was busy with the baby and didn't set the timer—she kept reminding me over and over to set the timer. She has gotten used to the routine, and now time-outs are easier for both of us.

~ *Jennifer C., Covington, Georgia*

Keeping Kids in Time-Out Away from Distractions

We use the center of the floor in the kitchen for time-outs, and it works great for our 26-month-old. It's away from distracting things like toys and TV, and doesn't interfere with any regular routine. My day-care provider turned me on to this, and keeping consistent with each other helps my son understand that a time-out is a time-out no matter where he is. We use the kitchen timer to keep track.

~ *Valeri L., Camarillo, California*

I made the bottom step of our stairs the "naughty step." Every time my daughter got the slightest bit naughty, I'd sit her on it firmly and tell her what she had done was wrong. It worked like magic. She doesn't move until she's said, "Sorry, Mummy" (which now takes about 10 seconds).

~ *Parent Soup member Kathryn199*

I do day care in my home for one- and two-year-olds. I have one corner of the room padded with pillows and blankets. I call it the "Comfy Corner." Whenever anyone is unhappy, they must go to the "corner." The only rule is that they must stay there until they feel better. When they are finished with their fit, they may come out and join everyone else who is happy. Although it sounds simplistic, it really works. It gives them a chance to blow off their steam without interrupting everyone else. I have my time-out in a different place so they don't feel as though they are being punished for crying or becoming angry. These are both normal emotions that toddlers should be allowed to express. Most of my children stop crying as soon as they realize that they are going to go to the "Comfy Corner."

~ *Jennifer D., Cincinnati, Ohio*

Do you have a playpen? If so, try putting him in it instead of his room for time-outs. Put the playpen in the middle of the room where he can't get his hands on anything to throw. That's what I do with my two-year-old, and it seems to work.

~ *Kristi G., Concord, California*

Denying Them an Audience

I would remove the child and place him in his room when he throws his tantrums. Children's temper tantrums tend to be about getting attention.

KIDS SAY THE
DARNEDEST THINGS

My son thinks nothing of slapping his 10-month-old sister. I tried time-outs on the couch and in his room. Needless to say, I got tired faster than he did, since I would have to physically carry him to his room. So we embarked on a new method of punishment: pacifier retrieval. I took his pacifier from him and put it in a cabinet. Then I told him he would not have it for five minutes, I then set the oven timer. They were a very long five minutes. We went through this three times until he caught on. One time, he was determined to get the pacifier, so he went to the playroom and got one of his chairs, crying all the while. When he came down the hallway he said to me, crying, "Excuse me, Mama." The etiquette lessons I'm teaching are definitely there.

~ Lisa W., Hudson,
New Hampshire

If you move him to his room and put him in his crib (if he is still in one) or on his bed and leave the room, you have removed his audience. After he calms down I would go back in the room and talk about it, discipline the tantrum then, when he is calm and ready to accept your teaching.

~ Parent Soup member kmmc

My husband will take our two-and-a-half-year-old daughter upstairs when she starts crying or whining (the kind of crying that comes after being told "No"). He places her on her little chair and tells her she can come back down when she is finished crying. She always comes down in about a minute and tells us, "I'm done crying now"!

~ Susan D., Bradford, Massachusetts

Make the Most of Time-Outs

Make sure you're not overusing the time-outs. I used to make the mistake of saying, "Time-out!" after every little infraction. It loses its effectiveness unless you use it sparingly. Now I try to use it mainly if my kids do something physical, like hitting. I try to use other consequences for different misbehaviors (for example, if they are shouting at me because they want something, I turn around and walk away, or pretend that my ears can only hear appropriate tones of voice). I've even started letting some of the smaller stuff slide, even though it might drive me crazy, because I don't want to be constantly focusing on what they do wrong. If you spend more time concentrating on what they're doing right, so will they.

~ Laurie M., Merrimac, Massachusetts

TOOTH CARE

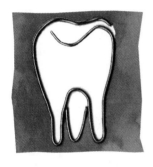

Many kids just don't like to brush their teeth—or have anyone else do it for them, for that matter. As one Parent Soup member says, "They just don't really understand that putting this big stick that tastes weird in their mouth and moving it around in an orderly fashion is good for them." Of course, it is possible to teach your son to brush his teeth. See if some of the tried-and-true tips below don't help clean the pearly whites in your house.

The Problem

Q: My two-year-old daughter refuses to brush her teeth. We've tried pleading, making a game of it ("Here, help Mommy brush her teeth"), and refusing to let her out of the bathroom until she brushes (of course, I've caved in on that because I want out of the bathroom myself). She will sometimes let me wipe her teeth with a washcloth, but lately she's resisted that, too. I've so far resisted the urge to tie her up and sit on her, but the thought of cavities and dentist bills has me considering it. Any ideas?

~ *Anne L., Cedar Rapids, Iowa*

Teaching by Example

A: Our dentist has told us that there isn't a real urgency to get your child to brush until she turns three. He says that it's sort of like potty training—you can't really force them into it. He did say, however, that when it does come time for them to brush, you should have the child in the bathroom with you while you're brushing your own teeth. Let them watch you do it, several times. Their natural curiosity will encourage them to mimic Mommy and Daddy, and eventually they will ask if they can brush too. Also, when they do ask, allow them to do it on their own for the first few times. After a few times, ask if you can help them do it a little bit faster.

~ John W., Brook Park, Ohio

A: Try using bubble-gum flavored toothpaste and use it for yourself, too. Put him on a stool in front of the mirror with yourself at the same time and tell him to do like Mommy does. Eventually he will start to imitate you. My son started off the same way and now copies me.

~ Randi H., Fort Lauderdale, Florida

Let Them Practice on Someone Else's Teeth
A: I have my two-year-old brush my teeth while I do his. This works pretty well. I also have had him do his stuffed Elmo's mouth while I do his.

~ Dana D., Campbell, California

Try a Different Brush
A: My three-year-old was the same way. Then for Christmas I found a battery-operated toothbrush. He loved it so much, we have now moved up to the children's Oral B rechargeable. (Don't use the adult version, it's a little too powerful.)

~ Lisa M., Bixby, Oklahoma

The Fountain of Tooth

A: We recently bought one of those drinking-fountain attachments for our bathroom sink. Now my two-year-old loves brushing his teeth, because he gets to drink out of the fountain, too.

~ *JoEllyn M., San Diego, California*

Keeping Them in the Bathroom

A: Sit on the toilet seat with your child standing between your legs. Cross one leg over the other (so that she is in the "triangle" created). Lean her head back. Brush. She won't be able to escape and she will get her teeth brushed. Of course, the other option is to make sure she drinks a glass of water before bed and that you just offer the option of her brushing when you brush your teeth. Not making it a fight may do the trick.

~ *Tarrant F., Gainesville, Georgia*

Try Giving Her Control

A: What I found to work was to give my daughter control of the toothbrush and let her "do it herself" for a few minutes first. Then, about the time she starts getting bored and is ready to put the toothbrush down, I say "Almost finished? Let Mommy have a turn!" I think this has helped her to feel like she has some independence and responsibility, yet I still get to make sure it's done right.

~ *Lisa K., Tucker, Georgia*

The Art of Distraction

A: Wrap some gauze around your finger and take your toddler on your lap for story time. While she's busy looking at the book, gently rub her teeth with the gauze. For older children, encourage them to make "mouth bubbles" when they brush their teeth. They'll learn that vigorous brushing makes the best bubbles.

~ Susan H., Syracuse, New York

TOYS

At their best, toys stimulate young imaginations and provide hours of entertainment. At worst, they cost a lot of money only to wind up stuffed in the back of a closet or, more painfully, underfoot. Here, Dr. Greene shares his ideas on the best bets for toys that your kids will love.

How Can You Find the Best Toys for Toddlers?

Q: My daughter is two years old. What are the best toys for children this age?

~ Laurie P., Hoboken, New Jersey

DR. GREENE'S INSIGHT

A: Play is a child's work, stimulating her growth and development. Activities such as television, or fancy toys that perform while she watches, can artificially satisfy her inborn desires both for play and for adult attention, thus robbing her of joy-filled opportunities for growth (in much the same way that processed, partially hydrogenated snack foods can replace the magic of a ripe peach). To find clues as to the best toys at any age, turn off the TV, put away the passive-play toys, and watch your child. Many kids will begin to play spontaneously, using whatever is at hand; take note of what they choose to play with. Others will be directionless or frustrated; interact with them playfully, and their choices will begin to emerge. Spontaneous play gives us important clues to the cutting edge of a child's development. With this in mind, here are some ideas that will provide hours of child-directed play for many two-year-olds:

- Kindergarten blocks. Natural wood blocks come in a variety of shapes and sizes for creative building.

- Sorting toys. Sorting is one of the most important intellectual tasks for two-year-olds. A simple sorting toy can be made out of an egg carton and some buttons (make sure the buttons have open holes, in case the child gets one in her mouth—they shouldn't be used unsupervised). Have the child put the red buttons in one receptacle, the blue in another, etc. Then, dump them out and put the round buttons in one, the square in another, and so on. As she learns how to organize the same information in several different ways, it will prepare her to receive and organize the massive information influx over the next year.

- Dolls of all sizes, animals, puppets, toy telephones, toy buildings, simple vehicles (cars, trucks, and trains), old clothes, and simple costumes—all of these can encourage vibrant, imaginative play. Again, observe your child. Some kids would love to pretend with a toy lawn mower, others with a kitchen set, and others wouldn't like either.

- Balls of all shapes and sizes, connecting toys (large stringing beads), digging toys (bucket, shovel, and rake), a sandbox, a beginner's tricycle, a children's keyboard (or other musical instruments), and large crayons

Which was 1995's most popular Barbie?
a. Malibu Barbie
b. Home-office Barbie
c. Pediatrician Barbie
d. Skydiver Barbie
e. Brunette Barbie

Answer: c

From *Parent Soup: The Game*

can all stimulate physical as well as intellectual and emotional development.

- Books. Reading together is a rich experience that supports language development and nurtures your bond with your child. Storytelling can also be quite powerful. Make your daughter and people she knows into characters for some of your stories. Use both everyday events and time-honored tales.

- Computer programs. As we prepare to enter the 21st century, our children need to be adept with computers. Many interactive computer programs now teach numbers, colors, shapes, and pre-reading skills. Children absolutely love these. This software is both far better and far worse than television. The programs are highly educational and promote the active involvement of children; they even satisfy children's desire for praise and attention (with cartoon characters dancing and singing when children figure something out). As such, however, they can be even more addictive than TV. Use them as an enrichment, but don't let them substitute for your praise, your attention, and your involvement.

Toys are powerful tools. But don't be lulled into the misconception that more is better. More toys, more lights, more sounds, and more money do not make for a happier or healthier child. Many studies have shown that even the most deprived environments are full of opportunities for play. If the toys are versatile and someone is willing to play along, children with fewer toys will often experience even more delight and creativity. Children need safety, freedom, loving attention, and praise. Most parents have had the experience of giving their child expensive gifts only to find the child more interested in the wrapping, the box, or some little party favor. Learn from this. Often the best toys are made from wooden spoons, cardboard boxes, tubes, pots and pans, and other safe items that she "discovers" around the house. And don't forget to play along with her. Play is an important part of a parent's growth as well.

Where Do You Put Them All?
Keep your child's baby bathtub and use it as a toy container. It's easy to store under a crib or a table and is sturdier than a cardboard box.
~ *Parent Soup member MallMedia*

Keep It Simple
I have found that you can buy all the toys on the market and children will want something else. My advice and experience with my 13-month-old has been to let her play with lots of different things. She has toys, but she will play with a microwave popcorn packet for hours and never get bored. At a restaurant, I will give her a few little toys but she will prefer to play with the menu. Most of all she loves laundry time, and will play with socks for hours!
~ *Parent Soup member Tis me1972*

WHINING

You know the tone of voice. All it takes is one "Mommy" in that nasally drone to get your attention. That's exactly what your daughter will hope it does. Any behavior that gets your attention is a good behavior in the eyes of a toddler. Even one that drives you crazy. You may want to do whatever it takes to stop their whining immediately, but giving in to a whined demand practically guarantees that your daughter will continue to whine when she wants something. Read on to find out how other parents have taught their kids that whining doesn't work.

The Problem

Q: My son is a constant whiner. I don't really know if it's just to get what he wants or if there is a reason behind it. He just whines about anything and everything. I can't tell if it started when my other son was born or if it is just his age. I'm getting stressed out, and I don't like to be constantly yelling at him, but whining is all he seems to know how to do. Is it his age, or something I'm doing?

~ *Parent Soup member JOKY2*

Watch how You React

A: I'd be willing to bet that your constant yelling is at the root of your problem. Your son is getting a lot of attention if you yell at him all the time—if I got that much attention for something, I'd do it a lot too! I feel that your best bet is to tell him that you can't understand him when he whines and then ignore him until he says something without whining. That way, you're reinforcing the good behavior (talking in a normal voice) and ignoring the bad (whining). It could be that this is all related to the birth of your second child, but even if it is, this method will still work if you do it 100 percent of the time.

~ *Everett H., Norwell, Massachusetts*

Another Use for the Time-Out

A: Whining can just drive you bananas, can't it? I have a four-year-old who, of course, does his best whiny voice when I am the most busy. The method that has seemed to work the best for me is one with which I was a little uncomfortable at first: I put him in a very brief (30-second) time-out. This brief time-out: (1) makes him aware that he's whining, (2) separates me from the whiny noise and thus calms me down, (3) gives him time and space to regain his "big-boy voice," and (4) is short enough that it is very different from "more serious" time-outs. The amazing thing is that it has worked! When he starts to whine, I just point to his time-out chair and he stops, midwhine, apologizes, and starts over again in a normal voice. Of course, it's not perfect all the time, but much better than it used to be!

~ *Parent Soup member amiamom*

Identifying and Avoiding the Causes

A: The whining at my house comes mostly when my three-year-old is sleepy or bored. I try to understand when the whining starts and take her on my lap or give her a quick hug. I've also found that the whining is sometimes in response to my asking her to "wait a minute." At this age, they don't understand time very much. To alleviate this, I try to attend to her needs as soon as possible without being a servant to her. One more thing—sometimes I tell her that I'm only going to respond to nice voices or ask her to ask me in a nice way. The same things don't work with her every time.

~ *Parent Soup member tjcmom*

Ignoring the Whiny Voice

A: My son was quite the little whiner starting at about three, and he still can be (at five) when he wants to be. When he goes into his little "whine mode," I remind him to use his "big-boy voice," and if he continues to whine, I tell him that I cannot hear him until he can talk like a big boy. Then I turn and walk away. He usually comes up behind me, taps me on the back of the leg, and tells me what he wants in that magic big-boy voice. If at all possible, I give him what he has asked for (within reason, of course), reinforcing that he has properly communicated what he wants.

~ *Parent Soup member anitalyn*

Could Whining Be a Reflection of Inner Turmoil?

Q: My sister and her three children, ages five, two, and four months, recently moved in with me after she and her husband separated. We are getting along fine, except with the two-year-old. She doesn't ask for anything without whining or crying. She is particular about her choices (i.e., the color of her bottle) and will carry on until she gets her way. I have told my sister that we can't give in to the child because if we do this behavior will never stop. My sister is going through a lot right now, and I think she gives in to the child because she can't deal with the crying as well as her marriage difficulties. I am at my wits' end and need some advice.

~ *Parent Soup member Lucy*

THE ELIUMS' POINT OF VIEW

A: How wonderful that you are there to help your sister through this rough time. We agree with your assessment of why your sister "gives in" to her two-year-old. Mothers in separation often feel extreme guilt for causing their children misery and want to make it up to them somehow. Your sister is probably too mentally, emotionally, and physically exhausted to deal with the many needs of her children right now, and her middle one may sense this more than the others and feel anxious about it.

Whining is an immature way of asking for help. Your little niece needs reassurance, lots of attention, and love to help her feel safe. If you do not give her what she needs, her whining, crying, and outrageous demands will only increase. We do not mean that she should have no limits or boundaries. She must learn to follow family rules even at your house to prevent this temporary situation from turning into a disaster—not good for any of you. However, she may need more hugs, rocking, kisses, attention, and involvement than the other ones. If you can relieve your sister from the little one's demands by taking her with you on errands, taking her for walks or to the park, or involving her in things you do around the house—cooking, laundry, making beds, for example—she will feel that she belongs and be less fearful about these huge changes that are taking place in her life.

It is very hard to be a middle child. Where does one really belong? The eldest often has special privileges just because they are older; the youngest gets more attention and care because they need it. Your little two-year-old niece needs a special aunt right now with lots of patience, understanding, and love.

What Do I Do if My Child Makes a Habit Out of Whining?

Q: Help! Our son is an incessant whiner and frequent crier. We have tried everything to curb his whiny ways, to no avail. My husband and I are at odds over how best to deal with this. I feel that whining is just a way to get attention, and even negative attention is still attention, so ignoring him is probably the best course of action. My husband agrees to a point, but even I can see that this approach has limited value and that something further needs to be done. Our son whines about everything—what to eat, what to wear, and when to go to bed. Our son is tremendously bright, inquisitive, and quite serious. He is also a perfectionist who has a difficult time dealing with the mistakes and foibles of everyday life.

~ *Parent Soup member SheSpends*

THE ELIUMS' POINT OF VIEW

A: Whining is a child's immature way of telling us that something is wrong or that he needs something. Unfortunately, whining can become a habit, as in your son's case. A whining child needs compassion ("I'm sorry the world looks so black"), encouragement ("I know it's hard"), and a big push ("When you say 'please,' you can have your dessert," or "After you're in bed, I'll read you a story"). Children under the age of seven must be given very few choices about things. They feel more secure when their parents lead them safely through the day. These years are the years when we must be up on our feet, actively helping our little one learn to control himself and his world. Taking a small child by the hand while you say, "Now it's time to brush our teeth," walking him to the bathroom, seating him on your lap, letting him put on the toothpaste, and brushing your teeth together works wonders to get around the whining.

Whining is also something a very young child does naturally when he is tired, afraid, or hungry, so you might say to your son when he whines, "Your whine tells me that you are feeling very little and that you need a nap. Maybe when you wake up, I'll have my big boy back again." This must be said without judgment, because when whining is confronted with anger, it simply escalates the situation. Very often, our children are the barometers for the condition of our family life, and if something is amiss, they pick it up. This could be tension between Mom and Dad, financial worries, worries concerning the illness of a loved one, and so on. To help your son with his whining problem, you may need to look deeply into your own relationships and concerns.

index